WONDER DRUG

WONDER DRUG

7 Scientifically Proven
Ways That Serving Others Is
the Best Medicine for Yourself

**STEPHEN TRZECIAK, M.D., AND
ANTHONY MAZZARELLI, M.D.**

ST. MARTIN'S
ESSENTIALS
NEW YORK

Published in the United States by St. Martin's Essentials, an imprint of St. Martin's Publishing Group

WONDER DRUG. Copyright © 2022 by Stephen Trzeciak and Anthony Mazzarelli. All rights reserved. Printed in the United States of America. For information, address St. Martin's Publishing Group, 120 Broadway, New York, NY 10271.

www.stmartins.com

Designed by Kelly S. Too

The Library of Congress has cataloged the hardcover edition as follows:

Names: Trzeciak, Stephen, author. | Mazzarelli, Anthony, author.
Title: Wonder drug : 7 scientifically proven ways that serving others is the best medicine for yourself / Stephen Trzeciak, Anthony Mazzarelli.
Description: First edition. | New York : St. Martin's Essentials, 2022. | Includes bibliographical references and index.
Identifiers: LCCN 2022000931 | ISBN 9781250863393 (hardcover) | ISBN 9781250809056 (ebook)
Subjects: LCSH: Altruism—Psychological aspects. | Helping behavior—Health aspects. | Self-actualization (Psychology) | Mental health. | Mind and body.
Classification: LCC BF637.H4 T79 2022 | DDC 158.3—dc23/eng/20220401
LC record available at https://lccn.loc.gov/2022000931

ISBN 978-1-250-80904-9 (trade paperback)

Our books may be purchased in bulk for promotional, educational, or business use. Please contact your local bookseller or the Macmillan Corporate and Premium Sales Department at 1-800-221-7945, extension 5442, or by email at MacmillanSpecialMarkets@macmillan.com.

First St. Martin's Essentials Trade Paperback Edition: 2023

10 9 8 7 6 5 4 3 2 1

For our children

CONTENTS

Without data, you are just
another person with an opinion.

—W. Edwards Deming

Introduction

Anthony Mazzarelli here. But call me Mazz.

In 2013, I became the chief medical officer (CMO) of Cooper University Health Care—an academic health care system that includes an affiliated medical school, flagship hospital, a Level 1 trauma center, and one hundred other sites in southern New Jersey, now with $1.6 billion in annual revenue and around 8,500 employees. I was thirty-eight years old, which seems impossibly young in hindsight. Needless to say, I'd never been a CMO before, and Cooper had never had a practicing emergency medicine physician in the position before either. My qualifications were my experience as a doctor at the hospital, my law degree, and, I think, my ability to get along with others. I knew going in that the CEO and the board had taken a chance on me, and I dearly hoped they'd put their faith in the right person.

Shortly thereafter, in 2014, the CEO told me that she'd hired a top consulting company that deals with employee and physician engagement and patient satisfaction. "They're the best, and they're going to help us," she said.

I was all for it. I'm not going to refuse help when it's offered. So I met with the consultants and they gave me a list of things that we had to get our then five hundred physicians to do to make improvements. I remember jotting down "say thank you," "introduce yourself," "listen more," "don't interrupt," and "nod a lot." Boiled down, the message was that our faculty needed to show more compassion and to connect with patients and one another.

I listened and nodded (and didn't interrupt *once*) through the presentation, but the whole time, I was thinking, "I'm never going to be able to get the physicians to do this mushy stuff." Apologies to doctors, but we're not always known for our soft skills or at least not known for changing our ways with those niceties. (I can practically hear my medical school professors who believed customer service wasn't their responsibility, saying, "That's what nurses and social workers are for.") Our faculty were academic types, doctors who'd been doing it their way for thirty-plus years and, as the faculty of our medical school, have been teaching others that same way. If I gave them the new mandate, many, if not most of them, would roll their eyes and say, "I'm already compassionate" or "What a waste of time and energy." They'd brush away the advice of this consulting group like lint off their shoulders.

Compassion: *recognizing the suffering of others and then taking action to help.*

When I started medical school, compassion wasn't explicitly part of our curriculum. It wasn't the title of any lecture. It wasn't the answer on any test. As a student and as a doctor, I learned about compassion in the halls and patient rooms of our hospital. I've seen its power but felt its effects most deeply when I was on the other side of the equation.

In 2013, my pregnant wife, Joanne, and I rushed to the obstetrics (OB) department at Cooper in a panic. Joanne, a cardiologist, and I had reason to worry. Even though she was full term, days away from her due date, she hadn't felt the baby move for hours. The nurse tried to find the heartbeat and couldn't, but she never let on that she was worried. She remained calm and spoke to us in a soothing voice.

The OB physician came in rolling an ultrasound machine with her and introduced herself with the same calming, reassuring tone, somewhere between "I know this might be really bad" and "Everything's going to be okay." It seemed to strike the right balance, which was: "You're in the right place, and you're going to get the right care for right now."

But it wasn't going to be okay. Using the best technology we had, the physician couldn't find a heartbeat either. It's probably the hardest job an OB doctor has, telling the expectant parents that their worst nightmare was their new reality. My wife was pregnant with a fully formed baby, and there was no sign of life.

I'll never forget the absolute sorrow at that moment. I'd been in the exact same situation as a caregiver, but it was entirely different to be on the other side of it, to say the least. I have relived it hundreds, if not thousands, of times in my mind since, and I'll never forget or stop appreciating the compassion shown to us on that day. It reverberates and revisits and is more powerful than people (including doctors) realize. Every carefully chosen word, the reassuring tones, comforting touches, even the moment of silence when hope was lost, mattered deeply to us. It matters still. It will always matter. The pain of our loss is forever intertwined with gratitude, and it helps. When all is bleak, you search for any small light and focus on it.

Patients and families may not remember a doctor's or nurse's name or face, but they will remember the smallest comforts we offer. Those moments are part of the story. Kenneth B. Schwartz, cancer patient and founder of the Schwartz Center for Compassionate Healthcare in Boston, said that compassion "makes the unbearable *bearable*."

If I hadn't had the experience of losing a son, would I be as convinced that compassion *always* matters? I can't say. But I knew I approved of the consultant's recommendations, and that I needed to get our entire health care system on board. On a human level, I hoped to lead a team that always gave patients and their families the same care and compassion that my wife and I received that day. I also had a business mandate to make our system more efficient and profitable. Let's face it: the bottom line does matter. And if compassion could help us be more profitable, it'd be a win-win. The powers that be at Cooper believed it would. They expected me, their brand-spanking-new CMO, the youngest on record, to make it happen. If I didn't, they might want to kick themselves for hiring me.

I had a simple solution to a complicated problem: *call Steve.*

I wish that all of life's problems could be solved by calling Stephen Trzeciak (maybe they can?). This one definitely would. Along with being the co-author of this book, Steve is an intensivist (intensive care specialist) and was the head of critical care medicine at Cooper. His reputation as "the science guy" is well earned; he was our number-one National Institutes of Health (NIH) research grant recipient, the most published faculty member, our star researcher, our very own Super Nerd. Not only that, when I was just out of med school and a resident (a doctor in training) at Cooper, Steve was my attending physician (my teacher). We went *way* back. But even if we didn't have a professional history and friendship, I would have gone to him first to solve this problem.

My logic was, *Who else can turn the minds of our academic staff but its* most *academic member?* If Steve could harness his nerd power and get an avalanche of research that proved compassion would make our system run better than it had in decades, we'd have a stronger leg to stand on than just "the consultant said so." I knew we had very strong physician leaders across the health system who would follow the data and lead their people to do the same. My intention was to weaponize scientific evidence. We had to build a data bomb and drop it on the doubters. Steve would be our Oppenheimer.

Stephen Trzeciak here. Steve is fine.

Mazz called me in to talk about a new research project, a deep dive on compassion, empathy, kindness—anything and everything that fell under the umbrella of Not Being a Jerk—in the realm of health care. He said, "You're the science guy. Can you take this list of mushy recommendations and science it up, give me evidence that I can take to the medical faculty that being compassionate will help the bottom line?"

My first thought was: "Okay, I wasn't expecting that."

Second thought: "Do people really call me 'the science guy'?"

I call myself a "research nerd" all the time, because I really do *love* to start with a hypothesis, do experiments, gather data, and draw conclusions. The scientific method is how I approach just about everything in my life, especially my work.

At that time, my research had been focused on resuscitation, the science of almost dying. I had an NIH grant to study the optimal level of oxygen in the blood to avoid brain damage in cardiac arrest patients who'd been resuscitated via CPR and electric shock paddles ("Clear!").

But this research is probably only interesting to about 5 percent of doctors and few other people. As my research career evolved, I felt an internal need to put my energy and expertise into research that'd be meaningful across all specialties, not just my own. But I was stumped to figure out one subject that would be impactful for any specialist, primary care physician, or surgeon.

Compassion covered the ground on that score, so I found myself warming to Mazz's ask.

Beyond that, I felt a personal yearning to dig into this vein. Mazz didn't know that I'd been wrestling with some frightening and upsetting thoughts lately that touched on the subject of caring about and for other people.

Some quick background: I do critical care. In the intensive care unit (ICU), I often meet people on the worst day of their lives. My patients are as close to dead as you can be without actually being dead. Technically, I don't really "meet" many of my patients because they're usually unconscious when I show up. One thing I have learned after twenty years working in the ICU: life is *fragile*.

One day I had to tell a single mom that her nineteen-year-old daughter—her only child, best friend, and the center of her universe—was never going to wake up again.

On the drive home that day, I thought the unthinkable: *I don't know if I can do this anymore.*

I was numb. Burnout is as common as the cold among health care workers. It's real, and it's heavy. The main symptoms are depersonalization, emotional exhaustion, and a dark feeling that no matter how hard you try, you can't make a difference.

I was batting three for three there. I'd read that burned-out doctors were twice as likely to make medical errors. I knew quite well that medical error was a leading cause of patient death. Burnout played a significant role in doctors having one of the highest suicide rates of any profession.

I could barely admit it to myself, but some part of me feared that I was heading down a dark road and that I desperately needed to change direction, and soon. My poker face was glued on tight; my colleagues had no idea just how burned out I was. Quitting wasn't a serious consideration.

I have four kids and a mortgage, and being a doctor pays pretty well. But this problem had to be solved, or I might put myself and others at risk.

I did what I always do to solve a problem: science it. The best research on how to relieve burnout symptoms said to take nature hikes, do hot yoga, get a meditation app, take a vacation. Basically, to be a better doctor, I was supposed to get far away from the hospital and patients.

Escapism is built upon the belief that if health care providers spent *less* time caring for patients in favor of more self-care—"*me* time"— that burnout would evaporate, and good cheer would miraculously replace it.

Well, I wasn't buying it. It did not compute. The answer to workplace burnout could not be to run away from the workplace. How was that a sustainable strategy for me, as the head of my department? Something had to change *fundamentally* at the point of care to reverse my, and anyone's, disconnection, emotional exhaustion, and hopelessness.

At this critical point in my career, when I was trying to figure out a way to save it, Mazz tossed me a lifeline (although I didn't realize it at the time). If nothing more, our side project gave me something to think about besides my burnout.

Empathy: the ability to understand and share someone else's feelings.

I started with some key questions: What are the physiological and psychological effects of compassion and empathy? Can the effects of Not Being a Jerk be measured?

My scientific approach was to use a rigorous methodology, and not allow my personal feelings to influence my research. Along with being a doctor, Mazz is a lawyer too; he knows how to make arguments. I wore my agnostic scientist cap and remained unbiased.

Our exhaustive review of the scientific literature began on PubMed— it's the Google for health care. What Mazz and I thought would be a trickle of research turned out to be a raving, overflowing river of it. One study led to another, and another. In all, we reviewed more than a thousand scientific abstracts. We gathered the most relevant into what we affectionately call *The Curator,* a supergeek spreadsheet of data that grew from a handful of research studies to more than 280. No one had ever compiled all the research on this subject in one place before.

At the time of their initial publication, people who read these papers on the effects of compassion probably found them incredibly interesting and perhaps also very impactful. They made ripples in the water, and some studies probably made a substantial splash. But with the methodology in our review—that finally connected all of the key studies—the ripples and splashes came together to form an unmistakable tidal wave of data that could potentially transform health care.

I'll condense a year of study into four words: Compassion moves the needle.

Doctors' and nurses' compassion was associated with better patient outcomes in almost every aspect of health care, from decreasing a patient's perception of pain to counteracting stress-mediated disease, speeding recovery from serious illness, increasing patient adherence to treatment—the list goes on. Suffice it to say, Mazz now had his data bomb to drop on the old-school academic faculty members. They couldn't deny the overwhelming evidence that compassion would boost the metrics he'd been asked to improve. Mazz and I both knew these physicians and their ability to change their management of patients based on evidence-based medicine. They prided themselves on providing the best practice in medical care. Now we had the data to make the case for a change in the approach to patients based on science—with data that used the same rigor in its production as the medical journals they all read and rely upon for technical excellence.

Along the way, as I read study after study, I felt a stirring of hope. The evidence was clear: the cure for my burnout was *not* to escape. **I could boost my resilience and protect myself from burnout by making deeper human connections.**

When I started medical school in 1992, I remember being taught the strategy of not getting too close with patients or their families. Not connecting or caring too much, my teachers said, was an emotional shield. Mazz describes this lesson as a part of "the hidden curriculum" that doesn't appear in medical textbooks. But it's learned by medical students through socialization with senior doctors in the halls and on-call rooms of teaching hospitals. The thinking was that too much compassion, too much caring, would overwhelm, along the lines of "Don't get too close, or you might get bitten." Here is the problem: when you actually look into the scientific literature, you see a different signal.

Imagine our surprise when we uncovered a preponderance of evidence that signaled that the association between compassion and burnout is actually *inverse*. Low compassion; high burnout. High compassion; low burnout. This suggests that more human connection can be good for you and that the protective shield for doctors is actually to have doctor-patient relationships that are more meaningful and fulfilling. We should care more, connect more.

I'd always thought of myself as a compassionate doctor. In hindsight, though, I was probably a bit remote, sticking with the clinical applications (the dials, monitors, and computers in the ICU, the science-y stuff) and not giving my full attention and care to the humans connected to the machines. Was that the reason I felt so exhausted? **The counterintuitive finding here is that caregiver compassion not only can improve outcomes for patients, it can transform the experience for caregivers as well.**

I decided to test this out by doing an experiment—on myself. I was the only study subject. In scientific literature, a study's number of subjects is denoted by the symbol "n." So for my experiment, "n=1." The title of my informal study: "Does Compassion Transform Experience for the Caregiver?"

One bit of research I'd found was that it takes only forty seconds of compassion to make a difference on both sides of the hospital bed. (Later, I did a TEDx Talk about this called "Healthcare's Compassion Crisis."[1]) So I started, very intentionally, devoting an extra forty seconds (at least) to speaking supportive words to conscious patients and to family members. I endeavored to connect more, not less. I cared more, not less. I leaned in, rather than pulling back. It was tricky at times, because, as I've said, many of my patients can't hear or see me. I had to make a mental switch, to put the care back into the health care I provided. And not just with patients and families, with the people I worked with who were also super stressed and overworked.

Very quickly, on my new protocol, I started doing my job better. I got excited about being a doctor again. And that was when the fog of burnout began to lift. Being intentional about compassion changed everything—inside the hospital walls and outside.

Burnout is not limited to the health care profession, of course. The compassion crisis is everywhere we look. Most of us—Mazz and me included—were not raised to scan our world, constantly searching for opportunities to care for and serve others. Most of us scan our world for problems coming in our own direction and for ways to serve ourselves. It's not our fault we were socialized and conditioned to put our own needs first. But what Mazz and I have learned over our four-plus years of research on this subject is that by serving others, we reap tremendous benefits ourselves.

When the two of us began our side project, we never set out to change people's hearts. We were out to change their *minds*. There is bona fide science in the art of medicine, and the science is strong. We wound up changing our own minds, and our mission in life.

We started living by the strategy of being compassionate as best we could, to recover and protect ourselves from burnout. We presented our findings at Cooper, convinced the faculty to try the new way, and tested its effectiveness. Subsequently, a consumer market research company found through focus groups and other methodologies that when the general public thought of Cooper, caring and compassion were the first things that popped into their minds. In a meeting of our physician leaders (service line chiefs and department chairs), they overwhelmingly voted for compassion to become one of the core values for our health system, and we made it official shortly thereafter. And, year over year, the *financial* performance of our health system improved as patient experience and physician and employee engagement continued to rise. *Compassion in action!*

Around that time, I (Steve) became the chair of the department of medicine, and shortly afterward, Mazz got promoted to co-president and CEO for the entire health system.

The story grew bigger than our patch in South Jersey. Believing our research and conclusions would benefit the entire medical profession, we wrote a book called *Compassionomics: The Revolutionary Scientific Evidence That Caring Makes a Difference.*[2]

Our new focus put our work on a different trajectory. Along with being CEO, Mazz started speaking on CNN, NPR, Fox News Radio, Sirius XM, and other outlets about the (medical and financial) power of compassion. My research now focuses on compassion and empathy tools. My previous work about oxygen levels and so on was great for getting grants, piling up citations, and adding lines to my CV. But it wasn't really making anybody feel better.

We decided: we're not old, but we're too old to work on anything but what matters the most.

The book got into the right hands. Health care providers and other readers did their own n=1 experiment—tested the compassion hypothesis for themselves—and found the same results I did, that it helped them immensely. Emails and letters telling stories of life-changing turnarounds poured in. This got us thinking and pushed us to ask: **This cannot just be true for health care providers . . . Could our findings be a universal that applies to *everybody*?**

That is a big reason for why *this* book came to be. My n=1 experiment generated an observation (boosted well-being), and reading about that triggered a bunch of other health care providers to replicate my experience, so then there were more data.

The logical next step in our research was to transition from health care providers to everyone—from compassion for patients to serving (all) others and altruism.

Altruism: selfless concern for and serving the well-being of others.

Health care providers respond well to upping compassion for those who are suffering. Those of us who are not health care providers might respond well to upping altruism, serving others around us (who are not necessarily suffering). We decided to do another synthesis of the evidence to test the hypothesis that serving others is the best medicine for oneself in the general population. If giving behaviors helped health care workers be resilient, would it do the same for *everyone*?

I was a philosophy major in college and Mazz has a master's degree in bioethics, so we've been trained to ask the Big Questions.

What is the key to emotional and physical resilience?

Relationships.

What is the key to better relationships?

Giving of yourself. You don't lose anything by serving others, you only *gain*. **Giving is powerful therapy for the giver, any giver.**

In *Compassionomics,* the Big Question was: *Does compassion really matter?*

Yes. And we had the data to prove it. Now, after two more years of curating studies, testing it in our own experiments, and sharing it far and wide, we have very compelling evidence that serving others is the best medicine in *any* environment.

So that brought up a few Big Questions that still needed answers:

What if everything you've been taught about happiness and fulfillment is wrong?

What if the secret to success is not what you think?

What is the evidence-based way to live your life?

Conventional thinking is to focus on ourselves, to self-help. (How's that working for you, by the way?) It doesn't add up. The bulk of scientific evidence points to a totally different paradigm, and it's been right in front of us all along.

The self-serving, self-help culture is *not* going to get you to true happiness, fulfillment, or success. But serving others will get you there, *and we can prove it.*

The paradigm shift we'd like to usher in: by serving others, your life will crack wide open in only the best ways. But—here's the mind-bender—if you do it only for selfish reasons, you might as well forget it. To benefit from what Mazz and I call the "Live to Give" mindset, you have to *mean it,* and we will show you the evidence. We're asking you to care, to really care, about other people, and to back that up with action. It's not a subtle "art." It's *hard science.* We have science-d the heck out of serving others, and if you want to rewire your brain for joy and alter your physiology for longevity and health, you have to go all in.

We are not Buddhist monks in saffron-dyed robes on a mountaintop spouting off about karma. Karma might very well be a bitch. But until we have evidence-based research that proves it, we can't support that theory.

The Boomerang Effect—the belief that goodness comes back to you—might very well hit you square between the eyes. But until the data on it is reported in peer-reviewed scientific journals, we can't endorse it as an evidence-based life philosophy either.

Pay It Forward—the practice of doing something nice for someone to reciprocate a kindness done for you—is a pithy bumper sticker. We'd never advise people not to pay it forward, but as a science-based strategy, there are *no data available.*

Karma, boomeranging, paying forward are emotional, sentimental concepts. We humans take comfort in these concepts because they "feel" just. They give us comfort and a measure of control, as in, *If I'm a good person, I'll have a happy life,* despite knowing, and seeing in their own experience, that there is little anyone can do to protect oneself from the curveballs of life. There is no protection from bad things happening, even if you're a good person.

Serving others or giving of yourself isn't a deal you make with the universe. It's a way of life that lowers stress, fine-tunes your body's physiology, deepens relationships, promotes resilience to hardships, and can even help you earn more money.

Giving is not transactional though. It's transformational. Giving impacts living in a virtuous cycle of positive emotion and better health. People who have figured this out, either by new revelation after seeing the science behind it or perhaps the science just confirmed/supported something they always knew intuitively, are people Mazz and I call "Live to Givers."

People often come to altruism for moral and ethical reasons. They see a plea on TV to send money for starving kids with flies on their eyes or shelter dogs shivering in a cold cage with Sarah McLachlan singing in the background. The emotional appeal is aimed straight at your heart.

But another approach, the one we're pitching, induces altruism just as well: reason. For a recent study, scientists from Harvard, Princeton, and Brooklyn College showed their 975 participants one of the following pitches—an emotional appeal, a rational appeal, a combination of emotional and rational appeals, and none (the control group)—for a charity for impoverished kids.[3] The emotional appeal had a photo of the child living in poverty. The rational appeal used data and evidence-based arguments to make a case for donating. The participants in the study were then asked how much of a $100 allotment they would donate to the charity. You'd think that the emotional pitch about disease, suffering, with a picture of a child, would get the biggest donations. But the rational pitch with data about impact on people in need was just as effective.

In this book, we're appealing to your sense of reason, your mind. We're making a scientific case for focusing your life on serving others. You don't have to *feel* an obligation to do your part or to hedge your karmic bets. We're presenting an altruism protocol because it's proven to work.

Our style, if you will, is to look at familiar things in an unfamiliar way. We take concepts that are typically considered to be in the sentimental and emotional or moral and ethical domains, and we place them under the scrutiny of science. We can look at, for example, how being selfless in marriage or whether reaching across the aisle to find common ground is beneficial not only in meaningful but also in *measurable* ways. We can provide stats on how it matters, how much it matters, how it works, what biological mechanisms are triggered.

As medical doctors with the goal of *changing minds through science—* we only know what we know from data. And we have an avalanche of it that supports that if you Live to Give, you can have a longer, happier, healthier life with better relationships and more professional success. Everything you want out of life can be had by focusing your energy and intention on other people. Through altruism, you can transform into a new state of mind and body and become a new person.

We want to be clear. This is not a do-gooder book, it's a science book. And we're not do-gooders. We are physician scientists. You will get no "holier than thou" from us, for sure.

Science shows that giving is way better for you than grasping. And our job here is to deliver the message. Serving others can be a wonder drug. It's effective treatment for scores of conditions, and there are essentially no side effects.

If you are in a dark place, just stuck in a rut or feel lost, we prescribe serving others. We'd prescribe it to every single person on earth. We'd pump it into the water supply. Since we haven't figured out how to do that (yet), we offer you this book instead.

Wonder Drug is perhaps the most counterintuitive "self-help" book you're ever going to read. We're going to teach you how to let go of the goal of helping yourself, and in so doing, help yourself.

Part I is all about the Epidemic of Self-Interest we're facing right now. Our Me Culture has been conditioned into us from a young age. Children start life with the impulse to care about the well-being of others and are indoctrinated into the "you do you" mindset as they get older, face competition, and have to make choices about the kind of life they want to have. "Follow your bliss" sounds innocent enough, but the underlying message is to be self-serving. It's actually our natural state of mind to want to do for others. Our bodies were designed to reinforce that behavior in physiological rewards. But to get those benefits, we have to undo and unlearn the ruthless dog-eat-dog mindset, and embrace serving others to grow.

Part II presents the Cure, all the ways that serving others makes you better. We'll go through it all: how altruism benefits your physical body, your mental health, your happiness, and your professional success. For now, know that your brain—the activation of neural pathways—changes on altruism. When you connect with other people, you get hits of reward center hormones—endorphins, dopamine, oxytocin, and serotonin—that make you feel good. Your fight-or-flight stress response is thwarted by serving others, and, in case you don't know, chronic stress is a major cause of chronic systemic inflammation that can lead to heart disease and cancer.

Here is a brief preview list of potential health benefits from serving others:

- Longer life
- Better control of blood pressure
- Fewer cardiovascular events, like heart attacks and strokes
- Better functional status in the elderly
- Less chronic inflammation
- Slower aging
- Better willpower and physical stamina
- More energy
- Better sleep
- Less depression
- Less anxiety
- More happiness and fulfillment

In your professional life, a servant-leader mentality earns you the loyalty and devotion of colleagues, as opposed to "winning" their enmity, bitterness, and resentment with a greed-is-good "screw you" approach. Live to Givers actually have more success and make more money. In terms of your personal relationships, altruism makes you sexier in the eyes of potential love interests, and a better partner in marriage.

Part III is the Prescription. We prescribe seven ways to take your giving "medicine" and change your life, starting immediately. These strategies are your prescription for all-cause physical and emotional discomfort and pain, and hold the power to heal. And none of them are hard to swallow. They're more like a spoonful of sugar than colonoscopy prep. Science shows you don't have to create major upheaval in your life and surroundings to Live to Give. You don't need to sell all your possessions, move to a third world country, and haul water from a distant well. In fact, our first strategy of the seven is to "Start Small" by incorporating micro acts of compassion into your daily life. And then the strategies build until your outlook on life—and your experience of it—is wholly transformed.

It bears mentioning that the barrier to entry into giving mode is small but seismic. By reading this far, you've already begun the process of making a "personal paradigm shift." A personal paradigm is a belief or a framework for how to live. A personal paradigm *shift* is rethinking that belief and reframing your mindset. To change your life, you will have to change some paradigms—namely, the ones that you've been conditioned to believe, like "Winner takes all" and asking, "What's in it for me?" By wrapping your mind around new concepts, like "We're all in this together" and asking, "How can I help?" you will create a shift that will carry you through crisis and into a more generative, fulfilling life.[4]

If you're not "feeling it" yet, *that's okay*! You don't need emotion to change your mind or behavior. You only need to trust in science and keep reading. By the end of the book, you'll be an amateur Data Nerd (hey, nerd means enthusiast, and there's nothing wrong with that!). Like you, we didn't create the scientific literature on the subject. All we did was curate it for you, reach emotion-free, evidence-based conclusions, and share the real secret of success as an act of giving from us to you.

We'd like to make this point very clear: We're not perfect specimens, to be sure. We are just works in progress with selfish moments. Plenty of them. But we see the power of serving others now, and we're doing our best to try every day to follow the science and taking action to serve others by following the evidence-based prescription outlined in these pages.

Mazz here again.

Here's a story from the Cooper hospital files to illustrate our point. A late-middle-age male patient was hours from death with a sudden brain bleed. His daughter's wedding was just weeks away. She knew that his dying wish would be to be there at her wedding. So our amazing nurses made it happen, right then and there, and put together an impromptu wedding. They got creative and used IV tubing for rings and used an old pound cake from the back of the break-room freezer to make the ceremonial cut. The flowers came from a willing donor on another floor. One of the nurses was an ordained pastor, which was lucky. He jumped in to officiate the wedding.

Everyone who was there said that their hearts broke for the family, but their hearts were also filled. Any of the nurses and doctors who gave up their time and energy to pull this off could have said, "My shift is over. I'm too tired. It's not my job." But the entire unit banded together and did their part to do a great thing for a dying man and his child. Each one of those people was focused on the daughter, her fiancé, the patient, not on himself or herself. It was more work for them, but there is no way they didn't get something out of it or love being a part of it. They'll remember that day in the ICU for the rest of their lives, and every time they tell the story, they'll have that same feeling well up in their chest and benefit from it. And this wasn't a one-off. Another impromptu wedding happened recently with a COVID-19 patient.

As leaders, we're working hard to help make Cooper an organization that thrives on being other-focused. If people are happier and feel like they make a difference, they have more energy and bring a higher level of effectiveness to the job.

I find that serving others is so helpful to me that I schedule hours in the emergency department (ED). As CEO, I don't have to practice medicine or see patients at all. But I've found that going into the ED and connecting with patients keeps me in a Live to Give mindset. Bam, I'm back in compassion mode, with a renewed sense of purpose. I'm reminded that even small things like taking a patient's history has the capacity to be meaningful beyond measure.

During the winter of 2020–21, we had wave after wave of COVID-19 patients, and we were all wrung out. We worked incredibly long hours, I would make rounds throughout the hospital with our staff, hoping that my compassion and energy would be contagious in a good way. Caring for people, dealing with their anxiety, listening to them, and interacting with them was the wonder drug I used to give me strength and help me work longer. Much more effective than Red Bull. I used the science of compassion to get me through the greatest health care crisis of our lifetime.

Steve again.

I'm striving to get better at serving others every day in my life, not only at the hospital but everywhere, with everyone. I don't get it right all the time. But as I think about it, and what I would tell my kids, is, "The more you're just in your own head, the more screwed you are." That's not my opinion, belief, or religion. I'm not preaching to you. I'm presenting scientific fact.

There's only one message that you can synthesize from the sheer amount of data. So if you want to live an evidence-based life, you have to focus on other people and not just yourself. And if you don't want to take your medicine, then don't be surprised if you stay stuck in your rut, feeling totally burned out. Altruism is a powerful therapy to cure your *life*. Adherence to prescribed therapy is everything in medicine. And, by the way, compassion makes patients more adherent and more likely to take their pills! Another way it heals.

You might be wondering what we hope to achieve by writing this book and presenting these data and this treatment plan. We're not writers; we're curators and teachers. So what, exactly, are we trying to teach?

Back to asking Big Questions:

What is the key to good health, happiness, and fulfillment?
Serving others. And again, we've got the goods to prove it.

Life's most persistent and urgent question is, "What are you doing for others?"

—Dr. Martin Luther King, Jr.

Perhaps this Big Question from Dr. King will become even more persistent and urgent for you once you see all the data assembled in the pages to follow. We hope it'll inspire you to sign on to a scientifically proven way of doing small things every day to serve others and watch your life transform as a result.

Our bigger hope is to increase the amount of global compassion and care through science. If we measure outcomes on a population basis, serving others can change the world. The best medicine for both individuals and the population is to ask, "How can I help others?" and to put in the time and effort to do it. If enough people become Live to Givers, a lot of the problems we see in society today could get solved.

So you can either be part of that vision and have that same goal, or you can just have the goal of using our treatment recommendations as the best medicine for yourself. That's okay. Even attempting to Not Be a Jerk is a good thing for you and the people who populate your corner of the world. It'll break down the bubbles, throw ladders down into the foxholes we've been living in, and let us climb out and breathe in the clean, cleared air.

What a relief and joy that will be.

PART I

THE DIAGNOSIS

An Epidemic of Self-Serving

It is well to remember that the
entire universe, with one trifling exception,
is composed of others.

—John Andrew Holmes

1

It's Not You, It's *Me* Culture

In modern U.S. history, there were periods when the cultural ethos of our nation had us serving others and devoting ourselves to the greater good. The Greatest Generation fought to end tyranny during World War II in the 1940s. Civil rights protestors risked their lives for social justice in the 1960s. The hippies and anti–Vietnam War protestors brought about a cultural revolution based on peace, love, and understanding.

But as the Summer of Love wound down, after we'd boomed enough babies, our collective consciousness took a decisive turn inward. Author and cultural critic Tom Wolfe defined the 1970s as "the Me Decade" in a 1976 article in *New York* magazine, kicking off what became a Me Half-Century. Our ideals began to shift away from the idea that we depended on each other for our health and well-being, toward bootstrap individualism, upholding personal achievement as the ultimate success.

The Me Decade dovetailed into the Greed Decade of the 1980s, with the unofficial mascot of suspender-loving financier Gordon Gekko, from the movie *Wall Street*, who famously coined the mantra "Greed is *good*." Grabbing and grasping for personal wealth in the '80s flowed into the unbridled entitlement of the 1990s, aka the Self-Esteem Decade, when everyone got a trophy and our own feelings and needs came first. During those years, books about the toxicity of self-focus and rampant brattiness started to pop up, notably the bestseller *The Culture of Narcissism,* by historian and social critic Christopher Lasch.

By the turn of the twenty-first century, with the widespread use of the internet and social media, we took to posting incessantly about our lunch, creating YouTube channels, and uploading a million selfies. Broadcasting our own point of view became a national fixation. It was literally reflected on the Mylar "mirror" cover of *Time* magazine in 2006 that named "YOU" Person of the Year. All this selfie-ness didn't improve our relationships. The opposite. "The biggest totem to interpersonal misunderstanding is the selfie stick," said Nicholas Epley, human behavior expert and author of *Mindwise: Why We Misunderstand What Others Think, Believe, Feel, and Want.*

Me Culture evolved again to take on a holistic, mindfulness bent by "living *your* best life," and "following *your* passion." "Self-care" has been elevated as the panacea for whatever ails us. The influencers and soul patrol espoused that by forever working on ourselves, we'd find happiness.

Every generation has its version of "I'm doing me." We have been immersed in Me Culture, in its various permutations, for fifty years, doubling and tripling down on all-about-me-ism. And that'd be swell, if the scientific data showed that it had any health benefit.

The truth is, it's *not* all about you. It never has been. And by fixating on ourselves, we can actually harm ourselves. Self-serving culture has trained us to take care of number one and "our own," and screw everyone else. But this attitude has left us feeling alone and empty, and it's triggered an anxiety epidemic. You'll see the evidence of that throughout this book. Research has found that the more people focus solely on themselves, the worse off they may be in almost every metric that can be measured: physical and mental health, emotional well-being, and professional success.

THE HIDDEN DANGERS OF MINDFULNESS

We're not bashing self-care and mindfulness per se. Meditating on kindness and compassion is incredibly beneficial to one's health. But there are risks with the self-care approach if it's only about taking more and more "me time." Of course, taking time for yourself is vitally important. Getting off the hamster wheel or slowing down in the rat race are un-equivocally good for you. We all need work-life balance, for sure. But the question is, what do we do in that respite time?

According to the National Institutes of Health, double the number of Americans (21 million) are doing yoga today than they were twenty years ago.[1] Eighteen million are meditating. The self-care message that mind-body practices can reduce stress has clearly been received. We like walks in the park and downward-facing dogs as much as the next guy. But so many self-care choices are increasingly isolating. Yoga and meditation, as we commonly do them in America, are often solitary pursuits. Not to say that team sports are better than yoga. They are about working together and sharing goals and experiences though. In yoga class, your mat is your island. In a room full of people, you are alone in your breath, mind, and body. Same thing with app-style meditation. It's all about you and your eight-minute journey inward, accompanied only by a lilting, disembod-ied British voice on Headspace, with your headphones or earbuds block-ing out the rest of the world.

In terms of happiness and success, exclusively self-focused self-care is just not as effective as other-focused other-care. Looking *outward,* mak-ing human connections, serving and caring for others—the opposite of looking *within-ward*—has proven stress-relieving benefits. **Science sup-ports that a key to resilience is *relationships*.** In decades past, we found uplift and resilience in our families, our friends, our relationships. But now, it's just us and our phones.

The trend toward solitary pursuits is likely, to some extent, to be a result of technology. We spend more time staring at screens, detached, functionally alone, than ever before. It's likely hurting us, and our kids. According to a San Diego State University/University of Georgia study[2] of 1.1 million U.S. adolescents from 1991 to 2016, their psychological well-being decreased sharply and significantly after 2012 when wide-spread use of social networks exploded. Predictably, the teenagers who spent more time on social media, texting, and gaming—and less time doing *anything* else, like sports, face-to-face interacting, homework— had the lowest well-being scores. The happiest kids spent the least amount of time in front of screens.

Well-being: the state of being comfortable, healthy, or happy.

We live online too. We recognize all the good that comes from that version of connectivity. But there is a downside to having so much information at our fingertips. When we're engaged with our devices, we're not making the human connections that actually give us a sense of well-being. With their eyes glued to screens, our kids are learning to be excellent gamers, but they're not learning how to relate and connect with other people.

Needless to say, while our kids are gaming and texting—and getting more depressed—so are adults. We can be sitting in the same room, all on our phones, and we might as well be on different planets. Isolation and loneliness is crushing our human spirit. Despite our obsession with self-care and devotion to wellness, we aren't doing so well. According to various reports:

- Thirty-five percent of Americans over forty-five are chronically lonely.
- Only 8 percent of Americans report having meaningful conversation with their neighbors.
- Only 32 percent of Americans say they trust their neighbors, and only 18 percent of millennials.
- Depression rates are rising.
- The suicide rate has risen 30 percent since 1999. Forty-five thousand Americans die by suicide every year.
- Among teens over the last several years, the suicide rate has risen by 70 percent.
- Seventy-two thousand Americans die from opioid addictions per year.
- Life expectancy in the U.S. is falling, not rising.

In what is likely the longest-running scientific study ever conducted (eighty years and counting), the Harvard Study of Adult Development (aka the Harvard Grant Study, named after the research's benefactor) began tracking the health of 268 Harvard sophomores, beginning in 1938 and checking in with them regularly over time. (Note: all the original study subjects were men because Harvard was still all male back then.)

The researchers followed the trajectory of their lives, with the aim of identifying the key factors responsible for good health and happiness. Only a handful of the people initially enrolled in the study are still alive, but the results over the years paint a clear picture of the importance of human connection in health, vitality, and longevity.

Robert Waldinger, M.D., the current study director and the fourth to hold that title, who is a psychiatrist at Massachusetts General Hospital and professor at Harvard Medical School, summarized the findings in a TEDx Talk[3]: "Good relationships keep us happier and healthier . . . and loneliness kills. When we gathered together everything we knew about [the study participants] at age fifty, it wasn't their middle-age cholesterol levels that predicted how they were going to grow old, it was how satisfied they were in their relationships. The people who were the most satisfied in their relationships at age fifty were the healthiest at age eighty."

Meaningful relationships were not only the key for good health and longevity but also for the Grant Study subjects' well-being. After decades of rigorous investigation, in what we think could be one of the best lines ever in academia, George Valliant, the study director for forty years, said, "The seventy-five years and twenty million dollars expended on the [Harvard] Grant Study points . . . to a straightforward five-word conclusion: 'Happiness is love. Full stop.'"

Meaningful human connection is *protective.* What is the mechanism by which human connection can impact our health? In short, being lonely causes a similar response in the body as being under extreme stress all the time. For example, it raises the level of the stress hormone cortisol circulating in the blood, and over time loneliness can contribute to chronic systemic inflammation—a factor linked to bad things like cardiovascular disease and cancer. As Frankenstein's monster put it poetically, "Alone bad. Friend good."

Prosocial behavior: voluntary actions that are intended to help or benefit another individual or group of individuals. You can think of prosocial behavior as kindness; for example, helping, sharing, donating, cooperating, volunteering.

Antisocial behavior: voluntary actions that harm or lack consideration for the well-being of others. In short, antisocial behavior is aggression, hostility, disruption, criminality.

Solitary pursuits, even well-intended ones, don't necessarily strengthen relationships. Relational pursuits, like volunteering, joining, giving, helping, are prosocial. Prosocial behaviors, attitudes, and activities can lower stress and improve health and well-being, far more so than delving deeply and exclusively into the self *by yourself.*

SELF-INTEREST STARTS AT THE TOP

To examine egocentricity in our culture, researchers at the University of Michigan analyzed[5] 226 presidential State of the Union addresses from 1790 to 2012. In each, they searched for pronouns that emphasized self-interest, such as "I," "me," "mine," and mentions of their own family members. Even "we" and "us" were considered self-interest keywords because citing collective success was an example of bragging on your own people. Other-interest keywords were "you," "he," "she," "friend," and "neighbor," words that weren't directly self-referential or boastful about the given leader's personal or familial achievement.

For 1790 to 1946, the tone and language of the annual speech was decidedly other-interested. The shift toward self-interest happened in the 1950s, but it really skyrocketed in the '70s. You would think Jimmy Carter, famously altruistic in his post-presidential life through his work for Habitat for Humanity and other charities, would give other-focused speeches, but his addresses used an abundance of egocentric language. Egocentric language was high in Ronald Reagan's State of the Union speeches as well. And who wins for the *least* self-interested language since the '70s? George W. Bush. Not that his speeches were overwhelmingly other-focused. They had neutral language.

The researchers used the State of the Union address as an example of the clear shift toward self-interest in politics, but they also noted studies that reached the same conclusion via telltale self-interested language in books and popular songs. But the president sets the tone for the country. The "I, me, mine" language of our leaders influences and informs the rest of us. Call it trickle-down *egonomics*.

In individual homes, parents set the tone, and they influence their children. For a recent Harvard University Graduate School of Education study[6] of ten thousand middle- and high-schoolers from thirty-three different schools, researchers asked the kids to rank what mattered most to them: (1) achieving at a high level, (2) their own happiness, or (3) caring for others. Nearly 80 percent made achievement or happiness their number-one choice. Twenty percent picked caring for others. The majority of the students believed their peers all felt the same way. In terms of their core values, the majority of the students placed "hard work" as their top choice, with "fairness" and "kindness" lagging far behind.

The big disconnect—what the researchers called a "gap"—appeared between what values parents *thought* they were prioritizing to their kids, and what the kids actually picked up. The parents claimed they were trying to raise caring children and that they prioritized morality and ethics over achievement, but that was not the message the kids were really receiving. The researchers' most striking finding: **80 percent of the kids believed that their parents put a higher value on achievement and accolades than they did on caring for others.** You can almost hear the dinner table conversations, with parents always asking, "Did you ace the test . . . win the game . . . get a part in the school play?" but never asking, "Were you a good kid today?" The vast majority of adolescents don't believe their parents *really* care about caring, perhaps, *because they don't see them do it.* Two-thirds of the students believe that doing well academically is their teachers' top value too. Only 15 percent thought their teachers valued "promoting caring in students."

Adolescents who don't prioritize caring—and why would they, since they likely don't get that message from their teachers or parents?—rate low on empathy and are less likely to volunteer, help a stranger, or tutor a friend. They'll be stuck in self-interest and they can't get out, effectively stunting their emotional growth and cutting themselves off from the Live to Give behaviors and attitudes that can lead to a happy, healthy, successful long life.

Sara Konrath, Ph.D., a leading social science researcher from Indiana University who specializes in philanthropy, recently ran a meta-analysis[7] (looking at all the stats from every study on the subject she could amass) of research on the adult attachment style of 25,000 college kids from 1988 to 2011. Without getting too deep on the subject, adult attachment style indicates how you relate to others now, but it's usually based on how your parents treated you as a small child. The healthiest attachment style is "secure" or being trusting, open, and loving in relationships. Less-healthy insecure styles are "dismissing" (saying, "I don't care" about relationships), "preoccupied" (being demanding, dependent, and clingy) and "fearful" (being too afraid of getting hurt to get involved). Konrath found that **secure connections are on the decline, dropping from 49 percent in 1988 to 42 percent in 2011.** Insecure connections are increasing, with the biggest jump in dismissing style, defined by having an attitude of not caring about making connections.

In another meta-analysis,[8] Konrath synthesized data for more than thirteen thousand U.S. undergraduate college students and found that their dispositional empathy—understanding the feelings of others or, simply, being able to put yourself in another's shoes—was "sharply dropping" from 1979 to 2009, and the decline had picked up speed over time.

Because empathy is often a prerequisite for giving behavior, this study speaks directly to the state of compassion in America among young people. A 2016 Pew Research survey[9] found that one-third of Americans do not even consider compassion for others to be among their *core values.*

After fifty years of Me Culture, we may be losing the ability to care.

RETURN TO SENDER—OR NOT

A unique measure of altruism is called "unplanned helping behavior," a random act of kindness or compassion that is spontaneous, often anonymous, with no apparent benefit to yourself. A classic example would be helping someone carry a stroller up the subway stairs or returning a lost wallet.

In 2001 and 2011, researchers fanned out to thirty-seven diverse urban centers in the United States, and twenty-six in Canada.[10] In each location, they "lost" sixty letters in stamped envelopes, with clearly written addresses. The letters were left in plain view on the sidewalk, in stores and phone booths (fewer of those in 2011), in busy parts of town with lots of foot traffic on sunny days. In 2001, a total of 3,721 letters were lost; in 2011, 3,745 went astray. Each letter was marked with a code to indicate where it'd been lost. Once the letters had been distributed, the study author, Keith M. Hampton, of Michigan State University, just sat back and waited for letters to be returned to the neutral-seeming addresses in Des Moines, Iowa, or Brandon, Manitoba.

The overall return rate in 2001 was 56.5 percent. The United States had a slightly higher return rate of 58.7 percent compared to Canada's 53.6 percent.

The story changed in 2011. The overall return rate dropped to 50.3 percent, with the United States falling 9.2 percent. Canada's rate stayed essentially flat. In ten years, the United States' unwitting study participants were nearly 10 percent less helpful. We're losing one percentage point in helpfulness per year!

Some theories about why we were more helpful in 2001: The author cited research that suggested the terrorist attacks on 9/11 increased Americans' civic engagement and prosocial helping behaviors (at least for a while). According to a U.S. General Social Survey, our trust in others hit a low point in 2012. Poverty rate and income inequality were high following the Great Recession, and public distrust led to a decrease in unplanned helping behavior. But, again, Canada didn't see a significant drop, and they felt the effects of the recession too.

Apart from horrible events and their fallout, possible explanations like fewer post office boxes didn't really pan out. The areas didn't see a drop in pedestrian traffic or change that much population-wise. By all indications, we're losing the will to make a tiny time sacrifice to do a solid for a stranger.

GO YOUR OWN WAY

How does one generation compare to another, in terms of caring?

Some enlightening reveals come from San Diego State University, where researchers compared values and priorities between Baby Boomers, Gen Xers and Millennials.[11] The younger generations ranked extrinsic (outside yourself) goals like money, image, and fame as more important than Boomers did when they were young. What's more, Gen Xers' and Millennials' "concern for others" (a category that included being charitable, having empathy, and pursuing a job that helps the society) and their "civic orientation" (being engaged in social justice, politics, and environmental concerns) fell from Boomer levels too. Although Boomers are thought of *by Millennials* as being self-interested, the data suggest that the reverse is more likely to be true.

Why are younger generations more self-focused? Perhaps we've trained them to be! We preach it. Have you attended a college graduation ceremony in the last fifteen years? Speakers are bound to offer advice, and the bottom line is often some version of "follow your bliss." Encouraging young minds to value their worth, find their true voice, and pursue their heart's desire might sound great at first listen. But if you cut away the flowery verbiage, what you're left with is yet another version of "you do you" and "indulge yourself."

Scott Galloway, professor of marketing at New York University's Stern School of Business, bestselling author and entrepreneur, once publicly excoriated the countless guest lecturers that fed students the "follow your passion" advice. "*What bullshit!*" he said. "Things that are 'passion'—luxury, food, entertainment, sports—those are massively over-invested. Less than one percent of the people who are passionate at those things are able to make a living at them."

We all know stories—some true, some urban legend—about the aspiring chef who loved grilled cheese and made a fortune in food trucks. Or the comedian who got famous doing YouTube skits and landed a series on Hulu. "There are a lot of well-publicized wins around people who follow their passion and become fabulously wealthy," Galloway continued. "I find that people who are telling you to follow your passion are already rich. And they typically got rich following their 'passion' of software that services health care scheduling. That was their passion? Their passion was getting rich so they could get a fast car and marry someone who's better looking than them."

That last part sounds a bit cynical, but Galloway is famous for not mincing words. His advice for his students: Your job is to find something you are really good at, something of value to others. Then do it for ten thousand hours to, with grit and perseverance, become great at it. By then, the economic accoutrements, relevance, prestige, and camaraderie that follow greatness will make you "passionate" about whatever "it" is. And remember money is not an end, it's a means. Think of money as the ink in your pen to write your altruistic life story or the fuel to make your story burn brighter.[12]

What story? That's for you to decide. Galloway teaches that the stories that bring fulfillment are the ones that involve serving others and building deep and meaningful relationships.

Steve recently trained his high school–age daughter in some research nerd skills by analyzing the language in graduation speeches of U.S. News & World Report's top-ranked colleges and universities. Using a meticulous methodology, she went sentence by sentence, and pared away anything that wasn't direct advice from speaker to the newly minted college graduates. Was the advice "you do you" or "help somebody else"?

Guess.

Less than 25 percent of all instructions to new graduates were about serving others. Much of the advice was the equivalent of "You're the bomb. You can crush the world, just find your passion, work hard, and you'll kill it!"

Wouldn't it be awesome if someone got up to address graduates at an Ivy League school and said, "You don't have to crush or kill the competition to get ahead. You don't have to be rich to grab the more attractive mate. In fact, stomping, etc. will actually hurt you, and prevent your success. You'll be much happier—and probably even make more money—if you gave up selfish goals and set out to help other people"? That speaker might be booed off the stage! A message of "making it" by serving others is not necessarily what ambitious young people are used to hearing.

And yet, telling them to pursue their "bliss" can cause a lot of stress and anxiety. Not everyone knows what their passion is, especially when they're twenty-two years old. It makes it seem like they *should* know, and if they don't, they're awash with doubt and fear. Some wonder how a passion for DJing in fraternity basements can translate into a lucrative career or give them a sense of deep fulfilment.

Without a meaningful mission, true fulfillment may be impossible.

Sara Konrath, Ph.D., wrote in a well-researched essay called "The Joy of Giving," "Over time, giving makes people see that they have an important role to play in relieving others' suffering and making others happy. . . . Giving increases givers' sense of meaning and purpose in life. Studies have found that people with a defined sense of purpose in life live longer and healthier lives than those with a less defined sense of purpose."[13]

Knowing the answer to "What's my *why*?" gives you direction. Being clueless about your *why* creates confusion, anxiety, and lostness. Me Culture might have you think, *If I can get 100,000 Instagram followers, I'll be okay.* Racking up followers might be a *goal.* Getting thousands of likes on your selfies will provide your brain with dopamine hits galore. But boosting your ego is not a *purpose.* It doesn't answer the question, "Why am I here?"

When you are doing good for others and are really great at it, you have a purpose. With purpose, passion and success will find you.

Author and *New York Times* columnist David Brooks has been exploring this topic for a while now. In 2014, he gave a TED Talk[14] about the internal conflict we all deal with in our pursuit of either résumé virtues (achievement, accolades) or eulogy virtues (how people will talk about you at your funeral). Live to Give attitudes and behavior are actually a boon for both résumé and eulogy virtues. They make you more cherished and beloved by friends and strangers *and* impress the colleagues and bosses who will rally behind you and give you promotions and raises. (We'll go into the specific scientific evidence about that in later chapters.)

The available evidence supports the idea that if you're happy, you'll be successful. It's not the other way around.[15]

If we were going to give a commencement address, first we'd pass out

T-shirts that say, "Passion is not purpose." Then we'd tell grads to reject Me Culture concepts like following your bliss. Just don't take the bait. Starting out your life with self-interest and the objective of crushing, killing, whatever, is worse than "bullshit," as Professor Galloway said. It's terrible advice that can lead you down the wrong path. Of course, it's tempting to indulge your interests and your ego and believe that random "passion" is going to make you rich. But that false promise is a distraction from finding purpose that could be helpful for others and wildly beneficial for you.

As you'll see in these pages, to be healthy, happy, and successful, the evidence does not support "Follow your bliss" but rather "Live to Give, and health, happiness, and success will find you." You'll feel plenty of passion in being great at serving the greater good.

> If your dream includes just you, it's too small.
>
> —Ava DuVernay

WE HAVE UPLIFT

A particularly insidious aspect of Me Culture is hyper-individualism, the idea that the goal of life is your own happiness, sufficiency, and the lofty concept of self-actualization (being the best version of you). You walk alone, and you have to rely on yourself to get where you're going. Hyper-individualism is covered on page one of any book that advocates the Me Culture brand of self-care, that we have to prioritize our own experience, and constantly ask, "Does this give me joy?"

In David Brooks's 2019 TED Talk,[16] he said:

I had fallen for some of the lies that our culture tells us. The first lie is that career success is fulfilling. I've had a fair bit of career success . . . but it hasn't given me any positive good. The second lie is I can make myself happy, that if I just win one more victory, lose fifteen pounds, do a little more yoga, I'll get happy. And that's the lie of self-sufficiency. But as anybody on their deathbed will tell you, the things that make people happy are the deep relationships of life, the losing of self-sufficiency. The third lie is the lie of the meritocracy. The message of the meritocracy is you are what you accomplish. . . . The emotion of the meritocracy is conditional love, you can "earn" your way to love.

While we pursue personal goals to achieve our own happiness and fill the empty feeling inside, we become blind to the needs and desires of other people, as well as numb to our "deeper longings," as Brooks put it, a sense of connection to others. Most world religions share the tenets of service and compassion and give people that sense of belonging to something bigger than themselves that feeds their souls.

The vortex of hyper-individualization, though, sucks us in with a lie, that if you achieve status and so-called success, you will receive love and feel happy. But by using society as a mirror to reflect your own worthiness, you hand off your self-worth to others. Somehow, we think happiness is our individual responsibility, while also depending on societal acceptance and validation to feel good about ourselves. Is happiness in our control or out of our control? Both? Neither? The contradictions of hyper-individualism take an emotional toll. We're confused about the source of fulfillment and no matter what we do to earn conditional love, it'll never be enough. No matter one's status, if we're focused solely on our individual happiness, we'll still feel alone, empty, and insecure.

Brooks wrote in his memoir *The Second Mountain: The Quest for a Moral Life*, "Eventually, most people realize that something is missing in the self-centered life. One way or another, people get introduced to the full depths of themselves, and the full amplitude of life. They realize that only emotional, moral, and spiritual food can provide the nourishment that they crave."[17]

Giving and helping others is a spiritual food that nourishes.

Once you get to a certain age, you can look at a few of the people you grew up with or knew back in the day and see how hyper-individualism made a mess of their lives. Their focus was so sharply and unwaveringly on themselves that they ruined relationships, flamed out in their career, and wound up lonely and bitter.

If you think of the happiest people you've ever known, always in a good mood, always smiling, they're invariably other-focused and part of something bigger than themselves. They have a glow about them that you do not totally understand, but you know you want some of the secret that they hold.

Many of us believe that if we only had more time and money, we would be happier. In fact, abundant research has found that *giving* our time and money makes us happier. By giving, we gain a priceless sense of community and belonging. Sara Konrath wrote in "The Joy of Giving," "Over repeated giving interactions, people start to meet like-minded others, feel more connected and less lonely, and increase their sense that others are there for them. In themselves, **social connections predict healthier and longer lives.**"

Think about it: almost every movie you've ever seen that could be described as "uplifting" has the same basic plot. It starts with a main character who is lost and alone. But once he or she experiences an intensive merging with a ragtag crew of fellow lost and alone souls, and they unite in a common cause to right wrongs, they find purpose and belonging. In the end, the characters have learned and grown, and they're joyful in their togetherness. The audience leaves the theater with a "feel-good" smile on their faces.

Uplift, the feeling, comes from joining together to do something for the greater good. You don't get that same warm glow from watching a movie about some entitled jerk who makes a fortune in Bitcoin. You might leave the theater fantasizing about what you'd do with some Bitcoin billions, your Gulfstream, and a gold-plated toilet. But do you *really* want to be the star of that hollow Me Culture movie? You'll probably get stabbed in the back by an underling before long.

Or do you want your life to be an uplifting We Culture story about banding together, making friends and allies, and doing amazing things that makes the whole world rejoice? We want to be in *that* movie, the one where dozens of people give you high fives as you get out of your fighter jet and one of the people you saved the day with, who was a former rival, has some light banter with you about who would be whose wingman.

One last quote from Brooks: "I now think the rampant hyper-individualism of our current culture is a catastrophe. . . . The whole cultural paradigm has to shift from the mindset of hyper-individualism to the relational mindset. The current historical moment has normalized selfishness, self-preoccupation, leaving us divided and alienated. We are down in the valley."

Fortunately, we can climb out of the valley. Our culture might be stuck in first-person gear. We've been indoctrinated to believe in it. But we can strip Me Culture away by reverting to our true human nature. We were not born to live and struggle alone. We were made for one another.

If you want to go fast, go alone.
If you want to go far, go together.

—African proverb

Survival of the Kindest?

Me Culture appeals to our sense of personal empowerment. We have a romantic attachment to self-sufficiency. The word "independence" was the United States' very first declaration, after all. The rough-and-ready American ideal is personified by the cowboy, the loner on a horse who doesn't talk much but does what he has to do to survive.

It's no wonder that, as Me Culture really took hold in the 1970s, the quintessential movie star was Clint Eastwood. He was the embodiment of "rugged individualism." All of his westerns from 1973's *High Plains Drifter* onward told the story of a mysterious drifter with questionable morals who always left heartache and a high body count in his wake. The Eastwood eye squints and pithy one-liners sent a clear signal to fans about what it takes to be brave and strong: don't show you care, don't get entangled, shoot straight.

In his 1859 breakthrough work *On the Origin of Species*, Charles Darwin wrote, "It hardly seems probable that the number of men gifted with such virtues . . . could be increased through natural selection." Exactly! If you're allergic to relationships and prone to gun battles, you probably won't live long enough to reproduce. And yet, many fierce individualists seem to believe that looking out for number one is the key to their survival.

By the way, Darwin didn't actually coin the phrase "survival of the fittest." His contemporary, English philosopher Herbert Spencer, came up with it. Spencer believed that history would forever be shaped by brawny types. (We know how wrong that theory is now; Tim Cook, Elon Musk, and Jeff Bezos aren't exactly cowering under the boots of professional wrestlers.) Darwin himself rejected the idea that strength or "fitness" ensured survival. He believed that the values of empathy, compassion, and altruism guaranteed sociological success. "Those communities which included the greatest number of the most sympathetic members would flourish best and rear the greatest number of offspring," he once wrote. A community that nurtured and supported each other would thrive and grow; a community that feared and reviled each other was bound to die out. A tribe of Live to Givers who sacrificed for each other, said Darwin, "would be victorious over most other tribes; and this would be natural selection."

In his book *The Compassionate Achiever: How Helping Others Fuels Success,* Christopher Kukk, Ph.D., studied Darwin's conclusions about the evolutionary necessity of compassion. He wrote, "[Darwin] calls compassion 'the almost ever-present instinct' when a fellow human witnesses the suffering of another. . . . [He] believed that compassion was a natural instinct that we all share. The bumper-sticker way of teaching and labeling Darwin's ideas as exclusively focused on the 'survival of the fittest' is not only misleading; it completely misses his idea that humanity's success hinges on its level of compassion."

A more accurate description of Darwin's core concept is "survival of the kindest." Kukk wrote, "Groups consisting of mainly 'survival of the kindest,' compassionate people will succeed more than they fail."

Our species started out in small tribes and grew into large civilizations, not because we fought to the death over scraps of meat, but because we shared our woolly mammoth steaks around the campfire and helped each other. Anthropologist Margaret Mead, when asked to pinpoint the first sign of civilization in ancient culture, didn't point to an artifact of a tool. It was proof of medical intervention, specifically a fifteen-thousand-year-old femur bone found at an archeological dig that showed signs that it'd been broken and had healed. Instead of leaving the ancient patient where he fell to be eaten by predators, someone in his tribe had gotten him to safety and cared for him until he healed.

"Helping someone else through difficulty is where civilization starts," said Mead.

The Crush-Kill-Destroy impulse of high-testosterone males is what American biologist Edward O. Wilson called "the Paleolithic curse" that harms society and prevents humans from making connections that enable us to survive and thrive. But if humans behaved like Dirty Harry or Pale Rider, society would break down. We'd be living in an apocalyptic world of every man, woman, child, and horse for themselves. If we lived in a state of constant competition with each other, we'd still be defending our caves with sharp sticks. But by cooperating, sharing, and caring as a species, we've advanced and endured. As Wilson wrote in *The Meaning of Human Existence,* "Within groups selfish individuals beat altruistic individuals, but groups of altruists beat groups of selfish individuals."[1]

Aiming for individual success puts your focus on yourself. Aiming for group significance puts your focus on others. The Buddha said, "In separation lies the world's greatest misery; in compassion lies the world's true strength." It seems obvious. And yet, culture perpetuates the myth that being a ruthless loner makes you strong, and that caring for others makes you weak and vulnerable. If you don't care, you are somehow protected.

But Darwin called it, long (long) before Clint Eastwood and Me Culture. We were biologically designed to help each other, and to benefit from serving others as a species *and* as individuals. The idea that competitive gladiator survival of the fittest behavior is evolutionary is actually incorrect. **Helping is evolutionary.** You see it in nature everywhere, in the animal kingdom, among species that hunt in packs or send out warning calls about nearby predators. Look at bees! Look at mushrooms! A vast mycelium network of fungus colonizes tree and plant roots and helps them share nutrients and communicate with each other about environmental dangers. Our human nature is to help each other too. The fact that it feels good to serve others is a sign of an evolutionary advantage for helping.

Cooperation flows from our following that baked-in impulse, and chaos is the inevitable result of ignoring it. By going against our species's "ever-present instinct" for compassion, as Darwin put it, and buying into the culture of self-interest, we are making ourselves anxious, depressed, and sick. Our human species was born to be caring and kind to each other; we evolved successfully because of it. It makes no sense for culture to push self-interest at this point in history when raging viral forces are at work to isolate us and therefore to make us weaker.

We have been duped into believing Me-ness will make us happy. By falling into that trap, we are denying our innate We-ness. The "survival of the fittest" bullies might believe that they should only look out for number one. But if we follow our true nature of "survival of the kindest" and look out for numbers two through seven billion, we will not only survive, we'll thrive.

> I tell my daughters . . . being a strong man includes being kind. That there's nothing weak about kindness and compassion. There's nothing weak about looking out for others.
> — President Barack Obama

BORN TO BE GOOD

High on the list of life skills parents try to instill in their kids: "It's fun to share!" It might not always seem like little humans are naturally inclined to play nice. We can think of some incidents at our own homes when our saying "Take turns!" might as well have been spoken in medieval French, for all the good it did. Children might be thought of as self-centered because they are exquisitely in touch with their needs and desires. But that does not mean they're selfish. The evidence shows that kids as young as two get more joy from giving than they do from getting.

An illustrative study[2] to support this was designed by a team of researchers led by Canadian social psychologist Elizabeth Dunn, Ph.D., at the University of British Columbia. For the experiment, the team brought twelve healthy toddlers under the age of two into their lab and introduced them to a few cute stuffed animal puppets. The toddlers were told that the puppets liked treats, and then the researcher fed them a Teddy Graham or a Goldfish cracker ("the toddler equivalent of gold," Dunn said), while the researchers playacted the puppet making yummy sounds.

Once the toddlers and the puppets sufficiently bonded over their mutual love of Goldfish crackers, the researchers placed empty bowls in front of the kid and the toy. The child was given eight crackers and asked if they would like to share some of their treats with the puppet.

Throughout this process, experts on facial expressions watched the toddlers closely for their emotional response. **The kids exhibited happiness when they received treats, but they demonstrated *even more happiness* when they gave their treats to the puppets, especially when they removed a cracker out of their bowl and placed it in the puppet's bowl themselves.** The study concluded, "By documenting the emotionally rewarding properties of costly prosocial behavior among children in the second year of life, this research provides foundational support for the claim that experiencing positive emotions when giving to others is a proximate mechanism for human cooperation and prosociality."

Toddlers were the perfect subjects for studying the inherent joy of "costly giving"—personal sacrifice. They were too young yet to be socialized about sharing, and blissfully ignorant of Me Culture influence. Their joy in giving away their own precious resources supports the idea that humans are born to serve others. We are hardwired to feel good about giving.

THE UNIVERSAL REWARD

Our mothers always say, "It's better to give than to receive." Turns out, Mom's advice plays out scientifically.

Dr. Dunn, an OG in the field, has conducted landmark research stretching beyond the borders of North America. A series of studies[3] by Dunn and her colleague Michael Norton, Ph.D., of Harvard Business School examined the emotional benefits of giving money away in 136 countries, rich and poor alike. Methodologies varied. One study asked subjects to recall past incidents of being generous, and to rate how happy it made them feel. Another asked Canadian and South African participants to either buy items for charity or for themselves and found that people were happier to shower others with gifts and cash than they were about buying things for themselves, regardless of cultural or economic context.

The entire world is alight with "warm glow," the feeling people get when they open their wallets and hearts for others. Warm glow is a universal reward, and a personal benefit. Dr. Sara Konrath's research[4] has determined that **between 86 and 90 percent of cultures that have been studied have shown that people receive physical health and well-being benefits from giving to others.** Researchers studied[5] hierarchies of values for people across more than sixty different nations (including the United States) over six continents (sorry, Antarctica) and found that giving to others was overwhelmingly considered the number-one value, "a universal," more precious than power, achievement, or pleasure.

Positive affect: the propensity to experience positive emotions and interact with others and with life's challenges in a positive way.

Researchers at Harvard measured[6] "social capital" in 142 countries and concluded that high levels of community trust and support— helping friends and family, volunteering, being a generally trusting person—were associated with greater life satisfaction and positive affect among 95 percent of the planet's population. **Independent of age, gender, income, religion, marital status, and education, subjects who self-reported high levels of social trust (having someone to count on, and being someone others could count on) were happier and less stressed out than those with trust issues.** It didn't matter if the subjects came from first, second, or third world countries. Feeling supported by a community and trusting that if you are in need, others will come to your aid makes people happier.

It might seem like a "no, duh" finding from the big brains at Harvard. But, then again, there are still plenty of people around the world who would advise putting trust in "our own" only. Emotionally, distrustful types are left out in the cold. By expecting the worst, they might protect themselves from betrayal. But they'll never bask in "warm glow" or feel the joy of connection despite the risks.

YOU KNOW WHAT HAPPENS WHEN YOU ASSUME . . .

An unfortunate universal truth of humankind is that we tend to make assumptions about others, including underestimating their altruism, falsely believing that they (whomever "they" are) aren't as pure as we are. Negative assumptions are often based on stereotypes. For example:

We assume one political party is more compassionate than the other.

The political climate in the United States couldn't be more divided, in part because of the assumptions Democrats make about Republicans and vice versa. It's only logical that, if you are a member of a political party, you ascribe to some of the ideology and values it upholds. The illogical part is assuming that, if your party is good and kind, then the other party must therefore be evil and cruel.

During the 2016 U.S. presidential campaign, researchers at Pennsylvania State University set out to determine whether different political party members stereotyped each other about how compassionate they were. In five separate studies,[7] some in person and some online, respondents consistently stereotyped Democrats/liberals as being more compassionate than Republicans/conservatives. Democrats, by the way, were more extreme in this opinion than Republicans. However, when members of both parties were assessed on their own personal values and beliefs about compassion, the results were pretty much the same across the board. The research showed that, as individuals, Democrats were no more or less compassionate than Republicans. Perceived differences, not reality, exaggerated political stereotypes.

We assume women are more empathetic than men. Researchers at the University of Oregon tested[8] this stereotype by having college students complete empathy tasks, like describing another person's emotional state. Women tended to be more accurate than the male subjects, especially when they were empathizing with other women. For another study of 108 men and women ages seventeen to forty-two, the subjects were again tested on their empathy skills, but this time, half were told that they'd receive payment for accuracy. The other half, the control, were not offered payment. Dangling cash as motivation worked. The empathetic accuracy of both men and women went up when they were promised payment, wiping out the previous study's gender difference completely.

On the one hand, it's nice to know that men, when motivated, can be just as empathetic as women. On the other hand, it's unfortunate that the men in the study (#notallmen) needed motivation to tap their empathy powers. Women just do this automatically with no expectation of extrinsic reward. Just saying. According to the women we discussed this finding with, they said their gender is well aware that caring and feeling for others is its own reward (#yesallwomen).

We assume the upper socioeconomic classes are more intelligent than lower socioeconomic classes. In terms of emotional intelligence and empathy, this stereotype is dead wrong. A University of California–San Francisco study[9] found that lower socioeconomic class individuals scored higher than their hoity-toity counterparts in empathetic accuracy, measured in how correctly they judged the feelings of other participants and picked up on facial cues in photos. It's been hypothesized that going through adversity (for example, poverty) makes people more sensitive and empathetic to the plight of others.

WHAT'S IN IT FOR THEM?

Although this assumption doesn't relate to stereotyping a particular group, it might be the most damaging of all. Research supports the notion that humans often view the entire world as if it were a used car lot. We see ourselves as the hapless buyers, and everyone else as a shady dealer who's motivated by self-interest and will do whatever it takes to come out ahead. Call it the skeptical "What's their angle?" automatic assumption.

Princeton University researchers tested[10] just how much people overestimate others' self-interest by going for the jugular. Okay, not exactly the jugular, but it did involve blood. The college student study subjects were given an information packet that included a dire warning about record lows in the American blood supply. Half of the subjects were urged to give blood and informed that the American Red Cross would pay donors $15 for the service. Half of the subjects were urged to donate but promised no payment. All of them were asked whether they would give blood, as well as how many of their peers could be expected to donate as well.

Sixty-three percent of the participants in the no-pay group agreed to donate; 73 percent of the blood-for-money group agreed. According to the researchers, that 10 percent difference did *not* indicate that a cash incentive made much of a difference in the subjects' willingness to give blood. Tell that to a car crash victim in the emergency department! We need all the blood donations we can get.

As for the estimation of the cash incentive's influence on their peers—the "What's in it for them?" self-interest assumption—the participants predicted that twice as many of their peers would give blood for money than donate for free. **Even if the majority of the participants volunteered to give their own vital fluid freely, they assumed that most of their peers would only be induced by the money.**

In a survey of Harvard undergraduates, students said their university valued "success" above all else. Their perception was of a cutthroat community of people clawing their way to the top. Students did not think that Harvard embodied compassion and didn't see this as a value that the school stood for. In fact, they ranked "compassion" near the bottom of the list of Harvard's attributes. However, when students were asked about their own individual values, "compassion" was at the top of the ones they personally held.

The students overwhelmingly said they were altruistic themselves, but their university (comprised of these same students) were not? What a striking disconnect! The students might be as altruistic as they believe they are, but they sure lacked awareness about how their peers felt about themselves. Harvard students drastically underestimated their peers' care and concern for others. As a result, Harvard asked their new freshmen enrolling in the Class of 2015 to take a pledge to help make it an institution where "the exercise of kindness holds a place on par with intellectual attainment."[11]

It's too bad that we expect others to be more self-interested than we are or than they are. That has to change. Essentially we are asking you to adopt a mindset that matches the way people actually are in the studies, rather than cynical assumptions. It shouldn't be a hard lift. If we all start assuming the best about each other, it'll be easier to make the personal paradigm shift toward serving others. Instead of an adversarial "What's in it for them?" point of view, adapting to "How can we help each other?" would benefit us all, and make Darwin—the patron saint of adaptation—proud.

ASKED AND ANSWERED

The Bible says, "Ask and you shall receive." But the common misconception is that asking for help—or directions (you know who you are)—is likely a sign of weakness or an imposition to be resented or ignored.

Researchers at Columbia University tested[12] the hypothesis that people underestimate the likelihood of receiving help if it's asked for directly. For one study, researchers sent fifty-two college students out into New York City streets with clipboards in hand, with the objective of asking complete strangers to fill out a two-page questionnaire. Before they set out on this mission, the participants were asked how many strangers they thought they'd have to ask in order to get five completed questionnaires. On average, they estimated that it'd take twenty asks to hit their quota. For every single "yes," they thought they'd get three "bug off, kid, you're bothering me."

The estimates were off by a whopping 50 percent. For every "yes," they got only two "no"s.

They repeated the study with different requests, such as asking strangers if they could borrow their cell phones, escort them across campus to the gym, or give directions. Across all variations of the "direct ask" study, the stats were consistent. Every time, the **participants underestimated by 50 to 66 percent how often strangers would say "yes."** The study didn't measure how happy the askees were about helping, but they did help, more often than the students expected.

At first, we were surprised by the results, assuming that New Yorkers would be way too busy to stop and fill out a two-page survey with no incentive. Hand over your cell phone to a complete stranger? That sounds crazy. But we fell right into the assumption trap too. Upon further analysis, we looked back at the three most recent incidents of being approached on the street by young people in Greenpeace T-shirts, tablets and pamphlets in hand, asking for "five minutes of your time." We groaned inwardly yet stopped to talk . . . about half of the time. Directions? Probably 75 percent. But that cell phone thing? We are split on it ourselves. One would lend it, the other would definitely not. (It's more of a germ thing.) We won't tell you which one of us. Even we have limits.

KINDNESS IN TIMES OF CRISIS

Helping behavior is never more heroic, and evident, than in natural disasters. When tragedy strikes, humans rush in to help. We have all seen this after earthquakes and tornadoes when community members dig in the rubble for hours, days, weeks, to find the missing. Stanford University psychology professor and author of *The War for Kindness* Jamil Zaki, Ph.D., calls the impulse for individuals to band together in times of crisis "catastrophe compassion." This banding together is the rule, not the exception. It's natural and predominant. Stories that suggest otherwise—like accounts of survival-of-the-fittest ruthless behavior during Hurricane Katrina, for example—often turn out not to be true.[13]

John Drury, Ph.D., a social psychologist at the University of Sussex in Brighton, England, has researched[14] shared social identity among the survivors of natural disasters and other emergencies. If people have a common experience and identity because of having lived through it, they're more motivated to help each other. More community help is associated with better outcomes, such as faster recovery and less posttraumatic stress disorder (PTSD).

Solidarity makes us resilient. If we're all in it together, we're more likely to get through disasters in one piece.

EVERY FIGHT IS ONLY ONE ROUND

Classic scene from a teen movie: a circle forms around two kids as they square off, while the crowd eggs them on to fight. *The Karate Kid* canon affirms the concept of "bystander effect," the phenomenon of people being less likely to intervene in a fight, or any emergency, when we're in a big crowd rather than alone. The idea is that when there are others around, we might think it is somebody else's responsibility to intervene. When we are alone, and there is no one else to help, we respond.

Some of us have actually been tested in real life, and found out the answer to the question "What would I do?" in that kind of situation. The rest of us can only guess how we'd react. Me Culture would tell us that the risk of intervening would offer little or no reward. But our better angels—and our evolutionary instinct—don't care about risk-reward ratios. Our humanity makes us all gym teachers who are ready, willing, and able to break up the cafeteria fight before it gets ugly.

Researchers at the University of Copenhagen examined[15] the human nature of stepping up in real-life situations by collecting data from 219 actual conflicts that were caught on public closed-circuit surveillance cameras in the United Kingdom, the Netherlands, and South Africa. **In nine out of ten incidents, at least one bystander stepped up.** The 90 percent helpfulness stat held up in all three countries in the study's scope. What's more, the bigger the crowd, the more likely it was that someone would jump in, debunking long-standing beliefs about the bystander effect and our natural inclination to help first, regret it (or not) later.

We have been taught to assume that, in an emergency, help is not coming. But, in fact, it will come, 90 percent of the time.

THE PARABLE OF THE BAD SAMARITAN

The most famous case of the bystander effect is used as a prime example of the phenomenon. Too bad what's written about the case in the most popular undergraduate psychology textbooks isn't actually true.

Kitty Genovese, a twenty-eight-year-old bartender, was stabbed to death at 2:30 a.m. outside her apartment building in Kew Gardens, Queens, New York, on March 13, 1964. Her murder was reported in the *Long Island Press* and the *New York Times*. Both newspapers described the killing, and the even more shocking revelation that thirty-eight residents of Genovese's building watched from their windows for half an hour as the killer, a man named Winston Moseley, attacked the young woman not once, not twice,

(Cont'd)

but three separate times, and that none of the witnesses tried to help or called the police. They just let her die alone on the cold ground. According to the newspaper stories, the witnesses might as well have made popcorn and pulled up chairs to watch a murder from inches away, as if it were on TV.

The stories triggered national disgust and horror, and shamed the residents of Kew Gardens. It seemed hard to believe that thirty-eight witnesses would do nothing to help. And yet people just accepted the stories as fact. No one said, "I smell BS." People do underestimate kindness and altruism, as we've established. And the account came from the *New York Times*, the paper of record. If the *Times* said it was true, then it must be. An urban legend was born.

Discrepancies came to light at Moseley's trial. For one, Genovese was attacked twice, not three times. The two attacks happened at different locations, making it impossible for more than three dozen people to witness both. Sightlines at either site were limited too. What's more, witnesses who could hear or see what was going on *did* intervene. One witness shouted, causing Moseley to flee after the first attack. Other witnesses claimed that they called the police, who blew them off. (This was before the 911 emergency call system existed, and apparently, at that precinct, calls of distress weren't always taken seriously.) Plus, a witness did go to Genovese, and held the dying woman in her arms while they waited for the ambulance. Genovese was still alive when it arrived. She did not die alone.

These facts came up at the trial, but instead of rewriting the story of the gruesome indifferent witnesses, the falsehoods stuck and became undisputed "truth."

In 2007, psychologists Mark Levine, at the University of Exeter, and Rachel Manning, of the University of Buckingham, both in the United Kingdom, took another look[16] at the Kitty Genovese story. They went back to the archives, reinterviewed witnesses, reexamined the trial testimony, and refuted the myth that good people did nothing when a member of their community was being stabbed to death at their door. What Levine and Manning found fascinating, as do we, was how intractable the Parable of the Bad Samaritan has been.

Some experts who based their research of the bystander effect on this particular case have refuted the refuters, saying that the witnesses changed their story at the trial so they didn't look bad. But the actual evidence doesn't support that claim. The refusal to accept a more accurate version of the events has become a parable in itself. Because we're conditioned to believe that people are inclined not to help each other in emergencies, we might hesitate to do so if a savage stabbing were to take place outside our own window.

The science says otherwise. It's not a simple question of "What would I do?" Bystander intervention is more nuanced than that. Levine had explored a number of factors[17] about the topic, and found a range of reactions:

In a "street violence scenario," friends are quicker to step up than strangers.

If the witnesses identify with the social status and gender of the victim, intervention is encouraged by the presence of a group.

If the victim is a woman, a larger group of female witnesses is more likely to help than a smaller group.

If more women are in the crowd of bystanders, they are less likely to help a stranger victim. But if there are a lot of female bystanders, men were quicker to intervene.

Guys might want to play the hero and rush in. Women apparently find strength in each other's presence. If you care about the victim, you're more likely to rally the crowd to help. There is no monolithic "bystander effect." Each case provides us with insight into group dynamics. But perpetuating the myth that all groups are heartless cowards in emergencies doesn't help anyone. It hurts us all.

YOU CAN'T TAKE IT WITH YOU

This chapter started with toddlers, and it ends with grouchy old men. You might think, knowing Grandpa as you do, that older men are set in their ways and their curmudgeon quality is not going to change.

Not so fast! Research has found that giving behavior increases in old age. Apparently, after a lifetime of self-interest, old-timers realize that the only joy worth a damn is found in serving others.

Ulrich Mayr, Ph.D., and his team at the University of Oregon[18] used functional magnetic resonance imaging (fMRI) machines to scan the brains of eighty participants between the ages of twenty and sixty-four. For one experiment, money was withdrawn from the subjects' personal bank accounts and moved into that of a charitable organization. For some, the cash transfer increased activity in the nucleus accumbens, a "reward center" in the brain. This activation occurred in 24 percent of the thirty-five and under subjects. But it happened for 75 percent of the fifty-five and older crew. Not only that, the older participants champed at the bit to give their money away to charity, volunteer to be studied for the experiment, and self-assess as agreeable and empathetic at a higher rate than their younger counterparts.

At sixty, people give a three times larger share of their income to charity compared to twentysomethings, and are 50 percent more likely to volunteer to serve others,[19] possibly because they have more money and time to spare. Maybe it's a status thing. Psychological motivation is hard to pin down. But Mayr's fMRI results show that the old-timers authentically enjoyed giving. Brain scans don't lie. However they might've behaved when they were younger, Mayr's senior citizen participants were genuinely happy to give to people in need. The older folks figured out over time, with trial-and-error and life experience, that helping others feels a lot better and is more significant than material acquisition and the trappings of so-called success. The important message to young people: skip the "getting" years of racking up glory and money. Go right to what old-timers have learned about significance by becoming a Live to Giver now.

For a Canadian study,[20] researchers rounded up 648 older people who scored low on agreeableness and had them do three weeks of loving-kindness meditation or kind acts exercises. At a two-month follow-up, the subjects were tested again to see if their baseline agreeableness changed. Both the other-focused meditation and the kindness exercises significantly reduced their depression, increased life satisfaction, and made the curmudgeons a little less curmudgeonly. Spoiler alert! This practice universally benefits everyone, not just cranky old men or select do-gooders.

There's hope for your Thanksgiving dinners yet! By learning how to be compassionate, Gramps can have a brighter outlook on life. By being kind (and patient) with him, you will reap the benefits of altruism too.

When we heed our human nature, our evolutionary imperative to give to others and help each other, we survive. If we are as giving as we were born to be, we thrive. If we can try to shift our low expectations about the kindness and compassion of others, we can become even more giving and grateful in return.

By giving, we get so much back. That's the paradox of altruism. Can you be genuinely other-focused, while gleefully receiving the personal benefits as well?

Short answer: yes.

Longer answer: chapter 3, coming right up.

Many of us think that compassion drains us, but I promise you it is something that truly enlivens us.

—Roshi Joan Halifax

3

The Giving Paradoxes

This book is about the amazing power of serving others, and the beneficial effects it has on your own physical and mental health, happiness, emotional and psychological well-being, and even your professional success. But the scientific evidence points to a very important *secret* about serving others and becoming an effective Live to Giver.

The secret lives in a *paradox*.

Paradox: a seemingly absurd or self-contradictory statement or proposition that when investigated or explained proves to be well founded or true.

For example, "Less is more." Less is the opposite of more, so how can it be more? One of us has recently sat through a Disney princess movie marathon with one of our kids, and less is definitely more in that situation.

Another is, "I can't live with or without you." Well, Bono, which is it? With or without? And if you can't live either way, why are you still breathing? (We kid Bono with the deepest respect; he is a true Live to Giver in his work to fight global poverty and disease.)

The premise of this book might seem like one giant paradox: serving others benefits *you*. And it absolutely does.

But there is another, very important, striking paradox, backed by rigorous evidence: to be at the top of your altruism game, you need to have a healthy dose of self-interest too, so you don't become a doormat. Doormats get trampled on and never make it to be effective Live to Givers.

In order to understand this, we will leave the doctor world for a moment, and go into the world of business. Specifically, we need to examine the research of one of the world's foremost organizational psychologists, Adam Grant, Ph.D., who has spent years studying how other-interest and self-interest impact job performance and occupational success.

TO BEST SERVE OTHERS, YOU HAVE TO TAKE CARE OF YOURSELF TOO

It's generally assumed that if someone is highly other-interested, that he or she is *not* self-interested. That would make sense if serving others were on a single continuum with extreme other-interest on one end, and extreme self-interest on the other, with most of us landing somewhere in between. As such:

Other-interest ←—————————————→ Self-interest

Grant found that highly giving people occupied the very top of the success scales. Interestingly, he found that they also occupied the very bottom of the success scales. What could explain this dichotomy? What made the most giving workers take such divergent trajectories in their success? In his book *Give and Take: A Revolutionary Approach to Success,*[1] Grant explained that there are actually *two* independent axes (plural of axis; not a pair of serial-killer accessories): one for self-interest and one for other-interest:

Low other-interest ←—————————→ High other-interest

Low self-interest ←—————————→ High self-interest

Grant's research shows that other-interest and self-interest do not exist on the same continuum at all. They are two completely separate and distinct mindsets. What this means is that if you're high on one, you are not necessarily low on the other. For example, high self-interest does not automatically mean low other-interest, and vice versa. Because they are independent axes, you can be high or low *on both.*

Those who are high in self-interest and low in other-interest are **EGOMANIACS** (our term, not Grant's). They are extremely selfish people, out only for themselves, and don't care about anyone else. Although being an egomaniacal power addict is a decent strategy for a Bond villain or Gordon Gekko, for real people in real workplaces, it's bound to fail. Everyone hates selfish, greedy jerks, and in the end, they don't get ahead. (Later on, we'll present the data that explain how we came to this conclusion.)

Those who are low in self-interest and low in other-interest are **SLOUCHES.** They couldn't care less about their own success or anyone else's. In fact, they don't really care about anything. Another term for them is apathetic.

People who are low in self-interest and high in other-interest are **DOORMATS,** for lack of a better term. This type not only bring fresh-baked cookies to the office, they also take on the overflow work that no one else wants to do. They let people walk all over them. Despite their service for others, they don't do well in the workplace either. For one thing, they're used and abused by Egomaniacs, and they're more likely to burn out.

People who are high in both axes are **LIVE TO GIVERS.** Grant calls them "otherish" in contrast to "selfish," and they are the most successful in the workplace. Grant's data shows this very clearly, especially in any occupation that requires teamwork, like service industries, sales, financial advising, politics, and even humanitarian work. People who are successful in harmonizing (or integrating) self- and other-interest will rise.

Live to Givers care about their own success *as well as* the success of their colleagues and the team at large. They sacrifice for others, while maintaining their own interest too. Their giving behaviors and attitudes are the most sustainable because they aren't emptying themselves out by giving in an unsustainable or unhealthy way. They keep some glory for themselves, and it fuels their ability to share it with others.

Researcher-storyteller Brené Brown says the secret to sustaining compassion, or what the most compassionate people have in common, is *boundaries*.[2] The most compassionate people have very clear boundaries that they insist others respect. They are very clear about what is okay and what is not okay, and they enforce that with the people in their lives. So it is radical compassion for others, predicated by well understood boundaries. The boundaries allow it to be sustainable.

Live to Givers realize that serving others also has beneficial effects for themselves, and they want those effects for themselves. Reaping the benefits is not *why* they help others; it is a byproduct of giving that they are all too happy to receive. And why not? Knowing that serving others is the best medicine for yourself does *not* ruin or prevent the beneficial effects of helping from happening. (We will show you data on that later.) Perhaps knowing that serving others also serves themselves makes them the most effective helpers and givers. The effect of being a Live to Giver is on the "live" part. It's the *how* they do so well at work, are effortless givers, and seem so full of energy, good health, and happiness.

Building upon the framework first described by Grant, and now updated and informed by all the data curated for this book, this is how we organize the four quadrants created by the two axes, with Live to Givers being the optimal for success:

	High other-interest	Low other-interest
High self-interest	Live to Giver	Egomaniac
Low self-interest	Doormat	Slouch

Grant calls both types that are high in other-interest Givers. They are at the top (Live to Givers) *and* the bottom (Doormats) of the success and performance chart. In any workplace, colleagues and managers who are Givers are preferable to Takers (Grant's term for those low in other-interest; our Egomaniacs). But if you are a Giver, you need some degree of self-interest to stop Takers from walking all over you. If extreme other-interested types can add a healthy dollop of self-interest to the mix, they can change from Doormats to Live to Givers, and enjoy greater success and longevity in their careers.

Now let's flip back from the business world to our world, medicine, to see that this paradox happens in health care too. Researchers at the University of Ghent, Belgium, set out to determine what factors can predict academic performance in medical students. The longitudinal study[3] of more than six hundred students tracked their performance and personality traits over a seven-year period. More than any other trait, the self-focused trait of conscientiousness—being diligent—was an "increasing asset" for the students. They always needed diligence in their studies to do well. But in later years when the students started working with patients in a clinical environment and needed to collaborate with each other in teams, **students who demonstrated other-interest traits—like extroversion, openness to helping, and agreeableness to assist classmates—performed at the highest level.** When they used the full force of their personality by helping other students *and* pushing themselves at the same time, they did the best.

To shine the brightest, turn your light on others.

Stop us before we paradox again.

Our vantage point is similar to Grant's. We are not only about workplace performance and "success," but also physical and mental health, happiness and fulfillment, and emotional and psychological well-being. The same combo—high other-interest *and* high self-interest—for the best outcomes in those categories still applies. Grant advocates that a healthy dose of self-interest is necessary to accept support from others. This is important because the ability to receive help from others fosters the ability to give help in return. Mutual help makes us more effective Live to Givers.

In a 2008 speech at the World Economic Forum, Bill Gates, founder of Microsoft and one of the wealthiest people on the planet, reminded us that Adam Smith—widely considered the father of capitalism and the author of *The Wealth of Nations,* who believed strongly in the value of self-interest for society—opened his first book with the following lines: "How selfish soever man may be supposed, there are evidently some principles in his nature, which interest him in the fortunes of others, and render their happiness necessary to him, though he derives nothing from it, except the pleasure of seeing it."

Gates went on to say, "There are two great forces of human nature: self-interest and caring for others." By harnessing the two great forces of self- and other-interest, which Gates called "a hybrid engine," you can ride them to the top and enjoy a long, healthy, satisfying life.

DON'T TREAD ON ME

Actual doormats have clear borders, whether rectangular, square, or in the shape of a cat head. Human Doormats need a healthy dose of self-interest to balance their giving and to define their boundaries to others and themselves. Endlessly giving or emptying your tanks without any concern for yourself can attract users who will take advantage, cause burnout, and lead to the erasure of self. Grant calls giving overextension with no protective self-interest "pathological" altruism, an "unhealthy focus on others to the detriment and total disregard of your own needs." Being low on self-interest while being high on other-interest can habituate Doormats to feeling uncomfortable about accepting any help at all. Without boundaries or support, it's no wonder they fall apart.

Some researchers say continuous giving with no concern for your own well-being—"unmitigated communion"—puts you at high risk for poor mental health. (The opposite behavior, continuous taking with no concern for others' well-being, is called "unmitigated agency," and is also harmful in different ways; think Egomaniac.) According to a Carnegie Mellon University study,[4] unmitigated communion is associated with "a negative view of self [and] turning to others for self-evaluative information." Relying on others for self-esteem leads to "overinvolvement with others and a neglect of the self," said the authors. Doormat-ism might sound sad and needy. But the unmitigated version is unsustainable, a clear sign of low self-esteem and a precursor for psychological distress.

Ninety-nine times out of a hundred, when we talk about compassion and altruism in media interviews, our headline advice is to get in the habit of asking, "How can I help?" In the case of unmitigated communion, we'd turn that around and tell extreme Doormats to start asking, "What about me?" to inch toward the center of the self-interest axis.

IS IT BETTER TO BE LIKED OR RESPECTED?

The term "badass" has incredible staying power despite its unsavory appeal in a literal sense. A badass is someone who tells it like it is, and is so good at what they do, they always win. Plus, they do it with a certain kind of cool (style points), but not always with politeness.

It is absolutely possible to be a total badass while being other-focused. The two are not mutually exclusive. To be other-focused, you will have to be a bit of a rebel, because We-ness is not always the societal norm. Also, altruism is not for the faint of heart. You might have to consider jumping in and breaking up fights between strangers, rolling up your sleeve and donating blood freely, and climbing rubble after an earthquake. To crack open your mind and really see another person's needs, you need to have wherewithal, grit, and some mental toughness.

Agreeableness—how positive, pleasant, and polite people seem to behave in social interactions—is one of the Big Five personality traits (along with extroversion, conscientiousness, openness, and neuroticism) that are partly innate. Adam Grant wrote in *Give and Take* that up to half of your agreeableness quotient may be hereditary. It's commonly assumed that agreeableness is on the same continuum as other-interest. The more other-interested you are, the greater your agreeableness (appearing warm, friendly, considerate); the less other-interested you are, the greater your disagreeableness (appearing cold, unfriendly, inconsiderate).

Grouping other-interest with agreeableness (and self-interest with disagreeableness) makes sense at first glance. Anecdotally, if you look at the people in your life who are the most generous and compassionate, the majority of them are probably sweethearts. If you look at the ornery people in your life, they're probably stingy with affection, time, and money. The benevolent, beautiful, bubbly, agreeable Glinda in *The*

Wizard of Oz was the do-gooder who helped Dorothy. The sadistic, ugly, cackling, disagreeable Wicked Witch of the West tried to kill Dorothy—*and her little dog too.* Archetypically, we associate agreeableness with being "nice," and disagreeableness with selfish disregard for others.

But linking agreeableness with other-interest doesn't work. Grant has found that there isn't a reliable correlation between the two.

In the workplace, Givers share credit, mentor, offer a hand up, and elevate the team for its collective success. Takers are climbers who only care about their own success.

Let's pause for a second while you make a mental list of the people in your workplace who are Givers and Takers . . . that didn't take long!

Now, some of the Givers on your list might also be grouchy, curt, rude, not someone you'd necessarily want to hang out with after work. Among the Takers, you might find some people who are charming, chatty, and nice (at least to your face). Being helpful and giving isn't necessarily about being agreeable and pleasant. In fact, the biggest fakers and schemers can be agreeable on the outside but motivated only by self-interest on the inside.

Agreeableness and other-interest are, again, *two separate, independent axes.* The agreeable–disagreeable continuum is a distinct third axis that is independent from other-interest and self-interest axes. With three axes at play, we've got a lot of possible combinations.

To mention a few, **those who are high in self-interest, low in other-interest, and disagreeable are TYRANTS.** In his lectures, Grant compares them to Cersei Lannister in *Game of Thrones.* They don't care about being liked or about what you have to say.

Those who are low in other-interest, high in self-interest, and agreeable are UNDERMINERS, perhaps even worse than Tyrants. Some would say that both types should be forced to walk naked through King's Landing while the citizens shout "Shame!" and hurl rotten vegetables at them. With Tyrants, what you see is what you get. Underminers are deceptive. They might applaud and encourage you, but they'll just do whatever is best for themselves. Insincere "Love it!" people are, in a way, wolves in sheep's clothing.

Those who are high in other-interest, high in self-interest, and

either agreeable or disagreeable are LIVE TO GIVERS. It might be more fun and easier on your nerves to be around agreeable people, but as Grant said in a TED Talk on the subject, "Disagreeable Givers are the most undervalued people in our organizations, because they're the ones who give the critical feedback that no one wants to hear but everyone needs to hear."[5]

A Live to Giver who is as disagreeable as the situation warrants is actually the *most* other-interested, because they're *giving* you a criticism for a reason. Through rigorous vetting and challenging weak ideas, they make themselves unpopular while pushing the team toward greatness. They're not going to just tell you want you want to hear. By telling the truth, they're looking out for others. By issuing sincere challenges, they elevate the team, even if they worry your last nerve doing it.

This fits with personal relationships as well. The people who love us the most tell us the hard truths we need to hear, no matter how much they might hurt. Truth-telling Live to Givers are not always easy to work or live with. But by giving honesty at the cost of likeability, they are sometimes the most giving of all.

THE EFFECTIVE GIVER

One last paradox: the more you try to give, the less impact you might actually make.

Some people give to any charity or person who asks for help. And some are more discerning about investing themselves in others.

Mazz knows a guy, we'll call him Bert, who is a very discerning giver. He's on the board of two charities that work toward finding cures for horrible diseases. Bert donates significant time and money to these causes. If you asked him for a donation to a different, equally worthy cause, he'd say, "Nope!" and make you feel bad that you even asked. Bert might come off badly by refusing to give to other charities. But he knows his mind and his heart. He's extremely committed to the two causes he cares deeply about, and

(Cont'd)

through his efforts, he's raised a fortune for them, brought about real change, and helped real people. Bert makes a real impact in his two orgs, and he's able to see the results of it.

Mazz knows another guy, we'll call him Ernie, who is on the board of every charity you can think of. He gives money to dozens of organizations that benefit health care, the environment, social justice. You name the charity, from the Red Cross to the United Way, he's involved with it, but probably only superficially. Ernie comes off as the nicest, most caring guy on the planet. But Ernie's impact is minimal. He's "all show, no go," and is less likely to get the Live to Give benefits of his altruism, since it's only for appearances.

The discerning grouch who says "no" most of the time might actually be the more effective giver.

The indiscriminating sweetheart who says "yes" to everything might actually be the less effective giver.

FINALLY, AN OXYMORON

An oxymoron is like a paradox because it's a contradiction. The difference is, a paradox is a statement or an action. An oxymoron is a description that juxtaposes two words that seem to cancel each other out.

Jumbo shrimp.

Bittersweet.

Instant classic.

Silent scream.

And . . . **altruistic egoism.**

Egoism: being motivated by your own interests and desires.

Hungarian-Canadian endocrinologist Hans Selye, M.D., wrote the 1956 book *The Stress of Life*, popularized the term "stress," and connected the dots between stress and health. He's also credited with originating the term "altruistic egoism." Selye realized decades ago that being other-focused could buffer the effects of stress on health and benefit not only the receiver but the giver too.[6]

There is a whole domain of philosophy around altruistic egoism, and the examination of whether or not altruism (the belief in and practice of selfless concern for the well-being of others) is really other-focused versus another mode of egoism (being motivated by self-interest). Can there be such a thing as public-interest or other-focus if everything we do always comes back to how it makes us feel?

Bob Buford wrote in *Halftime: Moving from Success to Significance,* "I am committed to practice 'altruistic egoism.' (Altruistic egoism means gaining personal satisfaction by helping others. It . . . counts as greatest gain the goodwill of one's neighbors)."

The philosophical debate about whether true selflessness is even possible raged between social psychologists C. Daniel Batson, Ph.D., who believes that pure altruism *does* exist through empathy, and Robert Cialdini, Ph.D., who believes that we suffer when we witness others' pain, and we only help them to make ourselves feel better. It's a circular debate that always seems to end in a stalemate. (We'll pick up the discussion over motivations for altruism in a later chapter.)

What does "pure" altruism look like? Mother Teresa? Using all of the Infinity Stones to wish Thanos out of existence, but dying in the process like Ironman? Even that, one could argue, could be seen as a selfish act if the sacrifice relieved Tony Stark's own pain at the idea of the world ending, and secured his legacy as the savior of Earth.

We really don't spend too much time thinking about philosophical arguments, or an other-focus purity test. We're science guys. We care about the evidence behind the health benefits of giving, caring, connecting, uplift, empathy, and compassion. And there are a *lot,* for you and for whomever you shine your light on.

Perhaps you've heard the phrase "zero-sum game." The best way to explain it is to picture a cake. Maybe it's chocolate. Maybe it's carrot. Let's go with chocolate. Say your friend eats the entire cake. One person gets cake; one person doesn't. That's the zero-sum game: 1 winner—1 loser = 0.

In a "non-zero-sum game," both you and your friend have your cake and eat it too. Plus, you put on a movie or the big game, laugh, maybe have some wine (Steve) or a beer (Mazz), and reward hormones light up both of your brains. One person's happiness doesn't mean that someone else must be unhappy. By giving, everyone gets the goods plus more: $1 + 1 = \infty$.

In a Live to Give world, we all get cake.

Altruism—pure or egoist, who cares?—is a non-zero-sum game. The "We" wins, every time! It's bi-directional, meaning it works both ways. The giver and the receiver benefit when one person helps and supports another.

As a wonder drug, other-focus is unlike any available treatment because, unlike prescription medications, there are essentially no adverse events, no long list of warnings in tiny print on the label or spoken at unintelligible speed on TV commercials. The safety profile is 100 percent clean. There is nothing wrong with knowing and appreciating that helping others with a giving heart also helps you. No moral failing in basking in "warm glow." No harm, no foul in doing good for others while enjoying the byproducts (like preventing burnout and reducing stress) of your genuine caring for another human being.

The vast majority of messages that you hear today, especially if you're young, are about getting to the top. Having that self-focus locks people inside their own heads. It's all about you.

But after you reach the peak, you realize that there's no *there* there. And then you see a more purposeful mountain to climb, what David Brooks calls "the second mountain," that of doing what you can to bring happiness, help, and joy to others.

We often tell people to just skip climbing that first mountain entirely, and go directly to the second. Just skirt the base of Mt. Selfish, and start your ascent of Mt. Selfless, and the data shows your entire life will be more meaningful, healthy, and happy. The view at the top of that mountain is much nicer, and maybe you have brought those you impacted along with you to enjoy it together.

To get there-there, you don't have to grapple with the debate of egoism versus altruism. The only conscious choice to make is to invite other people into your consciousness in a balanced way. Let in their needs and thoughts without letting them trample all over you.

And then, you'll be a Live to Giver, as agreeable or disagreeable as you want to be, which, as you'll see on these pages, is what promotes health and happiness, according to science.

You might have reached Live to Give status already. You might be depressingly far from it. The best way to find out? Turn the page and take the "How Self-Serving Are You?" Quiz.

One of the most powerful forces in human nature
is our belief that change is possible.

—Shawn Achor

How Self-Serving Are You?

Take the quiz below to find out.

Using the scale, please rate your level of agreement or disagreement next to each of the following twenty statements. Please answer with as much honesty as possible.

STRONGLY DISAGREE	DISAGREE	UNDECIDED	AGREE	STRONGLY AGREE
1	2	3	4	5

____ 1. Helping others is usually a good use of my time.

____ 2. If the opportunity presents itself, I enjoy doing what I can to help people in need.

____ 3. If I found a wallet in the back seat of an Uber, I would try to return it to the owner.

____ 4. Helping the people I love is one of the greatest joys in my life.

____ 5. In an emergency, like if someone were hit by a car, I'd try to help the person in need in any way I could.

____ 6. If a friend called and needed me right away, it would feel wonderful to drop everything and help.

___ 7. I believe that doing volunteer work for humanitarian causes is very rewarding.

___ 8. I would stop to give directions to lost out-of-towners.

___ 9. Volunteering my time gives me a warm feeling.

___ 10. I believe that donating time or money to good causes is important.

___ 11. Helping senior citizens is everyone's societal responsibility, even if they're not in our own family.

___ 12. Teaching compassion should be part of the curriculum for preschoolers.

___ 13. I want to donate my organs when I die.

___ 14. If I received a mass email asking for volunteers for community and school events, I would sign up.

___ 15. Helping people makes me feel at peace with myself.

___ 16. If a person behind me in the checkout line had just one or two items, I would let them go ahead of me.

___ 17. Helping people in need makes me feel proud, but it's not something to brag about.

___ 18. Helping others does *not* make them dependent, it gives them breathing room to help themselves.

___ 19. If a natural disaster struck, I would contribute money to help the victims.

___ 20. Donating to the homeless is just the right thing to do.

SCORING

Add up all of the point values of your responses. The score range is 20 to 100. The higher your score, the more other-serving you are. The lower your score, the more self-serving you are.

- **Below 60:** F

- **60 to 69:** D

- **70 to 79:** C

- **80 to 89:** B

- **90 to 100:** A

___

This quiz was adapted from the "Helping Attitude Scale,"[1] developed by Gary S. Nickell, a professor of psychology at Minnesota State University-Moorhead, in 1998. Our modified version is an update of the original; the spirit of the quiz is little changed from Nickell's original. After careful consideration, we've decided it's the best assessment tool available on other-focus because it addresses action *and* emotion.

Serving others is necessary to be a Live to Giver. You're not required to risk death to help strangers or loved ones. But if you see smoke billowing out of your neighbor's window, an other-focused person would stop in their tracks and call 911.

Emotions come into play because if you enjoy serving others, find it rewarding, and feel "at peace" through prosocial giving, you're more likely to continue doing it. The vast benefits of giving come from *consistent* behaviors and attitudes. There is no Insta-Give app. Serving others is a way of (long, happy, healthy) life.

When Nickell performed his initial validation of the scale with 409 undergraduate students, their average score was 79.56. The standard deviation was 8.73, meaning that, on a symmetrical "bell curve," 68 percent of the scores were between 70.83 and 88.29.

Out of a potential score of 100 (which only the Dalai Lama would get), a score of 79.56 is a solid C+, very nearly a B-, which sounds perfectly average to us, and a good assessment of other-service in the general population.

Our best guess is that if we took this quiz prior to doing our research, we would be somewhere in the C+ or B- range on serving others as well. Dammit, Jim, we're doctors, not do-gooders! But that was before we learned that scoring higher benefited us so profoundly. Since then, we've upped our empathy accuracy (feeling the feelings of others) and compassion (responding to others' feelings with action) to fall into a solid B, B+ range.

So? How'd you do?

If your score was, shall we say, *disappointing* (flashback to bringing home a C on your report card, and your mom saying, "I'm not *mad*. I'm *disappointed* . . ."), buck up, people. Other-focus is just like algebra in one super-cool respect: if you make the tiniest effort to learn how to do it, you can improve your grade. You are not doomed to be a C student at Live to Give University for your entire life. By reading this book and adopting the strategies in it, you can get higher marks in altruism before the semester is out, and still reap the benefits.

ONCE A JERK, ALWAYS A JERK?

Maybe you got a C or lower on this quiz. In that case, you might be wondering, *Am I just a born-to-be selfish type, destined to be miserable and die alone?*

We can put that grave concern to rest.

Neuroscience has looked at the "nature versus nurture" issue for some time. The "nature" idea is that we're born with personality traits, and those baked-in qualities can't be changed. If that were true, we'd be wired to be a certain kind of person based on our genes. Personality would be destiny.

The "nurture" idea is that we can be taught or trained to develop certain skills and minimize other behaviors. By that reasoning, personality would be a decision.

Everyone learned in school about genetics, and that our DNA determines a lot about who we are, e.g., our eye color. On the quirky side, we were taught that tongue rolling—being able to turn your tongue into a U or, for the truly gifted, a W—is a genetic trait, so only a select few of us will ever be able to do it.

Right now, as you are attempting to roll your tongue, we have some breaking news to report: it turns out that your junior high biology teacher was completely wrong. Not only have scientific studies shown quite clearly that tongue rolling is *not* an inherited trait, but they have also found that tongue rolling can actually be learned.[2,3,4]

When Steve told his kids this cold, hard truth, his daughter said, "You mean I'm not special?"

Of course she is! But not about that. (Sorry, Isabel.)

Steve says his wife, Tamara, is in the 99.99th percentile for having a "giving nature." We all know people who seem to have been born with a heart of gold. We also know people who seem to be naturally uncaring, born with a heart of stone.

There is evidence that, to some extent, one's capacity for caring does come from genetic predisposition. For a recent study,[5] researchers went to Twinsburg, Ohio, for an annual twins festival (called "Twins Days Festival: The Largest Annual Gathering of Twins in the World!"—like Coachella for people who once shared a uterus) and asked 296 attendees to fill out a well-validated survey about their willingness to register as an organ donor and other altruistic behaviors. Each question was measured on a five-point scale.

Sixty-five percent of the identical twins—pairs with the same DNA— had the exact same willingness to be an organ donor.

Of the fraternal twins—pairs with similar DNA like any siblings, but not the same—33 percent were perfectly aligned in their opinion of organ donation.

Would they help a lost stranger? Identicals were in agreement 63 percent of the time; fraternals, only 24 percent.

Would they give money to a stranger? Identicals agreed 51 percent of the time; fraternals, only 29 percent.

Would they give up their seat on a bus? Identicals agreed 46 percent of the time; fraternals, only 24 percent.

Attending a festival for twins? Both identical and fraternal twins at the festival agreed 100 percent of the time . . .

The majority of twins who share the same DNA were in step some of the time, but definitely not all of the time. The fraternal twins didn't seem to agree on much of anything. Only 16 percent gave the same answer about donating to charity. They seemed to be even less in sync as random pairings on the checkout line at Trader Joe's.

Professor of psychology at Stanford University Jamil Zaki, Ph.D., estimates that genetic inheritance from parental DNA accounts for only about 30 percent of innate capacity for caring for others. Seventy percent of your ability to give (emotion, time, money) is the result of nurturance.

As for inherited gifts, we are undoubtedly born with natural talents. No one in the scientific realm is debating the existence of exceptional innate abilities. We were not all born with Michael Phelps's body type and exercise capacity, true. But we can all learn to swim a little faster, with intention and lots of practice. We were not all born with the musical genius of Alicia Keys, but we can all learn to play a simple tune on the piano, again, with intention and practice.

Nearly *anything* that you want to do, you can learn, including other-focus. No one is "wired" to be selfish to the core. Thinking only of one's own gain is not woven into the fabric of anyone's soul. Contrary to what you might've heard, you are not "a generous, giving person" or for that matter "a greedy, selfish person." We're all just people who get to make choices about our behavior. We are not zebras. We can change our stripes as willfully as we change our shirts, if we believe change is possible.

"I am who I am" and "It is what it is" are not evidence-based scientific conclusions. Writing off altruism because you think of yourself as a natural-born self-focused person is a cop-out. We understand that one's sense of identity is ingrained (if not innate), and that change is scary. It's steering into the unknown without a map. People will believe just about anything that lets them off the hook from doing the hard work to change, even if they know they'll benefit from it.

We are science guys and we only present scientific fact. The fact is, the preponderance of evidence confirms that you *can* change your mind. Literally. **Empathy, compassion, and other-focus are skills, not traits.** Skills can be developed if you are willing to make that conscious decision. Being intentional about it is not only allowable; it's necessary for change to occur.

That's not a challenge or a threat. It's a promise of what can be.

Compassion . . . is a commitment. It's not something we have or we don't have—it's something we *choose* to practice.

—Brené Brown

THE BRAIN CAN BE TRAINED

You were probably taught that the human brain is a glob of fat, white and gray matter, nerve cells, and blood vessels, and you would be right. But, in terms of how the brain grows and changes, it's more like a muscle. If you only did "arm day" for several months, your guns would be huge, but the rest of you would be unchanged or diminished. If you exercised parts of your brain—like the regions for positive affect and connectedness—they would get stronger and bigger, and the unexercised parts—the regions for negative affect and detachment—would shrivel.

The brain can be toned and honed to be fiercely altruistic. When you drop everything when a friend asks for help, your brain swells for other-service. If your friend calls and you *don't* help, your brain's selfishness muscle gets stronger. A man who knew a lot about other-focus, but very little about beefing up (or beef), Mahatma Gandhi, once said, "Compassion is a muscle that gets stronger with use."

Neuroplasticity: the brain's ability to form and reorganize synaptic connections, especially in response to learning and experience, or during recovery from injury.

Neuroscientists first discovered neuroplasticity, the organ's incredible ability to change and grow, by studying patients with brain injuries, like a stroke or an accidental impalement with a knitting needle through the eye (such things do happen, you have no idea what we've seen in the emergency department over the years).

Quite extraordinarily, the brain can form new connections between neurons (brain cells) to compensate for damaged tissue. Neuroplasticity explains why some patients are able to recover from illness and injury and become functional again. Not overnight, but it can happen. The brain is not a brick, it's more like a lump of clay that can be reshaped, at least to some extent.

In recent years, neuroscientists have learned that the brain can adapt to far more than just a physical injury. It changes due to new situations and challenges, environments, and demands for performance.

Neuroscientists once believed that, after a certain age, the brain was "fixed," that old dogs could not learn new tricks. But **a healthy adult brain is dynamic. It can undergo neurogenesis (new brain cell formation), with only modest decline with aging, throughout our lives.**[6] Claiming you're too set in your ways to become a Live to Giver is an excuse. It's not supported by biological fact.

The malleable brain research has ushered in a real paradigm shift in the field. New avenues of study: looking at how the brain is shaped through repeated, specialized thought and behavior. Speaking of avenues . . . ever been to London? The city is a maze of narrow, twisting streets, like Diagon Alley in the Harry Potter books, but even more confusing. Wizened cabbies there know the maze like the back of their driving gloves. They have navigated the streets so many times, day after day, they just know—by second nature—where to turn and what shortcuts to take.

Researchers from University College London used MRI scans to study the brains of experienced taxi drivers in that city,[7] and found that the cabbies' posterior hippocampi, the spatial relations and spatial memory part of the brain, were significantly *larger* than those of non–taxi drivers.

You could believe that the cabbies were born with larger posterior hippocampi, realized they were intrinsically better at navigating, and thought, *I know what I'll do! I'll drive a cab in London!* But that seems far-fetched. A more plausible explanation is that daily exposure to the demands of complex navigation *changed the structure of their brains*. In response to constant use, that area of the brain grew larger. This study turned the idea of a "fixed brain" on its head (as it were).

Change causes growth. We find this to be particularly fascinating, because science has also shown that **growth causes change.**

THE MIND CAN BE TRAINED

Carol Dweck, Ph.D., and her colleagues at Stanford University have studied the cause and effect of learning new things. In her book *Mindset: The New Psychology of Success,* she explains how a vital part of learning new things is knowing that you *can.* Belief in change makes change possible.[8]

According to Dweck, many people believe that successful learning is based solely on innate ability. She describes such people as having a restrictive theory of intelligence or a "fixed mindset." Others, who believe that successful learning is based on hard work, training, and perseverance, are said to have an expansive theory of intelligence, or a "growth mindset."

"Fixed mindset" people believe their abilities are set-in-stone traits. They dread failure because they believe that it exposes their inherent lack of ability. As a result, they do not eagerly take on new challenges because of their fear of failure and looking or feeling stupid.

"Growth mindset" people understand that their abilities are skills to be nurtured. They do not fear failure because they recognize that is how learning happens. You need to work at it. As a result, such individuals are inherently more eager to take on new challenges and grow in their abilities. Dweck's research has shown that, over time, people with a growth mindset are more likely to be successful in whatever they are trying to accomplish.

And this isn't just true for math or geography but also our ability to care for others. A whole series of studies by Dweck and colleagues found that people who hold a growth mindset about empathy (the "I think I can" little engines) really do put significantly more effort into being empathetic, compared to people who hold a fixed mindset (the "I am what I am" crew). The growth mindsetters worked harder at being empathetic because they had a stronger interest in improving their behavior.

A person's mindset powerfully affects whether they make an effort at all. If you believe you can change, then you are motivated to realize it.

War for Kindness author Zaki, *Mindset* author Dweck, and Karina Schumann, Ph.D., at Stanford—an all-star team, kind of like the empathy Avengers—worked on a study[9] about whether mindset affected empathy when it's hard to maintain and muster. There's a lot of suffering out there. People feel distressed when they see so much need and then check out. Too painful; can't look. "The United States as a whole is . . . displaying an empathy deficit," they described.

Over a series of seven studies of measuring subjects' empathy during demanding tasks—listening to people's sad stories, aiding cancer patients face to face, engaging someone with conflicting political views—the team found that those with a growth mindset who believed empathy is a skill to be developed were able to make a stronger effort and keep trying to relate to those in need, even when the going got rough. The subjects with a fixed mindset who believed empathy is a trait tended to give up sooner. What's more, when the researchers educated the subjects about the growth mindset and convinced them that improvement was possible, they wound up trying harder, listening closer, and ultimately doing more and caring more. It's what we hope to do with this book. As Dweck said, "*Becoming* is better than being."

HOW LONG DOES IT TAKE?

Becoming an other-focused person is not a "one and done" prescription. The apt metaphor would be eating broccoli once and thinking that it'll give you good health and longevity. As doctors, we can assure you that it doesn't work with broccoli or altruism. To change your brain and nurture a giving mindset, you have to really immerse yourself in it.

To study the power of immersion and its effect on the brain, scientists seek out subcultures with unique focus. Hence, to study the brain's navigation skills, they scan a bunch of London taxi drivers. To study the impact of compassion on the brain, they commune with Buddhist monks in Tibet.

Tibetan monks are more compassionate than you, and us—even more than Steve's wife, Tamara. Yes! It's true. In their preparation to become monks, they spend more than ten thousand hours meditating on loving-kindness and compassion for others. They're not just casually meditating for relaxation by counting their breaths or using the Calm app. It's a bit sacrilegious to say, but the Tibetan monks are hard-core when it comes to compassion meditation, and their immersion does change their brain function.

Richard J. Davidson, Ph.D., and his colleagues from the Center for Healthy Minds at the University of Wisconsin–Madison studied some of the most experienced Tibetan monks—the "outliers of the outliers" in how much time they spend fully immersed in meditation. Specifically, these monks are the world's experts in a technique called "loving-kindness meditation" (LKM) to increase one's compassion.

Using 256 tiny electrodes attached to the head and measuring brain electrical activity with a test called electroencephalography (EEG), Davidson and colleagues found that compared to control subjects, these compassion adept monks had brain waves that were literally off the charts.[10] There is a particular type of brain wave, a gamma wave, that is seen on an EEG during moments when differing brain regions are firing in harmony, such as when you have an exhilarating "Aha!" moment of extreme insight. Typically, when gamma waves are observed they are only fleeting, found in isolated brain areas, and their amplitude is rather small. When the monks were in "compassion mode," they generated EEG data that was unlike anything Davidson and colleagues had ever seen before in their lab, or in *any* lab. The monks' gamma waves were much stronger and more sustained than normal subjects' and they were in synchrony across widespread brain regions.

The most interesting finding: when the monks *stopped* meditating on compassion, the gamma wave activity decreased but it was still markedly greater than control subjects', independent of any specific mental activity. This difference persisted even when the monks were sleeping![11] Davidson and colleagues were seeing, for the first time, an enduring transformation of the brain that was the result of thousands and thousands of hours of intentionality and practice in meditation on loving-kindness and compassion. It changed the monks' brains . . . it changed who they *are*. Cool side benefit: expert practitioners of compassion meditation get a plumping up of the gray matter in the emotional regulation regions of the brain,[12] so they feel chill too.

Fortunately, you don't have to quit your job, move to Lhasa, climb a mountain, and meditate with the monks to get some of the LKM benefits, like emotional control and brainwave fireworks. Davidson found brain changes in regular people after taking a two-week training course in compassion.[13]

If two weeks seems too long, how about one week?

A study[14] from Sonja Lyubomirsky, Ph.D., and colleagues at the University of California–Riverside randomized 280 subjects into three groups: (1) those who read news articles that said doing kind acts is good for your own happiness; (2) those who read articles that said doing kind acts is good for others' happiness; and (3) those who read neutral articles (the control group). Then all participants were instructed to perform kind acts and keep a record of them. After a week, their happiness, well-being, and connectedness levels were compared to their pre-study scores. The participants who read the articles that said kindness was good for oneself showed the biggest increases in every metric, like positive affect, life satisfaction, connectedness. The people who benefited from their kindness did too, no doubt. The study was all about *framing*. With the right framing, if you are trained to believe you'll benefit from serving others, you will.

If one week seems too long, how about six hours?

In two studies[15,16] from professor Tania Singer, Ph.D., and colleagues at the Max Planck Institute for Human Cognitive and Brain Sciences in Germany, researchers used fMRI brain scans to measure participants' neural response to videos of people in distress before and after a six-hour course in compassion training. Pre-training, while watching the upsetting images, the subjects' brain regions associated with negative affect (feeling bad) lit up. **After compassion training, the participants' brain regions associated with positive affect (feeling good) lit up brightly.** The conclusion: cultivating compassion is not only possible, it strengthens one's resilience and makes witnessing hard things easier to endure. Compassion is a coping strategy for dealing with distress. If it genuinely feels good (or at least eases your own distress) to help a sick or lost stranger, attend to a friend in need, or run into a burning building, you're more likely to do it.

Just six hours, less time than it takes to watch every episode of the first season of *Tiger King*, can fundamentally change who you are. Six hours is enough to become more of a Live to Giver, at least a little bit.

"WOULD YOU LIKE TO SIT?"

You're on a crowded subway or train, and by some miracle, you manage to snag a seat. You settle in, nodding apologies to the left and right for the tight squeeze, thinking, *Yes! I bow to the subway gods!*

And then at the next stop, a pregnant woman, a frail old man, or a guy on crutches enters the train. In a split second, your brain makes a decision to ignore the person in greater need of a seat or to get up and offer your seat to her or him.

We did a highly unscientific poll of our wives and close friends about whether people always give up their seat for pregnant women. We assumed men would fight each other for the chance to make this gentlemanly gesture. But no. "The people who jump to give up their seat for pregnant woman are other women," one friend told us. "Especially less pregnant women." One told us that she was days from giving birth and waddled onto a crowded train. Not one person even looked at her. She experimented by groaning loudly and clutching her belly. And still, people kept staring at their phones, in their own little worlds.

David DeSteno, Ph.D., professor of psychology at Northeastern University in Boston and author of *Emotional Success: The Power of Gratitude, Compassion and Pride*, and his team set out to determine if enhancing compassion would make people more willing to give up their chairs for those in obvious pain.[17] For their experiment, they asked participants to do a three-week training course on Headspace in either mindfulness meditation or cognitive skills (the control group).

Then the participants were asked to come to the lab to be measured for cognitive ability. In the waiting room, there were three chairs, two of which were occupied by actors hired by the research team. The participant sat in the last unoccupied chair and waited to be called in for testing. Little did he or she know that the test had already begun.

The waiting room door opened, and in hobbled a woman on crutches and a large walking boot, another actor. She played up clear signs of physical discomfort, just to be sure that there was no ambiguity about whether she was in pain.

(Cont'd)

As DeSteno and his team predicted, the participants who'd done the mindfulness meditation training gave up their seats more frequently than the control group, apparently increasing their compassion reflex. The researchers also found that the participants' level of empathic accuracy—correctly decoding the emotional experience of others—did *not* change after three weeks of mindfulness training. If it had, maybe they would have seen through the ruse and sussed out that the woman on crutches was faking and was probably having a blast pretending to be in agony. (Best side gig ever. It's enough to make you want to go back to grad school.)

Our Cooper colleagues Drs. Brian Roberts, Sundip Patel, and team published a systematic review[18] of the effectiveness of compassion training for physicians in the journal *PLOS ONE* (full disclosure: Steve co-authored the paper). Of the fifty-two studies they included in the review, 75 percent found that compassion training moved the needle in physicians' empathy and compassion. Some of the behaviors studied were sitting rather than standing while talking to patients; clueing in to patient's nonverbal emotional cues; making eye contact; validating, acknowledging, and supporting patients by saying things like, "I hear you," and "I'm here for you." When docs are trained to be compassionate, their behaviors change. Their patients report feeling seen, heard, and well cared for.

That's the goal. Care more, and everyone feels better.

If you have ever given up your seat on a train or in a waiting room, how did it make you feel? Did you get a hit of "warm glow" that was so powerful you had too much energy to sit anyway? If you did *not* get up, did you have to divert your gaze and stew in your own selfishness? Did the pregnant lady shoot daggers at you? How did *that* feel? Energy sucking? Just *bad*? Perhaps next time you're given the opportunity to be compassionate, you'll take it.

YOU DON'T HAVE TO DOWNLOAD HEADSPACE
(UNLESS YOU WANT TO)

"It's not who you are underneath. It's what you *do* that
defines you."
—Rachel Dawes in *Batman Begins*

Feeling more compassionate, empathetic, and other-focused is fabulous. Committing to mindfulness meditation is a fine idea. Certain areas of your brain will mushroom with positive affect.

But it's *the doing,* the taking of action, that really changes your core essence over time.

We will go deep on specific actions to take to serve others (and therefore yourself) in Part III of this book. For now, know that small actions add up to *big change* in your sense of self, how you interact with the world, and how the world and everyone in it perceives you.

By focusing on behaving as if you were .001 percent as compassionate as our monk friends in Tibet, you can make a difference in someone's life. And by "someone," we mean *you.* Your own life will be different, better, longer, happier, healthier. In the words of the immortal goddess Nike, *JUST DO IT.*

Attention self-labeled "selfish person": forget defining yourself that way. Labels can be peeled off. By *doing* prosocial acts, you are hereby relieved of the burden of thinking a certain way about who you are. Giving often and well causes a cognitive dissonance. If you are giving, then how can you be a selfish person? Your brain will realign itself to make that dissonance go away by asserting a new identity, that you are an other-serving person.

Which came first, feeling like a giving person or behaving like one?

It doesn't matter. One brings about the other. Altruism flows from awareness, from tuning in to the world around you, and responding to what you see. Meditation and compassion training open the door and prime your mind to become more aware. But what really triggers changes in yourself, your world, and the planet is the *act* of giving.

We're not telling you how to feel. But we are telling you that changes in behavior precede and cause changes in attitude. If you behave kindly toward a person, you'll become kind and you'll cherish them. If you don't believe us, take Aristotle's word for it. He once said, "Virtues are formed in man by his doing the actions." C.S. Lewis, an author who understood the power of opening hidden doors to discover incredible new worlds, once said, "When you are behaving as if you loved someone, you will presently come to love him."

Opportunity by opportunity, giving takes hold. Little by little, every iteration of it accumulates until you are transformed. Through repetition of Live to Give thought and behavior, you are a bit more elevated. Your brain's synapse pathways for serving others will become stronger and more deeply embedded. The less you enact selfishness behaviors, the more those synapse pathways will eventually wither and die. You don't have to begin a compassion journey on a mountaintop. You don't have to donate a kidney. Just getting off your butt and giving an old lady a seat is an excellent place to start.

By the way, this concept is also true in a negative sense. Through repetition of dastardly thought and behavior, you are a bit more degraded. Criminologists say that people who commit murder don't start there. They work up to it by committing smaller horrors until they get to the most heinous crime.

On a normal level, every time you *don't* help a friend, call for an ambulance in an emergency, give directions, or donate to charity, you are strengthening your brain's synapse pathways for disregard and distance from your fellow humans.

The "empathy deficit" seems to be growing in our culture. But if we can steer ourselves ever so slightly in a giving direction as individuals, our thoughts and actions will benefit the whole world. As parents and guardians, we can teach the next generation by our example, and maybe they won't become burned-out egoists.

Each one of us has the power to bring the Era of Competitive Jerkiness to an end. Along with helping humanity, we can also help ourselves. Remember this framing: if you believe serving others is beneficial for your own well-being, it will be.

In the next five chapters we're going to show you exactly what's in it for you, physically, mentally, emotionally, and professionally. So frame on . . .

PART II

THE CURE

Serving Others

The most exciting breakthroughs of the twenty-first century will not occur because of technology, but because of an expanding concept of what it means to be human.

—John Naisbitt

The Brain and Body
When Serving Others

We've made a lot of claims thus far about the healing power of serving others, and we're going to make many more. These claims are not opinions. They're science-backed conclusions. And to fully understand the biology of *how* caring for, connecting with, and helping people makes you healthier and happier, you have to understand basic brain and body mechanics.

The body is a machine, and the brain is the smart computer that operates it. Giving behaviors and attitudes are the super-refined unleaded fuel that allows your body and brain to function at its best. When you "run on altruism," you get many of the same biological benefits of exercising, eating right, and getting a good night's sleep. The evidence shows that volunteering, focusing on others, and giving time and money might be as good for your body and brain as CrossFit and the Mediterranean diet.

We *can't* say that, on altruism, you can lose twenty pounds in twenty days.

We *can* say that altruism sets you up for a harmonious deluge of hormones and neurotransmitters that trigger good feelings and help prevent or reverse **burnout, anxiety, and depression,** forms of psychological distress that rob you of joy and life satisfaction.

We *can* say that there are bona fide associations between other-focus and **lower chronic stress and systemic inflammation,** which can be contributing factors to poor health, e.g., heart disease and cancer.

By taking your Live to Give prescription, you are setting up your brain and body to protect you from neuropsychological and physiological damage. Abundant research shows that if you perform *random acts of kindness every day,* it will not only reduce your stress, anxiety, and depression, but it will make you—as well as the person you've helped— feel calmer, healthier, and happier. By focusing on someone else, you can change your biology for the better from the inside out, from your brain down to your toes.

It's not magic, although sometimes it might seem like it is. This wonder drug does not come in a pill. But by serving others and focusing on *their* needs, you can safeguard yourself, boost your immunity, feel better, and perhaps even live longer.

THIS IS YOUR BRAIN ON EMPATHY AND COMPASSION

Reminder: "compassion" is defined as an emotional response to another's pain or suffering involving an authentic desire to help. It's slightly different from a closely related but distinct term: empathy. Empathy is the sensing, detecting, feeling, and understanding component, but compassion goes beyond empathy in that it involves taking action to relieve someone's pain or suffering to whatever extent possible.

The skill of being able to put yourself in someone else's shoes (empathy) has a psychological basis. We mentioned in a previous chapter that people who have faced hardships are more likely to empathize with others who are going through tough times. But feeling someone's pain has a physiological basis too. We literally feel each other's pain in our brains.

Renowned neuroscientists Drs. Claus Lamm, Jean Decety, and Tania Singer have found that distinct neural (brain) structures allow us to share the pain of another. Their meta-analysis[1] of dozens of fMRI brain scan studies conclusively found that the same neural structures were activated when people witnessed the pain of others as when they experienced pain themselves. Meaning, empathetic pain lights up the brain the same way as experiential pain. When looking at pictures of body parts "in painful situations," there was even stronger brain activity in the relevant regions than if pain were inflicted on the observers themselves.

No wonder slasher movies are so popular. Our empathetic ability allows us to feel the horror without actually being attacked with a chain saw. But there's another side to our extra empathy perception: empathy hurts, but compassion can heal.

In one German study,[2] the researchers showed videos of people in distress to participants while using fMRI scans to record their empathetic activation in the pain centers of the brain. Step two: half the subjects did a meditation course on compassion and relieving the suffering of others; the other half (the control) did memory training. Step three: all participants watched some upsetting videos again. On a purely emotional level, the compassion-trained subjects had a different reaction to the videos. As they were focused on compassion for others, they told the researchers that watching the suffering wasn't as painful as before. On the neural level, the brain activity was markedly different. Instead of lighting up the pain centers of the brain, the fMRI scans showed activity in brain regions usually associated with positive emotion, positive affect (feeling good), and affiliation (a sense of belonging), i.e., a "reward" center of the brain. Another German study[3] found similar results. **Subjects' brains lit up in reward centers while observing suffering after they were trained to focus on taking action with compassion.** We all know this experientially as well. We know that bearing witness to others' suffering is very uncomfortable and difficult to watch, but we also know, experientially, that it feels good to help people.

Focusing on giving, caring, and connecting rewires our brain to be able to feel good when we see people suffering, because we register it as an opportunity, a precursor, to help them, and helping feels good. That positivity allows us to see suffering without suffering ourselves. If you've ever wondered how nurses in pediatric oncology are able to handle their work, now you know. They have a high tolerance for empathetic pain because of their Olympic strength in compassion, trying to make a difference in the lives of their patients, even when the prognosis is bleak. Neuroscience shows that it protects and heals them emotionally from what is likely to be one of the hardest jobs on the planet. They aren't necessarily born with a greater capacity for compassion than anyone else. But by practicing it so often, they've turned an ability into a superpower.

Just to be clear: if you are compassionate, your brain is more resilient. It can block out the empathetic pain of witnessing the suffering of others to allow you to give meaningful help to people in need.

The reverse—witnessing the joy of others—*also* makes us feel good. Stanford University researchers did a meta-analysis[4] of twenty-five fMRI studies to find out if "vicarious reward" lit up the brain's happy places. They found a consistent pattern of neurological overlap: **watching other people's positive outcomes activated the same parts of the brain as when people experience their own victories.** When our social connections do well—and we don't fall into self-interested traps of jealousy and competitiveness—we all have cause for joy and celebration. So when we give to others in a way that brings them joy, rigorous neuroscience research shows it is actually a two-way street.

THERE, THERE

You know when you're upset, and someone pats you on the shoulder, and says, "There, there. It'll be okay," and you really do feel better?

That pain-reducing effect *is* all in your head—specifically, in your brain. Social touch, a pat, holding hands, a hug, can have analgesic (pain-relieving) powers. The really cool part is that the warm, fuzzy "there, there" comfort is actually bi-directional. It flows from the pat-er to the pat-ee and back again unconsciously and automatically.

An Israeli study[5] described this phenomenon as "brain-to-brain coupling." Romantic partners were assigned roles of being the "target" of pain or the "observer" of it, while their brain activity was recorded on EEG machines. As per usual with this kind of pseudo-sadistic study, pain was administered to the targets. All for the sake of science! (Who signs up for these studies? A special kind of altruist, we suppose.)

Researchers recorded couples' brainwaves during four conditions: (1) no touching, no pain, (2) no touching, pain, (3) touching, no pain, and (4) touching, pain. In the first three conditions, their brains showed minimal coupling or link of brain activity. But during the last condition—touching plus pain—their brains coupled in twenty-two different places. The researchers concluded that **when one partner holds the other's hand, the analgesic effect increases for both, and the observer's empathetic accuracy goes up.** They actually know how their partner feels, because their own brains are having the same experience.

Apparently, humans are a little bit Vulcan, like Spock on *Star Trek*. We can mind-meld to a degree, understand what others are going through, and take away their pain and our own, through the touch of a trusted other.

Touch makes us empathy lightning rods. It also calms our entire nervous system and can even protect us from disease. Researchers at Carnegie Mellon University examined[6] the association between hugs, stress, and infection. Four hundred and four healthy adults were administered a common cold virus and observed for two weeks. During this time, researchers interviewed them nightly about their "perceived social support" and tallied how many hugs they gave each day.

The stronger their connections to others, the stronger their resistance to infection.

Participants who gave the most hugs were the most protected from the cold virus. In fact, the **researchers found that 32 percent of the protective effect of social support against infection was directly attributable to giving hugs.** Among those who did get sick, doling out hugs was associated with a faster recovery.

This study dates back to 2014 and the use of the cold virus might seem quaint to our pandemic-hardened notions about infection and the danger of social proximity. One of the things we all missed so desperately during the lockdown in early 2020 was physical close-

(Cont'd)

ness. Our brains and bodies crave touch because of its stress- and pain-reducing qualities, whether we consciously realize it or not. With touch and closeness, we heal together. Without it, we suffer alone.

THE FANTASTIC FOUR

The human body's endocrine system produces and releases about fifty different hormones. These chemicals are like the body's postal service. They deliver messages via the bloodstream that trigger certain responses. For example, melatonin, a hormone released by the pineal gland in the brain, sends the message, "Enough scrolling through Facebook already! Go to sleep." Insulin, released by the pancreas, tells us to break down Ben & Jerry's and turn it into energy.

Four particular neurohormones—endorphins, dopamine, oxytocin, and serotonin—can work together and independently to turn any day into Valentine's Day, essentially stuffing your body/brain mailbox with messages of love and happiness. Activities that increase the Fantastic Four boost mood and well-being. The Live to Give prescription in Part III of this book ramps up production of all four of them.

ENDORPHINS, THE HELPER'S HIGH HORMONES

What do they do? Energize, calm, increase strength, decrease depression, enhance self-worth, take away pain and discomfort (often referred to as the body's natural opioids), bring "runner's high" and "warm glow."

When do they flow? Some endorphin-friendly activities are exercising, having sex, laughing, getting a massage, eating chocolate, and meditating.

How do you know they are working? During a good long run, you know that "I could go on forever!" feeling? That's endorphins at work.

The Live to Give link: The then executive director of New York City's Institute of the Advancement of Health Allan Luks originated the term "Helper's High" in a 1988 *Psychology Today* article.[7] Luks recounted a pair of studies of more than seventeen hundred female respondents who described the "stimulation" of volunteering that sounded a lot like the energizing effects of vigorous exercise. The most common responses from the study subjects to "How does helping feel?" were "high," "stronger/more energized," "warm," "calmer/less depressed," and "greater self-worth." Luks pointed out that helping others, and the endorphins that come with it, are an antidote to exhausting mental and physical stress. Endorphins—as well as oxytocin and serotonin (more on them in a minute)—serve to block the stress hormone cortisol. When endorphins go up, cortisol goes down, in a kind of hormonal seesaw. Per the study respondents, the Helper's High lasts longer than a runner's high. Endorphins stop flowing shortly when a run is done. But the women in Luks's article reported feel-good flashbacks whenever they *remembered* helping others.

As physicians, we recommend exercise at least three times a week for overall fitness. But to get an endorphin rush, you don't have to sweat at all. You can get the same radiant glow from helping others, and, therefore, yourself.

DOPAMINE, THE FEEL-GOOD HORMONE

What does it do? Produces a feeling of "reward" when you accomplish a task or goal; boosts mood, motivation, and attention; regulates emotional responses; creates reward-seeking feedback loops—chasing the same high over and over.

When does it flow? The brain releases dopamine when we eat food we crave, have sex, take risks, take recreational drugs. Some people call dopamine "brain cocaine." Caution: dopamine is addictive. If you crave dopa hits from gambling, gaming, or receiving likes on Instagram, you might have a problem. (As doctors, we advise that you might need to put the phone down!)

How do you know it's working? When you get a yummy "yes!" feeling after taking a big bite of chocolate cake, that's dopamine hitting you in the reward center of the brain and producing pleasurable sensations and feelings of euphoria.

The Live to Give link: Dopamine is a connection between doing good and feeling good. According to an Israeli study, our brains have a built-in reward system as well as the hardwiring to take actions that benefit others, regardless of whether they're related to us by blood or not. We make these costly giving sacrifices out of evolutionary need; strong societies survive, and we are stronger when we help each other. Giving gets rewarded; giving ensures species survival. To advance the plot, we get a juicy hit of dopamine when we do good as "grist for the evolutionary mill," wrote the authors.[8] The dopamine sensation is one of the underpinnings of habits and addictions, whether you get hooked on a substance, a feeling, or a behavior. The good dopamine feeling you get from altruism can, over time, get your brain hooked on serving others.

OXYTOCIN, THE BONDING HORMONE

What does it do? Produces feelings of love, trust, friendship, and an intense feeling of safety and belonging. It eases stress, reduces fear, restores calm, lowers blood pressure, reduces pain, promotes bonding, energizes, makes you feel confident. It can reduce circulating oxygen free radicals that are linked with heart disease and cancer, and can reduce chronic inflammation throughout the cardiovascular system, thus slowing aging at its origins.

When does it flow? The oxytocin trigger is closeness, like a mother in labor or breastfeeding an infant, lovers being intimate, friends sharing a moment. Also, it's released when you give of yourself (time, effort). Even witnessing acts of generosity can spike oxytocin.

How do you know it's working? If you feel loving and loved, calm and close, you are enjoying oxytocin's figurative hug. But it's neither fleeting nor instantaneous. It can take a while to build up, as a relationship deepens over time.

The Live to Give link: From Stephanie Brown, Ph.D., and colleagues, a University of Michigan review[9] found that the neurobiology of the infant-caregiver bond and altruism are similar. In both cases, one suppressed his or her own needs for the well-being of another. It doesn't matter if you are related by blood to the child or the receiver of service; what matters is perceiving the need of another, being motivated by sincere caring, and providing needed care. Any situation that meets those criteria produces more oxytocin. Once the "caring motivation" mechanisms are well greased, oxytocin continues to flow. It's the gift of love that keeps on giving.

More helping leads to more oxytocin and, in response to the inevitable bonding that occurs, more helping, a wonderful "virtuous cycle." Elizabeth Bernstein wrote in the *Wall Street Journal* article "Why Being Kind Helps You, Too—Especially Now," "When we see the response of the recipient of our kindness—when the person thanks us or smiles back—our brain releases oxytocin, the feel-good bonding hormone. This oxytocin boost makes the pleasure of the experience more lasting. It feels so good that the brain craves more."[10] This oxy addiction isn't harmful. It's healthy. Oxytocin strengthens the heart,[11] boosts the immune system, and may help prolong life,[12] along with providing all the warm fuzzy feelings.

SEROTONIN, THE PRIDE HORMONE

What does it do? Promotes wound healing, helps you relax and focus, regulates anxiety, stabilizes mood, gives you feelings of well-being, happiness, and confidence. The most commonly prescribed antidepressant medications like Prozac, Zoloft, Lexapro, and Celexa are selective serotonin reuptake inhibitors (SSRIs) and raise the level of serotonin in the brain.

When does it flow? It comes on whenever you feel important or proud of others that you helped. Your boss complimented you in front of other people. You made a wise decision that saved you money or benefited your family. Watching your kids perform in the school play or receive an award. Your star pupil or mentee reaches their goal.

British American author Simon Sinek calls it "the leadership chemical" in his book *Leaders Eat Last: Why Some Teams Pull Together and Others Don't*.

How do you know it's working? When you see your personal investment realized in another person you care deeply about, a feeling of pride bursts from your chest. That serotonin rush feels good and reinforces the relationship.

The Live to Give link: Stanford University School of Medicine researchers set out to explain why various species, not just humans, promote "group survival," even if it's costly for individuals within the group. So they studied[13] the social behaviors of mice. In short, they built a little mouse house with two rooms with a door in between. On day one, the mice hung out together in one room. On day two, the mice were put in the other room, but alone. On day three, the researchers opened the door and gave the mice the run of the place. The mice chose to hang out in the room they associated with togetherness and avoided the alone room entirely. Their tiny brains were also studied, and the researchers discovered that social connection released oxytocin, which, in turn, set off a chain reaction that released serotonin as well. It appears that the two hormones are linked in a complex interplay in a reward center of the brain, the nucleus accumbens. Since the mice get a double hit of happiness from feeling connected, they—and perhaps we humans—are more likely to "tend and befriend," and ensure species survival. Our brains are wired to reinforce strong social connections with good feelings, care of the Fantastic Four hormones.

THE DEADLY DUO

We have seen more serious illness and death than the average person, possibly more than most medical doctors because of the specialties we're in. Based on what we have observed in our careers, and the prevailing wisdom in our profession, two modifiable things that are likely to cut your life short are chronic **stress** and systemic **inflammation** (and also motorcycles). Serving others reduces both, for both you and the recipient of your kindness.

STRESS

What is it? Stress can be a catch-all term to mean anything that aggravates, as in, "Traffic stresses me out." Mental stress occurs when you feel overwhelmed, upset, worried, or angry at the trials of life. Juggling work, family, home, and health, and the resulting frustration and underwater feeling, is a major driver of the self-interest self-care de-stress industry.

Physical stress is our body's automatic response to a threat. When our body perceives danger, our adrenal gland releases cortisol and our sympathetic nervous system, aka "fight, flight, or freeze" mode, is activated. Picture those nature videos of gazelles' heads shooting up (freeze) when there is a distant noise of a lion rustling in the brush. Then they bolt like hell (flight). When we are chronically under stress, we are like the gazelles with our heads up in the air on high alert *all the time,* constantly ready to run. That can't be good.

How does it kill you? A chronic cortisol flood can weaken the immune system, raise blood pressure, and increase the risk of diabetes and heart disease. High mental stress is associated with depression, burnout, and unhealthy habits like smoking and substance use disorder that, over time, can cause serious health problems.

The Live to Give fix: Think of the Fantastic Four as an **anti-cortisol,** and serving others triggers their releases. Hans Selye, the grandfather of stress research, put forth the idea decades ago that helping others combats stress for the giver. Man, was he right. A lightning round of studies confirm the stress-buffering effects of altruism:

- A University of Massachusetts analysis[14] of 340 middle-aged and older adults tested whether volunteering lowered salivary cortisol. Indeed, on the days that the subjects volunteered their time to serve others, their cortisol levels were lower than on the days that they didn't. The researchers were so impressed that they recommended volunteering as an intervention for people who are living in stressful situations.

· A University of Pittsburgh study[15] set out to determine whether giving and receiving support to/from others made people less vulnerable to mental stress. To measure this, they used fMRI imaging to look at participants' brains while doing stressful tasks (for example, hard math problems) with the threat of punishment for inaccuracy hanging over them, while, at the same time, the researchers assessed how much the subjects gave or received support. Among the *givers* of support, their stressed-out brain activity went down, even more than those who received it. A University of Maine study[16] found similar results.

· Finally, in what can only be described as the cutest study[17] in the batch, researchers from the University of Miami and Duke University, supported by the NIH, tested the hypothesis that it's better (for stress reduction) to give than receive. Three times a week for three weeks, senior citizen participants received Swedish massages. For the following three weeks, the same subjects were trained to give therapeutic massages to babies (one to three months old) and gave massages three times per week. With which practice did they have lower salivary cortisol levels and report feeling less anxiety and depression? Giving massages, not receiving them. This study should be required reading for all new parents. The perfect antidote to their own stress can also be beneficial for the health of their own parents. Let Grandma and Grandpa babysit more often!

THE NERVE OF SOME PEOPLE!

The phrases "getting on my nerves" or "worrying my last nerve" are often used to describe being at the end of one's rope with stress, although the nerve in question is never specified. There *is* a nerve in the human body that, when stimulated and toned, can lower stress and raise positive feelings, like flipping a light switch: the incredible vagus nerve.

Vagus is Latin for "wandering," and that's exactly what this nerve—the body's longest—does. It starts at the top of the spinal cord in the neck, ends in the intestines, and winds around the heart, lungs, and liver along the way. Director of the Social Interaction Laboratory at Cal Berkeley and *The Science of Happiness* podcaster Dacher Keltner, Ph.D., extolled the virtues of the vagus nerve to *Scientific American*,[18] saying, "When active, it is likely to produce that feeling of warm expansion in the chest—for example, when we are moved by someone's goodness or when we are moved by an emotional scene in a movie or a beautiful piece of music." Its activation also deactivates the sympathetic nervous system (fight-flight-freeze), turns on the parasympathetic nervous system (rest-and-digest), reduces heart rate, increases oxytocin production, and lowers cortisol. It's been called the "nerve of compassion" with good reason. A well-toned vagus nerve is associated with care-taking, cooperation, empathy, and, as Keltner said, "emotions that promote altruism—compassion, gratitude, love and happiness."

University of North Carolina professor Barbara Fredrickson, Ph.D., famously described a well-toned vagus nerve as an "upward spiral" for positive emotions. Her research found that vagal tone has a direct, causal relationship with psychological well-being. Increased vagal tone leads to increased feelings of connectedness and it "facilitates capitalizing on social and emotional opportunities and the resulting opportunistic gains," she wrote.[19]

So how do you activate and tone the vagus nerve? Simple. Be a Live to Giver. According to a University of Toronto series of studies,[20] compassion does the trick. Participants witnessed others suffer while researchers measured their heart rate, breathing rate, and vagal activity. When they responded to the images by expressing kind words, their vagal activity increased and their heart rate and breathing slowed.

Research supports the idea that any small prosocial, altruistic behavior is like lifting weights to tone up your vagus nerve. And once you get on that upward spiral of elevating the happiness of others, you'll never want to come down.

CHRONIC SYSTEMIC INFLAMMATION

What is it? When you accidentally cut your finger slicing bagels, the skin around the cut gets puffy and red because blood rushes to the site to heal and protect it. Inflammation as such is the body's normal, healthy defense response to injury or infection. Systemic inflammation is an exaggerated version of this response. Your immune system thinks that your entire body is under attack and sends in white blood cells (immunity foot soldiers) to defend real or false threats. It's like your entire insides undergo the body's "red and puffy" response.

How does it harm you? Chronic systemic inflammation is associated with heart disease, stroke, diabetes, and even cancer.

The Live to Give fix: Helping others has anti-inflammatory effects. Dr. Barbara Fredrickson compared[21] "eudaimonic well-being" (having a higher purpose in your life) to "hedonic well-being" (just seeking pleasure for yourself) to see if one or the other reduced systemic inflammation. Eudaimonic well-being was found to reduce pro-inflammatory "gene expression," meaning the genes that produce inflammation were turned off. Hedonism didn't. We'd never begrudge people the occasional wild weekend in Cabo. Although tequila and nude beaches might warm the skin, finding purpose by helping others and giving support warms the heart—and, over time, can reduce potentially harmful inflammation on your *insides*.[22]

In another study,[23] researchers tested whether acts of kindness could decrease systemic inflammation. One hundred fifty-nine adults were randomized into groups and instructed to perform kind acts for four weeks in one of three ways: toward specific others, toward the world in general, and toward oneself. (A control group did neutral tasks.) **The only group that showed a reduction in inflammation markers was the one that was caring and kind to specific people in their lives. By strengthening their social bonds through kindness, they quieted down their inflamed internal environment, which could reduce their risk for health problems if sustained over time.**

Childhood psychological trauma has been linked to elevated inflammatory markers in the blood that persist into adulthood. But compassion training can reduce those markers for people who've had early life adversity (also called adverse childhood experiences [ACEs]), and the higher risk of physical and emotional problems that go along with it. Emory University researchers worked with seventy-one adolescents in the Georgia foster care system with high rates of ACEs, giving half of them compassion training for six weeks while half did neutral tasks.[24] Their saliva was collected beforehand and afterward. The subjects who engaged in compassion training and were acting on it saw a reduction in their inflammatory markers. So even if the deck is stacked against you and you have every reason to be bitter toward the world, by shifting your focus to the well-being of others, you can change your outlook and maybe even your insides. **The research suggests that these kids could be less likely to have adverse health effects later in life by starting to practice compassion and caring for others *now*.**

THE MOTHER TERESA EFFECT

Back in the 1980s, Harvard University researcher David McClelland, as legend has it, was inspired by the positive feeling of a small act of kindness—he helped an old woman cross the street—to study the impact of doing good on the immune system, his area of expertise.

His particular specialty was salivary immunoglobulin A (S-IgA), an antibody that is not as flashy as the Fantastic Four, but does vital work in the body as a defender against environmental toxins and infections. Without a robust response from protective antibodies, you'd be more susceptible to any virus or germ floating around out there.

McClelland rounded up 132 Harvard undergrads, and randomly split them into two groups. Half sat for a screening of *The Power of the Axis Alliance*, a movie about Adolph Hitler during World War II. The other half watched a film about Mother Teresa tending to the poor and sick in Calcutta, India.[25]

(Cont'd)

Before and after the screenings, McClelland measured the participants' S-IgA levels by taking swabs of their saliva.

The movie about Hitler aroused thoughts of power in the viewers' minds, and *reduced* their S-IgA concentrations. Thinking about Hitler can literally make you sick. "Power motivation" does nothing to help you or anyone else.

The Mother Teresa group's S-IgA levels significantly increased. Just watching her altruistic acts and being inspired by them changed the viewers physiologically, and these changes, if sustained over time, could enhance their ability to fight infections. McClelland credited "affiliation motivation," the human desire to belong, as the major benefit here. "[The hormone] increase was sustained an hour later when subjects continued to dwell on the loving relationships that characterized the film," he wrote. The more you care and are motivated to help, the healthier you may be.

The brain and body are hardwired machines that run better on caring and connection than on disregard and disconnection.

Over time, by activating a Helper's High on a regular basis and opening all the Fantastic Four (endorphins, dopamine, oxytocin, and serotonin) floodgates, you'll be rewarded with good vibes, confidence, euphoria, closeness, and a natural high.

By touching and hugging and being close, you boost your immunity and can lessen each other's pain.

By practicing compassion, you can protect yourself from the Deadly Duo of chronic stress and systemic inflammation. Just watching someone show compassion can boost the immune system.

And while all these mechanisms are humming along inside you, your other-focus also boosts the good feelings and health of the people you help as well.

Now that we've sorted out the *how*—body mechanisms triggered by altruism that put the wheels of good health in motion—let's continue down that road a bit to get to the *what* of helping. What, exactly, are the physical, mental, and emotional benefits? What are the effects of being a Live to Giver on the *outcomes* of health, wellness, happiness, and success?

We'll get to all of it in this section of the book. In the next chapter, we'll present the evidence of how helping others could help you live longer and healthier.

We must love one another or die.

—W.H. Auden

Physical Health Through Serving Others

Here's the thing about the science of health outcomes and longevity: re-searchers don't often look at young people. You made it to thirty? Good for you, but no scientist is going to show up at your house to ask you questions about how you managed to last that long. If you live past one hundred, they'll be lined up on the sidewalk outside.

So when we curated the research on how being other-focused impacts physical health and longevity, most of the studies are about older folks. It makes sense. If you were a researcher studying the effects of any activity on serious health events or mortality, you would want to study a population that has experience with both.

Readers over forty: you will probably find the information in this chapter absolutely riveting if you have a passing interest in not dying anytime soon, staying fiddle-fit into the golden years, and keeping your marbles.

Readers under forty: your age group gets some attention in this chapter, but not a lot. However, the data here are still very relevant to your life now. If altruism promotes longevity in older people, think about what it could do if you started early, as a young person! Don't wait until you're on Medicare to be altruistic. There is no scientific reason to think the effects would not be greater if applied to the total lifespan. For example, you don't want to wait until you have a heart attack before you think about heart health. The things that could have prevented that heart attack go way back into the years before you even thought seriously about your health.

Think of it like those ads from financial advisors you see pop up on social media. If you invested in Tesla, Amazon, and Google at the beginning, your investments would be worth billions today! Altruism is an investment that can compound year over year, providing "health wealth" when you really need it down the road.

LIVE LONGER

Currently, the life expectancy in the United States is 77.8 years.[1] Those of you who are older than that, congratulations! You have beaten the odds and are playing with house money. It's quite probable that, over your lifetime so far, you've had some Live to Give practices. For those of you who are younger than 77.8 years, we have crucial medical advice: scale back on self-focus and spend more time, money, and energy on making a difference for someone else as soon as possible. There is ample evidence that helping behavior is associated with lower mortality, which is a science-y way to say less likely to drop dead.

The effects of other-focus on longevity are not magic, like drinking from the Fountain of Youth. Nor are we offering just our opinions. The scientific evidence shows that being other-focused counteracts your stress. As we discussed in the previous chapter, stress-mediated disease can cause early death. The mortality risk reduction by altruism likely works by buffering stress-mediated disease and the related risks. A University of Buffalo study[2] assessed 846 participants' past year's stressful event history, as well as how much help they provided to friends and family members, and then tracked whether they died over a five-year period. **The highly stressed participants who did *not* provide a lot of help to others died at a predictable rate during that time, given their age. But the equally stressed participants who provided assistance to their loved ones had a lower mortality rate. Same stress, less death.**

By turning your attention light away from your own needs and problems, and redirecting it toward those of others, you might get more time above ground.

Stephanie Brown, Ph.D., now at Renaissance School of Medicine at Stony Brook University, has done fascinating research on altruism among the elderly, including a five-year study[3] of older married adults. Participants who regularly provided "instrumental support" (helping) for friends, family, and neighbors, and provided emotional support to spouses, showed significantly reduced mortality compared to their stingily supportive counterparts. After adjusting the analysis for all the measured factors that could muddle the analysis (for example, demographic, personality, physical and mental health status, and marital-relationship variables), giving support to others was still *independently* associated with lower mortality. However, being the recipient of all that love and attention, no matter how much it was appreciated, was not associated with longer life.

So, with your partner, it's better to be the one saying, "You're welcome" rather than "Thank you" if you hope to outlive your partner and/or stay well enough to care for them as they age. The data supports the idea that if you intend to die first—and fast—by all means, stop giving.

As for helping people you don't necessarily know, an Arizona State University meta-analysis[4] found that **volunteering in the service of others among people fifty-five and over was associated with a *24 percent* lower mortality risk** after controlling for other factors such as health status. Similarly, a study[5] of 1,972 elderly Golden State residents from the Buck Institute for Research on Aging found that people who were **"high volunteers"—giving their time to two charitable organizations—had a *44 percent* lower mortality risk than non-volunteers** after controlling for sociodemographic, physical health, and psychological factors.

Giving behaviors are also associated with lower mortality rates for many specific diseases (see the sections on heart health and cognitive function below). Here's an Emory University study[6] about end-stage renal disease—that is, people with kidney failure needing dialysis. Two hundred forty-nine patients on dialysis were assessed for their giving and receiving of social support to and from friends, family, and partners, as well as doctors, nurses, and fellow patients. Researchers checked back a year later and found that the giving scores among the survivors were higher than among the patients who died. Controlling for other factors, the results showed that the patients with the lowest giving scores were at the greatest risk of dying. However, receiving social support didn't move the needle in either direction, toward survival or death.

Most of the studies of volunteering and longer life focus on a self-selecting group of subjects who participate in giving behavior. It's always possible there are confounding factors (distortions or inaccuracies) that studies don't measure and therefore can't take into account. (Note: nearly all of the studies we cite adjust for such factors with mathematical models.) In this case, some might be things like, do volunteer types eat less junk food than non-volunteers? Do they tend not to live next door to toxic waste dump sites? Those difficult-to-measure mystery factors might tip the scales and impact their mortality risk regardless of volunteering.

To address this, researchers collected[7] nearly three years' worth of data about 300,000 cohabitating married couples on the grounds that married couples living in the same house should be similar on lifestyle factors that could affect the results. What they found is that **spouses who volunteer to serve others do indeed have a lower mortality risk. But their non-volunteering spouses who sleep in the same bed, eat the same dinner, hang out with the same friends, do *not* get the same longevity benefit.** This supports the idea that the decisive factor isn't address, diet, or the drapes. It's not something in the water. It's whether a person gives a little bit of themselves and winds up, perhaps unintentionally, getting more of what we all want: time.

THE TRUTH ABOUT TELOMERES

We hate to drop a mega truth bomb on you, especially if you aren't even aware that these body parts exist, but here goes: if your telomeres are in bad shape, you might age faster and die sooner.

- **What are they?** Your DNA is made up of chromosomes, like the Xs and Ys that determine biological sex. If you picture a chromosome as a strand, like a shoelace, telomeres are the plastic tips on the ends that protect the string from fraying.

- **What do they have to do with aging?** At birth, telomeres (Greek for "end part") are nice and long. But every time a cell divides to replicate itself, the telomeres on the cell's chromosomes get a tiny bit shorter. Eventually, telomeres dwindle to nubs and can no longer protect the integrity of the chromosome, and the cell can no longer keep going. The life of a cell is a microcosm of a human life. Eventually, we get too worn out to maintain our bodily integrity, and we die.

- **The Live to Give link:** Research has found that being a compassionate, loving, giving person is associated with slower telomere attrition. A University of North Carolina–Chapel Hill/Duke University randomized trial[8] in 142 middle-aged adults from Barbara Fredrickson, Ph.D., and colleagues assessed telomere length two weeks before and three weeks after the study subjects did a six-week workshop in either meditation (focused on the self), loving-kindness meditation (LKM; a practice devoted to the Buddhist tradition of focusing on unselfish love for other people), or nothing (the control group). They found that after controlling for demographics and baseline length of telomeres, telomere length decreased significantly in the control group and the self-focused meditation group, but not in the LKM group. They concluded that focusing on giving love to other people may buffer telomere attrition. Importantly, the effects on telomere attrition were observed after just twelve weeks of other-focused LKM activity. Researchers at Massachusetts General Hospital and Harvard Medical School did a similar study[9] with similar results.

- Look, nothing is going to stop time or halt the aging process. But focusing our mind on giving love to other people may be able to slow it down a bit. Isn't it worth a try?

HURT LESS

During the writing of this book, Mazz went through one of the most physically painful experiences of his life. Without getting into the gory details, he had a massive kidney stone, and it could only be neutralized by inserting a stent through a particularly sensitive body part, having the kidney stone lasered into pieces, and then each piece carried with a small basket out through the same sensitive body part. And the standard of care for this procedure is that several days later, at home, the patient pulls out the stent him- or herself from that same sensitive body part!

Yeah.

Mazz was able to tolerate it a bit better on one occasion by prescribing himself a hefty dose of other-focus. One day during that week, waiting in line at the hospital to receive his COVID-19 vaccination, he started to get a wave of intense pain, an eight on a scale of ten. Instead of focusing on the agony, he looked around for someone to help. Near him in the line were a couple of residents (physicians in training) he knew, one of whom had been a medical student of his.

He started asking them how they were doing, what was going right in their units, what could be better, how he could help, a leadership practice called "rounding." He took out his phone and started taking notes, fully engaging with the trainees about their needs. His pain didn't magically disappear, but the conversation and help he provided made it tolerable.

Other-focus is a readily available tool to control and reduce pain, in particular, if one volunteers to help others who are in the same miserable boat. In a British study[10] of adults with severe osteoarthritis or rheumatoid arthritis, the subjects volunteered to help other arthritis sufferers on how to cope with and manage their pain. In a six-month follow-up, the volunteers reported that their own arthritis pain was reduced. Not only that, they had a new, positive outlook on life from helping coach and support other sufferers.

Researchers at Boston College studied[11] the effects of transitioning patients with chronic pain into a new role, of voluntarily providing peer support to others with the same condition. Their pain was assessed three times: when they were patients only, during training to provide peer support, and during volunteering to help support other patients. Pain levels—as well as the associated depression and disability—dropped during training and volunteering. Subjects mentioned "making a connection" and having "a sense of purpose" in their follow-up interviews. What's more, the people who received the peer support also reported reduced pain. Both the giver and receiver benefit. Win-win. Not a zero-sum game.

A recent, very interesting study[12] published in the *Proceedings of the National Academy of Sciences* helps explain the neuroscience underpinnings behind altruistic behaviors having pain-relieving effects. The researchers used fMRI scans to see what part of the brain was being activated. Study subjects volunteered to serve or provide support for others and then were administered a painful shock. Post-giving, the activity in the brain's pain centers in response to the shock was reduced. The more meaningful the altruistic act, the less pain activity showed up on the scans. They found the same results in patients with chronic pain due to cancer. The secret is out: if you know you're in for some physical pain—like going to a boot camp workout or moving furniture—be sure to provide a meaningful service to others right before you go.

A gallant act of sacrificial love would be to "take a bullet" for your spouse. In a NIH-supported study,[13] researchers from the University of Colorado tested if making a chivalrous gesture to take a romantic partner's pain in their place would lessen the pain intensity for the knight in shining armor. So, the researchers had romantic pairs stand in front of a brick wall, and then fired bullets in their direction, making sure one of them jumped in front of the speeding bullet . . . okay, that didn't happen. We doubt such a study would pass a research ethics review board. What they actually did was give participants the opportunity to voluntarily take an electrical shock on behalf of their romantic partner (always with the shocks!). Then, the subjects received their jolt while the researchers looked at their brain activity on an fMRI scan.

In this study, all the knights in shining armor were women. **Twenty-nine heterosexual female participants' brains were studied in two conditions: (1) during a baseline pain challenge and (2) during an** "accept partner pain" condition. **The results showed that the gallant act reduced activity in the pain center of the brain, and it increased their positive thoughts and loving feelings.** They felt good about their sacrifice even if they still experienced pain. The more willing they were to take the pain, the less it bothered them. A loving gesture really can buffer pain. So if your partner offers to take a bullet for you, let them. It might help both of you.

HAVE A HEALTHY HEART

The leading cause of death in the United States is heart disease, with cancer in not-too-close second place.[14] If you have a bad heart, you've got big problems.

As doctors, we see so much heart disease, and patients look to us for advice. Along with quitting smoking and getting plenty of exercise, we recommend another scientifically proven method to strengthen the heart. Warm it up. To help ward off heart attacks, strokes, cardiovascular disease, and high blood pressure,[15] focus on others by volunteering, providing social support, or just getting out of your own head.

Young people study alert! In a paper published in *JAMA Pediatrics* from researchers at Mount Sinai School of Medicine and Northwestern University, researchers assigned 106 Canadian tenth-grade high school students without chronic medical issues to volunteer at an elementary school and work with little kids for two months; the control group was put on a waitlist. Remarkably, following the intervention, the volunteer group had reduced cardiovascular risk factors like lower inflammation blood markers, lower cholesterol, and lower body mass index, compared to the control group. Per the researchers, the adolescents "who increased the most in empathy and altruistic behaviors, and who decreased the most in negative mood, also showed the greatest decreases in cardiovascular risk over time."[16] See? It's never too early to start protecting your heart by serving others.

In a longitudinal Carnegie Mellon University study,[17] researchers took baseline measurements of both volunteering and blood pressure of their over-fifty-year-old subjects. Four years later, they checked the measurements again. After controlling for age, race, sex, baseline blood pressure, and major chronic disease (as per usual in all of these studies), the researchers saw a clear association with giving behavior and heart health. **The subjects who volunteered for at least two hundred hours over the previous year (roughly four hours per week) were about 40 percent less likely to develop high blood pressure compared to non-volunteers.** The subjects who served others reported higher psychological well-being and physical activity as well.

Ashley Whillans, Ph.D., now at Harvard University, asked 186 hypertensive adults how much money they spent on others, donating to charities and giving it away ("prosocial giving"). In the two-year follow-up, the big givers had better blood pressure numbers than the hoarders. For the second study, seventy-three subjects were given $40 by the researchers and told to spend it either on themselves or on someone else, on three separate occasions over three consecutive weeks. Compared to the self-spenders, the givers' blood pressure was lower at the end of the study period. Don't tell Big Pharma: According to these researchers, giving may be as good for your blood pressure as drug therapy. "The magnitude of these effects was comparable to the effects of interventions such as antihypertensive medication or exercise," wrote the authors.[18] The improvement was most pronounced when the subjects gave the money to people they love. Those kinds of small acts of giving can strengthen family ties, ventricles, veins, and vessels.

SELF-ABSORPTION: A HEART STORY

Back in the '80s, we had big hair, skinny ties, glam metal, and Atari. What a superfine era it was. While we were glued to MTV, social psychologist Larry Scherwitz, Ph.D., and colleagues, first at Baylor University and later at the University of California–San Francisco, were making important discoveries about self-absorption and heart disease.

In his first paper on the subject,[19] he compared participants with "Type A" personalities (intense, high-stress folks who are maybe a bit neurotic) and "Type B" personalities (chill dudes) by doing

(Cont'd)

a structured interview with them, and then putting them through blood pressure–raising trials, like plunging their hands in ice cold water, doing high-pressure problem-solving, and submitting to emotionally probing interrogations. While they did these stressful tasks, the subjects' blood pressure and heart rate were monitored.

Predictably, blood pressure spiked when the subjects reported feeling distressed. A major split within the Type A group emerged. Type A-ers who used an excessive amount of first-person pronouns ("I," "me," "my") during their structured interviews had markedly higher blood pressure spikes, emotional intensity, and extreme reactions to the tasks. The Type A-ers who weren't so self-referential were more like the Type B-ers in that regard and in having lower emotional intensity and lower blood pressure.

The scientists started out with the hypothesis that stress will raise your blood pressure (and thus heart attack risk) but wound up seeing a different signal in the data. **The bigger predictor of blood pressure spikes wasn't whether the subject was a tightly wound stress ball. A better "tell" might be self-absorption, as evidenced by being self-referential in the structured interview.**

In his next paper,[20] Scherwitz tested the hypothesis that Type A stressed-out people aren't necessarily at higher risk for cardiac events—for example, heart attacks. He and his team gathered 150 men who cleared benchmarks for Type A personality traits. There appeared to be no relationship between the subjects' neuroticism and existing coronary artery disease. However, when they counted how many times the subjects used "I," "me," and "mine" in their pre-study interviews, they found an association between self-references and coronary artery disease (CAD) of the heart. In his third paper,[21] a longitudinal look at 3,110 subjects, those with the highest mortality from heart disease were the ones who spoke most "densely" in self-absorbed language during their initial interviews.

Although these findings were not always replicated in later research using slightly different methodologies, the results are thought-provoking to say the least. It's a stretch to say editing your speech to avoid first-person pronouns will protect you from dying of heart disease. But if you shift your thoughts out of your own head, and instead think more about others, you just might do your heart some good.

KEEP YOUR MARBLES

By the year 2060, the U.S. cases of Alzheimer's disease are projected to triple to 14 million.[22] Many of us with elderly parents and grandparents are dealing with their dementia right now, and it can be devastating for all involved. There's an urgent need to find new ways to maintain cognitive sharpness for all of us, not just our current senior citizens but for all *future* senior citizens. Wouldn't it be great to know what to do *now* to avoid mental decline later? As it just so happens, there are lifestyle factors that may help you keep winning at *Jeopardy!* for decades to come. And you will *never* guess what they are.

An international meta-analysis[23] on the impact of giving behavior on dementia risk synthesized data from seventy-three separate research papers and found that **volunteering to serve others is associated with a big bag of mental goodies: not only reduced depression, better self-reported health, and better general functioning, but also better smarts related to preserved cognitive ability.** Like your tennis or golf game, cognition can be a "use it or lose it" proposition. Stay active in the world, connect and engage, meet new people, have new experiences, face new challenges, and your mind will thank you for it. A Brazilian study of some three hundred older people found that those who were the most altruistic kept the sharpest minds.[24]

Researchers from Johns Hopkins University School of Medicine conducted a randomized trial[25] of 128 sixty- to sixty-five-year-olds in a pilot program called the Experience Corps that placed older volunteers in public elementary schools to help out in any way needed. After eight months of clapping erasers, sharpening pencils, and playing tag at Baltimore grade schools, the senior citizens' cognitive performance increased significantly and the pep in their step (the all-important "walking speed" measure for elder wellness) stayed relatively bouncy.

With such positive results, the researchers hope that the Experience Corps idea takes off. The older folks will benefit from improved social, physical, and cognitive functioning. Public school teachers and administrators will have willing (and able) helpers. And the kids will benefit from the extra attention and boost their educational outcomes. Win-win-win.

STAY STRONG

We're not talking about septuagenarians lifting barbells at Muscle Beach. We mean strong enough to do basic daily activities. Loss of strength, flexibility, and stamina are common in middle age and beyond. After age thirty, humans can lose as much as 8 percent of their muscle mass each decade.[26] So it's important to take steps to maintain strength as we age if we hope to keep taking long walks with the dog, carrying groceries from car to kitchen, and hanging holiday lights on the eaves.

Research has found that altruism can actually make you stronger (at least a little bit). A study from the University of Maryland examined[27] the effects of altruism on self-control, tenacity, and personal strength in a couple of quirky experiments. For one, subjects held aloft a five-pound weight directly out from the side of their body, with a fully extended arm, for as long as they possibly could, both before and after they gave to charity. Next, the subjects were tested on grip strength before and after donating to a good cause. In both cases, the subjects kept the weight up in the air or maintained their grip strength measurably longer after helping others by giving their money away.

The author postulates that the participants experienced a form of "moral transformation" where they were energized by the experience of giving to others, resulting in extra stamina. Perhaps you have experienced something similar. When you know you are doing the right thing, it energizes you and makes you more persistent; it feels easier to persevere in your righteous pursuits with more strength, endurance, and tenacity. This explains why when you are doing something for a good cause, rather than just for yourself, you have a newfound extra boost of grit to push through difficult times.

When older people are dedicated to contributing to the well-being of others, especially younger generations (for example, sharing their wisdom with young people in a meaningful way)—a practice called "generativity"—they may gain in stamina and physical functioning. A University of Southern California study[28] of sixty- to seventy-five-year-olds assessed their generativity scores and their ability to keep doing activities of daily living (running errands, doing chores, cooking meals) on their own. **Greater level of generativity at the study's onset was associated with higher odds of better physical functioning over a ten-year follow-up period.** This shows that you don't have to give money or time; sharing something perhaps much more valuable—a lifetime of wisdom—can also be beneficial for the giver. And in this case, by sitting down and listening to Grandma's stories and advice, you might be giving her an opportunity to stay strong while receiving some of her wisdom at the same time.

Eric S. Kim, Ph.D., a health psychologist and social epidemiologist, currently at the University of British Columbia, has done extensive research at the intersection of altruism and aging. In one longitudinal study,[29] Kim and his team analyzed data from nearly thirteen thousand participants in a nationwide Health and Retirement Study of adults over fifty and looked at the relationship between changes in volunteering over time (four years) and physical functioning. After controlling for potential confounding factors, they found that **participants who did at least one hundred hours of volunteering per year—roughly two hours per week—had a significantly reduced risk of physical functioning limitations.**

This is the section about strength, not the death section, but it bears mentioning that Kim and colleagues also found that **one hundred hours of volunteering per year also was associated with lower mortality risk and a greater sense of purpose in life.** Two hours a week could potentially change the course of one's life, the wellness of a community, and the health of society at large. For the elderly, perhaps volunteering to serve others should be prescribed as commonly as Lipitor. Again, altruism is not "magic." Per science, it's just an evidence-based way to live.

ON PURPOSE

If you asked someone, "What's your purpose in life?" the answer probably would not be "a vacation in Maui." Daiquiris and snorkeling might be passions, and those passions might be worthwhile pursuits. But passions are often "selfish," meaning they benefit no one but yourself.

Passion is not purpose (we are seriously going to print T-shirts), as we explained before. True purpose is being involved with something bigger than yourself. It's devoting yourself to making improvements in your world—be it for your own family, your community, or the entire globe—some variation of "making a difference." You can look for purpose in your 401(k) and getting a corner office, but you won't find it there. True purpose comes from serving others in some way. And a wealth of research proves that having a purpose is good for your heart health and longevity.[30]

In all the studies about purpose in life to follow, the researchers used a psychometrically validated set of questions that probed one's sense of purpose. Researchers at the University of Michigan analyzed[31] the data from 6,985 over-fifty Americans who participated in a national cohort study (Health and Retirement Study) in 2006. Twelve years later, looking at which participants died, the researchers made their analytical adjustments, and found that stronger purpose in life was independently associated with decreased mortality. **Compared to those with the strongest sense of purpose, those with the least purpose in life had *double* the risk of death over the study period.** In another study, researchers at Rush University performed a similar analysis[32] among 1,238 senior citizens in retirement communities, their sense of purpose, and mortality, and reached essentially the same conclusion.

In health care, we talk about life span a lot, and possibly not enough about quality-of-life span. Many of us don't want to live to a hundred if we're incapacitated, unable to talk or walk or feed ourselves. Regarding stroke risk, Eric S. Kim and his team studied[33] 6,739 elder adults over a four-year period. They found that the greater their sense of purpose in their lives, the lower their risk of stroke. Another Kim study of the elderly[34] found that, **among 4,486 subjects, the greater their life purpose scores, the better their chances of maintaining grip strength**

and walking speed, two indicative factors of older adults' general functioning and health. What's more, each uptick on a validated six-point scale of life purpose was found to be associated with better health prevention practices—cancer screenings, for example—and 17 percent fewer nights spent in the hospital.[35]

For all of us, getting good-quality, adequate rest is crucial to our health. Can having purpose in life actually make you sleep better at night? Kim and his team studied[36] this topic among older adults, who, in general, are more prone to sleep disturbances. They analyzed the incidence of sleep disruption and life purpose in more than four thousand participants and followed up with them over a four-year period. You will be *shocked* to learn that, after controlling for potential confounding factors, **each level of higher purpose on that six-point scale was associated with a 16 percent drop in the odds of developing troubled sleep.**

No rest for the wicked, perhaps. But Live to Givers definitely do better in bed. And you can take that to mean whatever you think it might.

ON CONNECTION

There is abundant evidence that a lack of meaningful social connections is associated with poor health. This field of research—how loneliness affects health—isn't new. After James S. House, Ph.D., a University of Michigan social psychologist, and colleagues, published a landmark paper[37] in *Science* in 1988 on the topic, interest exploded and hasn't died down since. Recently, the surgeon general of the United States, Vivek Murthy, M.D., wrote a book about it called *Together: The Healing Power of Human Connection in a Sometimes Lonely World.* The data are so strong that the British and Japanese governments have created cabinet-like posts called the Minister of Loneliness (perhaps one of the saddest jobs ever).

Being a Live to Giver means focusing on others. It stands to reason—and is supported by evidence—that the more one serves others, the less lonely one will likely be (much evidence on that to come later). Conversely, if one is a selfish bastard, he or she is likely to have fewer meaningful relationships, be lonely, and be at higher risk for early death. No way to sugarcoat it. Loneliness *kills.*

Let's start with heart health and blood pressure, which might be going up right now as you tally how many close relationships you have. Researchers at the University of Chicago tested[38] the hypothesis that loneliness is associated with elevated blood pressure by performing a longitudinal study of a multiracial mix of 229 fifty- to sixty-eight-year-olds over a five-year period. They found that being lonely at the start of the study predicted increases in systolic blood pressure every subsequent year, independent of any other factor like age, gender, race, medication, and personality traits. A British meta-analysis[39] of **data from sixteen studies linked loneliness with approximately 30 percent higher risk of coronary heart disease and stroke.**

Per Julianne Holt-Lunstad, Ph.D., a psychologist at Brigham Young University and an expert in the impact of social isolation on cardiovascular disease, stroke risk, and mortality, "The epidemiological data suggest that having more and better quality social relationships is linked to decreased health risks and having fewer and poorer quality relationships increased risk."[40] She describes **the mortality risk of loneliness as similar to smoking about fifteen cigarettes per day and comparable to that of high blood pressure and obesity.**

You already know you might live longer if you ditch the cigarettes and cheeseburgers, but the evidence suggests you might also live longer if you spend more time investing yourself in service to others and building meaningful relationships. Or just get a roommate. In another meta-analysis,[41] Holt-Lunstad calculated that subjects assessed as being lonely had a 26 percent higher risk of mortality. If they lived alone, the risk increased by 32 percent. The phrase "I'm alone but not lonely" may not hold up. It's not a question of how you feel. It's about connecting and being around other humans. In the mortality study, it didn't matter if the participants subjectively believed they were lonely. The measurement of social deficit was objective, with researchers getting data on things like how often the subjects had meaningful interactions with other people.

In an example of yet another Live to Give feedback loop, investing yourself in close relationships makes you more fun and interesting to talk to, and therefore more likely to get and maintain those vital connections. Social connections may help ward off cognitive decline, according to a three-year study[42] in Spain of 1,691 middle-aged and senior citizen subjects. First, the researchers scored the subjects' social isolation and established their cognition baselines by giving them short- and long-term memory tests, making them recall a series of numbers forward and backward and assessing their verbal fluency. From the start, **loneliness was significantly associated with lower scores for cognitive function. Over time, the lonely subjects' cognitive function scores declined significantly more than the scores for subjects with meaningful connections.**

The same rapid decline has been observed with loneliness and physical functioning, especially in the golden years. Researchers at the University of California–San Francisco studied[43] 1,604 over-sixty subjects for six years. First, they got a baseline of social connectedness by asking questions like "Do you feel left out?," "Do you feel isolated?," and "Do you lack companionship?" and proceeded to follow up with them every two years for six years total. They also tracked the participants' mobility, ability to lift objects and climb stairs, and do activities of daily life, like putting away the groceries and cleaning up. After controlling for socio-demographics and physical and mental health factors, the **lonely subjects had a 50 percent higher risk of experiencing a decline in everyday-life activity skills compared to non-lonelies. And the bucket kicker: They were more likely to die during the study period too.**

Our prescription: invest yourself in relationships. Give. Help. Serve. Or maybe volunteer to help those lonelies who have no one to reach out to. Right now, or as soon as possible, call a friend, make a date, and on that date, be helpful. And then make it a habit. It can really be as simple, and profoundly impactful on your health, as that.

If you are feeling a bit distressed by this discussion about loneliness and health, you might find comfort in reading how to mitigate mental health problems by focusing on others. How lucky: that's exactly what you'll find in the next chapter.

If you want to lift yourself up,
lift up someone else.

—Booker T. Washington

Mental Health Through Serving Others

The last chapter about physical health focused on older folks because, rightly so, scientists target that population when they are studying negative events like heart disease, dementia, and mortality.

The research on mental health skews younger, for the same reason that physical health research skews older. Scientists target the under-thirtysomethings in their study of mental health because that population is so high risk for negative events like depression, anxiety, and burnout. To be clear, this chapter is not about happiness (that's coming up next), but rather about impact on diagnosable mental health conditions.

Millennials born between 1981 and 1996 are called Generation Anxiety for a reason. Generation Z-ers born between 1997 and 2012, aka Zoomers, have skyrocketing rates of anxiety and depression. The pandemic forced them into remote learning and canceled all their after-school activities. Kids were suddenly isolated and cut off from interactions at the time of life when they're supposed to be learning and developing their social skills. Thanks to COVID-19, older Zoomers graduated college into a dismal job market. No wonder a 2021 Centers for Disease Control and Prevention survey reported that 63 percent of eighteen- to twenty-four-year-olds had symptoms of anxiety or depression. Twenty-five percent were using alcohol and recreational drugs to mitigate stress. The same percentage reported having serious thoughts of suicide. Inexperienced with the hardships of life, and with their executive decision-making brain region, the prefrontal cortex, still under construction (it's underdeveloped until about twenty-five), these kids were hit especially hard by the pandemic. It set the table for a banquet of psychological disorders to come, since 75 percent of all lifetime mental illnesses start before age twenty-four, per the National Alliance on Mental Illness.[1]

It's not all bleak for the younger generations though. They have more tools than ever to combat pathological conditions like depression, anxiety, poor mood regulation, psychological distress, and substance use disorders. An important tool in the toolbox, the Big Buffer that lifts mood and minimizes symptoms for all of these conditions, is . . . (drum roll) . . . serving others!

Let's look at the evidence for specific mental health conditions one by one, and we'll show you how turning your focus to other people can help with them all.

DEPRESSION

We all have blue periods in life when we feel sad, are low energy, and can't seem to enjoy anything. Down times are often a reflection of life circumstances, which makes sense. Up to 6 percent of Americans deal with the "winter blues," aka seasonal affective disorder, each year. According to pre-pandemic data from the American Psychiatric Association, 17 percent of people (about one in six) will have major depression at some point in their lifetime;[2] 13 percent of eighteen- to twenty-five-year-olds will suffer an episode of it in any given year. Its symptoms are grim: sadness, emptiness, hopelessness, feelings of worthlessness, irritability, frustration, crying, loss of interest in things that once brought pleasure and happiness, sleep problems, exhaustion, appetite changes, and cognitive problems. Suicide and suicidal ideation (just thinking about killing oneself, even if they don't want to do it; thinking that maybe everybody might be better off without you) are at their highest rates since 2000 among young people.[3] During the pandemic spike, one in four eighteen- to twenty-four-year-olds contemplated suicide.[4]

A heartbreaking statistic, but true. And how long will the effects reverberate?

Self-focus can be an important contributing factor. In an extensive University of Illinois at Chicago meta-analysis[5] of the published literature, the authors found that self-focus is linked to negative affect (depressed mood), and this is especially true when we ruminate in self-focus, meaning we can't get out of our own head.

The standard tools for treatment for major depression include therapy, medication, and behavior modification. Research supports the idea that a prescription for serving others could also be considered as part of the regimen, especially for young people. **A Brigham Young University three-year study[6] of five hundred adolescents found that giving and helping strangers and family members was protective against depression and anxiety symptoms.** If giving behaviors are combined with character strengths like hope, persistence, gratitude, and self-esteem, the participants not only made it through their teenage years, they were more likely to avoid depression symptoms and thrive.

This is great news for parents and teachers who are looking for ways to help kids during those rocky years. Even the most psychologically distressed teenagers can benefit from becoming Live to Givers. A Wayne State University study[7] asked ninety-nine highly distressed teens to keep a daily diary for ten days of their moods and their helping behaviors toward friends. On their most kind-to-others days, the participants' moods sparkled. The more depressed the teens were at the start of the study, the stronger the association between giving to others and decreased distress symptoms.

With all the pressures of medical school, depression and burnout are known to run rampant in this field. Sad but true, this also makes medical school a sort of "lab" in which mental health interventions can be tested. A study[8] by Jennifer Mascaro, Ph.D., and colleagues at Emory University looked at how their psychological stress impaired medical school students' mood and related to their compassion skills. Second-year students were randomly given compassion training or put on a waitlist (the control group). As expected, the first group reported increased compassion for others, but they were also found to have decreased loneliness and depression. The students who were depressed at the start of the study reported the biggest boost in both compassion skills and personal well-being. The study authors concluded that learning to give to others benefits people who most need to break out of an "it's all about me, *and I'm miserable*" mindset in order to rediscover their compassion-ability.

Eudaimonia: *having a deep sense of meaning and purpose in life.*

Hedonism: *prioritizing and seeking pleasure for yourself.*

If you were to tell your best friend or partner, "I'm depressed," they'd probably suggest doing something fun to make yourself feel better. Take a vacation! Party on! But hedonistic pleasure-seeking behavior is actually *not* the way to lift yourself out of the blues. What *does* reset mood are eudaimonic activities—things that give you a sense of meaning and purpose in your life. Researchers at the University of Illinois at Urbana-Champaign tested the hypothesis that hedonic activities might lead to "ill-being," and eudaimonic activities set people up for "optimal well-being."[9] **They followed forty-seven high schoolers for a year and found that the Live to Give teens' depressive symptoms declined. The Live to Party crew's depressive symptoms increased.** Seeking pleasure might seem like a good strategy when feeling down. Pleasure feels good, but only for as long as you're doing it. And then you wake up with an empty wallet and an aching head, wondering what the heck happened last night, more depressed than ever. Many of us know this is true experientially (guilty!), and now we know it scientifically too. Find purpose by helping others and it can help lift you out of depression. Bonus: no hangovers.

Researchers in Finland, a country that, statistics show, is slightly more depressed than the United States,[10] followed 1,676 youngsters for fifteen years from 1997 to 2012 to see whether "dispositional compassion"—having an inner voice that tells you to do good and help others—prevented or lessened depression symptoms over time. **Not only did helping others lower the risk of depression onset and continued symptoms, it headed off "subsymptoms" like a negative attitude and performance problems in life and work.** The data support that if people are Live to Givers when they're young, they may enter adulthood with stronger mental health.[11]

IT'S ALL ABOUT "I"

According to marriage counselors, using "I" statements instead of "you" statements keeps touchy conversations from spiraling into heated arguments. For example, saying to your spouse, "I felt hurt when you ignored me at the party" is probably more productive than saying, "You were a total jerk tonight!"

In a different context, using an abundance of "I" statements has been associated with bad things, like depression. For a University of Pennsylvania study,[12] researchers compared the "distinctive features of language" like use of first- or second-person pronouns in three hundred poems by nine poets who died by suicide and nine poets who did not.

The suicidal poets—John Berryman, Hart Crane, Sergei Esenin, Adam L. Gordon, Randall Jarrell, Vladimir Mayakovsky, Sylvia Plath, Sara Teasdale, and Anne Sexton—used self-focused words, first-person pronouns, and were less likely to use communication words like "talk" and "listen." The study author concluded that their "I," "me," "my" language indicated a preoccupation with themselves and detachment from others.

The non-suicidal poets—Matthew Arnold, Lawrence Ferlinghetti, Joyce Kilmer, Denise Levertov, Robert Lowell, Osip Mandelstam, Boris Pasternak, Adrienne Rich, and Edna St. Vincent Millay—used fewer "I," "me," and "my" statements, more "you" language, and words about harmonious interaction with others like "share."

This is not to say that writing about oneself is a "tell" for suicidal tendencies (but it is a flashing warning sign *for poets*). Self-focus *can* predispose people to becoming lonely and depressed, which, in turn, can make them anxious and self-conscious. Researchers at the University of Michigan did two studies[13] about the intersection of students' self-image goals and their anxiety and social distress.

(Cont'd)

For the first study, 199 freshmen filled out a survey every week for twelve weeks about their self-image goals. **Those with egoist goals (like making sure "I" and "me" looked good) tended to have increased anxiety and distress. Those with compassionate goals (like being seen as a giving and helpful person) had decreased anxiety and stress.** The second study looked at roommate pairs and had them fill out once-a-week-for-twelve-weeks surveys about their self-image goals. It reached the same conclusions, that having goals about being a compassionate, supportive roommate predicted less distress. Chronic distress was associated with less compassion and more self-focused goals.

College is a challenging time. You're trying to get to know yourself and figure out your place in the world. On top of that, students are often forced to read poetry by suicidal writers, which is agony for all but a few English majors. An important lesson: There's no "I" in student. There is a "u," though, and when undergrads stop ruminating about their own anxiety and set goals about helping others, research supports the idea that they can reduce their risk of poor mental health (at least to some extent).

ANXIETY

Anxiety is a mood disorder, with symptoms including nervousness, tension, restlessness, trouble concentrating, and dread that something terrible is about to happen. Physical symptoms associated with cortisol flooding—the stress response—include rapid heart rate, sweating, shaking, insomnia, queasiness, and other gastrointestinal issues. Anxiety is like living on a tightrope. At any second, with one stiff breeze, you believe you'll go reeling into thin air, with a very hard landing.

Standard treatments for anxiety are medication, talk therapy, cognitive-behavioral therapy, or a combination of the three. Another intervention that could be considered is increasing purpose in life[14] through serving others and just being a kind person. A University of British Columbia study[15] of 142 adults with a high level of social anxiety found that just four weeks of doing kind acts—little things, like paying a compliment, writing a thank-you note, helping a stranger carry a heavy bag to their car, giving a small gift, letting someone go ahead of you in line at the supermarket—can boost positive mood significantly. Not only did the participants feel better about the prospect of interacting with others, they reported an increase in satisfaction with their existing relationships, and they were less likely to avoid socializing.

If you have social anxiety, you know just how hard it is to walk into a room full of strangers. A colonoscopy without anesthesia would be more comfortable. Non-anxious friends might say, "Just put one foot in front of the other!" They don't get it. But consciously and purposefully committing to helping others in small, innocuous ways that won't trigger a cortisol flood might help you walk into any room and feel okay about it. You might even be able to talk to people and enjoy yourself.

LOSS

Grief is a normal, natural reaction to losing a loved one, by death, divorce, or estrangement. It's also appropriate to grieve a lost job you loved, or to mourn for a neighborhood you've moved away from. We have all grieved for the loss of our normal lives caused by the pandemic. We often see people's grief in the hospital, given the specialties we're in. It can be painful to witness.

It's not considered to be a mental health disorder, but the symptoms of grief—sorrow, sadness, preoccupation with the death or loss, anger, longing—can be just as devastating and derailing as depression or anxiety. "Get over it" is not a solution. Grief shouldn't be rushed, but it can be treated and eased, if temporarily, through serving others.

Author and entrepreneur Bob Buford wrote in *Halftime: Moving from Success to Significance* about his son's death by drowning. He said he knew that people suffering from emotional illness are sometimes given a "prescription" to do acts of service or kindness for others because it helps them rise above their own problems. He found that the only thing that could pull him out of the depths of grief, albeit temporarily, was when he was focused on helping others. It served as a "decoy" for his emotional system. It also showed him a new way of being, and opened the door to his larger, other-focused self and life mission to spread the word about the power of giving.

Usually, when someone dies, the bereaved are on the receiving end of nonstop casserole deliveries. It's a nice gesture. People need to eat. But research supports that giving to others can also help the bereaved alleviate their grief, at least to some extent. Stephanie Brown, Ph.D, and colleagues studied[16] 289 adults who were grieving after the death of their spouse. **The surviving partners found relief in providing instrumental support—offering advice and practical help to others. By giving, their grief symptoms declined more rapidly in the six to eighteen months after their loss, regardless of how much help and attention they received.**

After a loss, or if you feel lost, research suggests that you have much to gain by giving to others who are also in need. The science is clear: healing can come from helping.

BURNOUT

Burnout has only recently been classified by the World Health Organization as an "occupational phenomenon" related to chronic stress. As mentioned earlier, the three components of the burnout syndrome are: (1) depersonalization—the inability to make personal connections, (2) emotional exhaustion, and (3) the feeling that you can't make a difference. Mental symptoms include irritability, dragging, snappishness, distraction, and doubting your accomplishments. Physical symptoms are extreme fatigue, headaches, and gastrointestinal problems. It's like trudging along in a hamster wheel that keeps spinning and spinning. After a while, you feel exhausted and disheartened by working so hard to go nowhere. Nurses and doctors talked about burnout often during the pandemic, when the tsunami of patients flooded in, wave after wave. At first, we had limited understanding of the virus and strategies to combat it. Of course we felt overwhelmed. Burnout is the perfect term, because you feel fried, emptied, like a building after a fire.

Having done his Super Geek deep dive into burnout in health care, which eventually became an impetus for *Compassionomics,* Steve conquered his own burnout by ignoring the conventional wisdom that says caring less is a mental health protective shield. Instead, he followed the knowledge he gained researching other-service—including a British systematic review[17] about empathy and burnout among health care workers that concluded that more empathy is associated with less burnout, and vice versa—and he made an effort to care more for his patients and connect more with colleagues. By practicing Live to Give behaviors, he was energized by compassion and empathy, reconnected with his purpose in life, and overcame burnout.

Of course, you do not have to be a health care worker to feel burned out. It's not exclusive to the "helping" professions either. The OG identifier of "burnout syndrome," Manhattan psychologist Herbert Freudenberger, Ph.D., observed it in many different types of stressed-out career-minded people. A universal remedy, across all fields, is compassion. "Empathy . . . helps to fight stress. When we actively try to understand others, we often begin to care about them. Compassion, as with other positive emotions, can counter the physiological effects of stress," wrote Kandi Wiens, Ed.D., and Annie McKee, Ph.D., leadership experts and senior fellows at the University of Pennsylvania Graduate School of Education, in their article "Why Some People Get Burned Out and Others Don't" in the *Harvard Business Review.*[18]

Robust research shows that a key to resilience and resistance to burnout is this: strong, intimate, close, caring *relationships.* When you are connected to people (rather than focusing solely on yourself) and are privileged to provide them with support and solace, you are more resilient when faced with stress and hardship yourself. Through activation of what University of California–Los Angeles psychologist Shelley Taylor, Ph.D., calls the "tend and befriend" effect,[19] a flood of hormones from the Fantastic Four (most importantly oxytocin but also endorphins and dopamine) quiets our sympathetic nervous system. Stress is tamed, and our ability to handle whatever life throws at us goes way up.[20]

Not to get all gooey on you, but science shows that a way to mitigate burnout in your own life is to pour love all over someone else's life.

And in the end, the love you take is equal to the love you make.

—Sir Paul McCartney

ADDICTION

When Mazz was in medical school, he won a prestigious summer internship serving at the Betty Ford Center in Rancho Mirage, California, one of the first residential rehab programs for alcoholics in America. Former first lady Betty Ford herself was his internship sponsor. One of the treatment tools at the center was the twelve steps of Alcoholics Anonymous (AA). At the time, as he was learning the steps, Mazz took a particular interest in their order. The first eleven steps—honesty, faith, surrender, soul searching, integrity, acceptance, humility, willingness, forgiveness, maintenance, and making contact—are mostly about looking inward and working on yourself. But the twelfth step is different. The last step is service, and it's about looking outward and committing to helping another person suffering from alcoholism. The experts in the twelve steps understand: if you finish eleven, you will most likely start drinking again. But when you make the commitment to serve as a sponsor (mentor and support person) for others who have gone through what you've experienced, you are significantly more likely to stay in recovery. Serving others can make sobriety stick, as confirmed by a Brown University study.[21]

What's the mechanism that makes this work? Serving others allows you to get closure (you were helped; helping someone else closes the loop) and accountability. If someone else's sobriety hinges on your own, you are more likely to maintain it. Taking on the care of a vulnerable person forces you to get real close, real fast; having another deep, intimate relationship is a good thing. Your recovery takes on a whole new level of meaningfulness when the sobriety, health, and well-being of another person hinges upon it.

GOOD, OLD TIMES

We've focused on the other-service mental health benefits on young people, but they work for older people too. Live to Give behaviors really can help change your outlook.

- A UCLA and Yale University study[22] found that focusing on others buffered stress about one's own worries. Study subjects kept a diary about it. On any given day, when the participants were out and about, doing good through prosocial acts, their well-being went up and negative feelings went down. The researchers concluded that prosocial behavior (for example, kindness for others) mitigates the negative effects of stress in everyday life. Other-focus doesn't *change* your circumstances. But the **research supports the idea that helping someone else in distress can help you forget your own worries, at least temporarily.**

- Researchers at Columbia University and the Massachusetts Institute of Technology studied[23] strategies for emotion regulation—that is, managing your own emotions. For three weeks, they ran an online interactive training program about regulating emotions in social situations. **The participants who used the most second-person language ("you") were most engaged in helping others with their problems, compared to first-person ("I") people who shared about or received help with their own issues.** The "you" group had lower depression, more gratitude, and increased perspective-taking of their own lives, leading to their greater emotional regulation and well-being.

- One more: for a University of Texas–Austin study,[24] researchers found that **over-sixty-five-year-olds who volunteered to serve others had lower depression levels than non-volunteers,** in part because it encouraged them to connect with other people. An interesting twist on their findings: when old-timers volunteered for religious organizations, they had greater mental health benefits than those who volunteered for secular causes. Perhaps this is because religions emphasize the righteousness of serving others, so the good acts are reinforced by doing, and the environment.

Mental health issues are like the out-of-wedlock children of an English duke. No one wants to acknowledge that they exist. If you or your child is depressed or anxious and needs help, you often have to go through the rigmarole to get insurance to pay for it—that is, if you can find a good therapist at all. And, unfortunately, there's still some stigma and bias out there about conditions that some people believe are "all in your head." (Fortunately, that stigma is beginning to lift. People are now seeing what should have been obvious all along: some people get diabetes, some get cancer, some get hit by a car, and some get depression, anxiety, and so on. We should look at all of these conditions through the same lens.)

Serving others is a mental health therapy that every single person can access. It's essentially free, so there's no need to do mortal combat with an insurance company to get it covered. And it's the only "medication" that has virtually zero negative side effects. If we turn the spotlight around and broaden our perspective beyond ourselves—getting out of our own heads—our well-being spirals upward. When people stop fixating on "me, myself, and I," and shift toward "How are *you* doing?" their anxiety, depression, grief, addictions, and obsessions can begin to fade.

Just recently, a friend of ours told us about her terrible, horrible, no good, very bad day. An important client took his business elsewhere, and our friend convinced herself she'd never work again and would most likely die alone on the street, homeless. At the depth of her anxiety, her sister called her in tears over a fight she'd had with her husband. Our friend instantly snapped out of her funk to help her sister. The simple act of shifting her focus to come to the aid of a loved one changed her entire outlook. Her mood went from cloudy to clear in a matter of minutes. She could have said, "I've got my own problems to deal with," and hung up. If she had, she might still be envisioning herself pushing a shopping cart of dirty blankets in Times Square. Instead, she jumped to help, calmed her sister, felt energized (Helper's High), and gained perspective on her own troubles. Her client didn't un-dump her. Nothing about her life changed . . . but her anxiety abated for a while.

Okay, that's enough about depression and anxiety and stress. Let's move on to far more pleasant topics.

Does giving make people *happy*?

Is "warm glow" the same thing as *joy*?

A giving heart is a full one, but does other-focus bring on a deep feeling of *fulfillment*?

Speaking for ourselves, we're *thrilled* to present the data on how serving others affects your emotions, coming right up.

The surest way to happiness is to lose yourself in a cause greater than yourself.

—Unknown

8

Happiness Through Serving Others

Before we get into the science about how you can give and serve your way to happiness, we need to discuss what happiness *is*.

There's the colloquial use of the word "happy," which most of us associate with a big smile, a sunny day, a warm puppy. Sometimes, that good feeling we equate with happiness is nothing more than a dopamine hit in the brain. NYU professor Scott Galloway said, "Happiness [as such] is just a sensation, just a dopa hit. You can get it from Netflix, Chipotle, or Cialis." Superficial happiness is temporary, lasting only as long as the funny movie, burrito, or sexual adventure. David Brooks describes that happiness can come from "a victory for the self" as we move toward goals or when things go our way, like when our team wins the big game.

Another word for happiness is "fulfillment," a term that might fall into the self-care, self-help domain. If you are chasing fulfillment, you might have to go around the block many, many times, and still never catch it. It can be elusive. The visual on fulfilment: picture an empty heart-shaped vase embedded under your ribs. Pouring love, purpose, and success into that vase (ful)fills it to the brim. Those "follow your bliss" college graduation speeches might mention a happy future in finding fulfilling work. But they're short on the *how* to find it and *what* that even means. We'll go into depth about fulfilling work in the next chapter about success. For now, just know that, vis-à-vis happiness, research suggests that you won't fill a yawning hollowness inside with mere dopamine hits, binge-ing episodes of *The Office,* or even winning the lottery.

And what about *joy*? Bestselling author and declutter expert Marie Kondo wrote in *The Life-Changing Magic of Tidying Up* to keep any personal object that "sparks joy," and to get rid of everything else. Kondo-ing joy equates happiness with objects that might make us feel secure, amused, comforted, proud, or confident. Decluttering your house or garage will give you a serotonin hit of accomplishment. But a wall of well-organized tools on a punchboard is not going to reduce your risk of heart disease, dementia, and stroke the way that Live to Give behaviors and attitudes could. In this sense, joy may just be that: a spark. It's not an eternal flame that provides a lifetime of "warm glow."

A happy word we'd like to associate with Live to Give behaviors and at-titudes is "transcendence" (that is, transcendence of self), or rising above a normal experience into . . . a higher plane? A righteous consciousness? Attunement with God? The transcendence version of happiness might not even feel good per se, but it is fuller and richer. Many times, while driving home after a long, hard day at the hospital, we've felt wiped out, completely spent. But along with the physical and mental fatigue is a sat-isfying certainty that we did our absolute best to try to make a difference for someone else, even if it wasn't possible to give them the outcome they were looking for. Steve calls this feeling "good tired." It's something like transcendence, in that you can float above exhaustion on a silver-lined cloud of serving others. Philosopher and physician Albert Schweitzer must have felt "good tired" in his day. He once said, "Life becomes harder for us when we live for others, but it also becomes richer and happier."

The opposite of "good tired" is "plain tired," when your day is nei-ther meaningful nor purposeful, evoking no happiness or anything else except fatigue and perhaps frustration. Day after day of feeling "plain tired" is what leads to burnout. But it can be avoided, by making an effort to connect with others in meaningful ways.

American psychologist and the director of the University of Penn-sylvania's Positive Psychology Center Martin Seligman, Ph.D., is a Big Question kind of guy, and he asks a whopper in his bestselling book *Au-*

thentic Happiness: Using the New Positive Psychology to Realize Your Potential for Lasting Fulfillment: "What kind of life makes people happy?"

He described three ways to go. The first is what he called "the pleasant life" of hedonistic pursuits. By seeking pleasure, you will feel superficially, temporarily happy. The data on this is clear, as we previously discussed, that hedonic happiness is fleeting. It doesn't come close to the well-being/ life satisfaction benefits of eudaimonic (having a higher purpose) pursuits, aka Live to Give behaviors.[1]

Dr. Seligman's second plane is "the good life" where happiness is found via engagement or deep concentration when everything else falls away, what Hungarian American psychologist Mihaly Csikszentmihalyi famously called "flow."[2] When in the "flow" zone, you are using your strengths and fully engaged in them. You could live in a rundown shack, but when you are actively engaged in doing what you're good at, you'll get a flood of positive emotions. David Brooks talks about flow as "the dissolving of self." When you are lost in your work or a cause, needling personal ambitions are forgotten. In freedom from self-interest, we feel happy.

Dr. Seligman's final (highest) plane is what he called "the meaningful life" of using one's strengths to serve others, finding a sense of belonging and purpose that creates the deepest, most long-lasting happiness. In his TED Talk[3] on the subject, Seligman described conducting a survey that asked participants, "To what extent does the pursuit of pleasure . . . [the pleasant life], the pursuit of engagement [the good life], and the pursuit of meaning [the meaningful life] contribute to life satisfaction?" The results of the initial survey—and fifteen replication studies—found that the pleasant life made "almost no contribution to life satisfaction," he said. The good life of engagement strongly contributed to life satisfaction. But the meaningful life made the strongest contribution of all. If you have meaning *and* engagement, he said, pleasure is like the cherry on top of the sundae. A combination of all three—in effect, ice cream, hot fudge, and the cherry—is "the full life." An empty dish without pleasure, flow, or meaning is "the empty life."

These findings are not just the musings or opinions of Dr. Seligman or his study subjects. It's what he, and other researchers, found through the same type of rigorous scientific inquiry that determines evidence-based medicine—for example, when to undergo surgery or what medications to take. And what they found in their research is that an unhappy life is empty of engagement and meaning.

As we've noted earlier, the pursuit of personal happiness is often solitary. It narrows your worldview to judging whether your own feelings are good enough. A narcissist can be happy about crushing the competition, landing an attractive partner, or making their first million, but that feeling lasts only so long before the egoist hunger grumbles again. A narcissist's heart-shaped vase has holes in the bottom. Fulfillment doesn't last.

Transcendence is surrender of the self at the service of others, but it's also using your strengths to help people in meaningful ways. You bask in a deep sense of belonging by making that effort. As we pointed out in the data, including the Harvard Grant Study, relationships are one of life's brightest joys, and the key to developing intimate deep connections is demonstrating genuine care and commitment. Feeling "good tired" means you've done right by others, and those positive vibes don't go away. Through deep commitments, transcendence accumulates over time, and it is built to last. It doesn't fade. It lingers and rises up every time you remember it, which inspires more helping behaviors. Your heart-shaped vase overflows.

Apologies to the Partridge Family, but you can't really "get" happy. Instead, the path to transcendence is *giving*.

I slept and dreamt that life was joy. I awoke and saw that life was service. I acted and behold, service was joy.

—Rabindranath Tagore

When you habitually shine your light on others, you radiate with your own inner light. The Giver's Glow is a side effect of sacrificial service. David Brooks wrote, "You can tell a person who radiates joy. They glow with an inner light, they are delighted by small pleasures. They live for others and not for themselves. They make unshakable commitments. They have a serenity about them, a settled resolve. They are interested in you, make you feel cherished and known, and take delight in your good."[4]

We have all met people like this. It seems like they never had a bad day in their life. If you talk to them, they will invariably invoke many of the traits of a Live to Giver.

THE HAPPIEST MAN IN THE WORLD

Neuroscience research shows that the most potent activator of brain circuits involved in the experience of human happiness is actually this: compassion for others. French scientist (and Buddhist monk) Mathieu Ricard is more than just an expert in compassion, he is a true outlier among outliers, having logged tens of thousands of hours over the course of his lifetime in meditation on loving-kindness and compassion for others.

When Ricard was studied[5] in Richard Davidson's lab at the Center for Healthy Minds at the University of Wisconsin–Madison, researchers found something startling. **After connecting 256 electrodes to Ricard's head and performing an EEG, as well as fMRI scans of the brain, they found that he was an outlier in one particular way that had never been seen before in their (or any) research. Compared to the data for 150 control subjects—regular people—Ricard was off the charts in his brain activity for *happiness*.**

The data were not merely a couple of standard deviations above the norm either. Ricard's happiness zone brain activity was so far outside the bell curve that he was in a world all his own. And for this reason, he became widely known as "the happiest man in the world."

What was he doing to make his data fly off the charts? Meditating on one thing and one thing only: compassion for others. Ricard considers compassion for others to be the happiest state, ever. The Dalai Lama concurs. He once said, "If you want others to be happy, practice compassion. If *you* want to be happy, practice compassion."

> The joy that compassion brings is one of the best-kept secrets of humanity. It is a secret known only to a very few people, a secret that has to be rediscovered over and over again.
>
> —Henri Nouwen

CAN MONEY BUY HAPPINESS?

Let's just get this subject out of the way.

People think that having money leads to happiness. Granted, the *lack* of money and the stress of financial insecurity can make it harder to be happy. Research shows that the average middle-class person is happier than the average poor person; the average high-earning person is somewhat happier than the average middle-class person. But once you have enough to pay your bills with just a little extra for fun and security, incrementally more money won't bring you more happiness.

A landmark 2010 Princeton University study[6] led by psychology professor Daniel Kahneman, Ph.D., found that **with increased annual income happiness goes up—but happiness levels off when income reaches around $75,000 annually (approximately $90,000 now). Above that threshold, they found no relationship between income and happiness.** Incidentally, the study also found that, contrary to the teaching of the Notorious B.I.G., "mo' money" does not necessarily cause "mo' problems," mo' unhappiness—or mo' happiness, for that matter.

So if you have enough to pay the mortgage, educate your kids, splurge on date night, take some vacations, and maintain a safety cushion, research suggests that there's not much difference in happiness between someone in a three-bedroom split level in Scranton, Pennsylvania, and someone in a fifteen-bedroom mansion in Palm Beach, Florida. Some subsequent research has suggested that there might be some degree of correlation between income and happiness above the threshold found by Kahneman and colleagues, but the effect, if present, appears to be quite small. That is, the variance in income at higher levels explains only a small amount of the variance in happiness.

In the next chapter, we'll explain how Live to Give behaviors actually help you earn more money, making it easier to get to the happiness income threshold, and above it. Scott Galloway wrote about the research on income and happiness in *The Algebra of Happiness: Notes on the Pursuit of Success, Love, and Meaning*. As we mentioned earlier, his take on it is that money is just "the ink in your pen" that allows you to write your life story—ideally, about making a positive impact on others that will wind up giving you purpose and, eventually, transcendence. In that case, being rich *can* make you happier than you would be otherwise because you may have more ink in your Live to Give pen. On the other hand, if you were to use money/ink to write the story of a life motivated by ego and pleasure, or not helping anyone else, it'll turn out to be a tragic story with a sad ending. We can't help thinking of Tony Montana in *Scarface*, in his sprawling mansion, surrounded by lavish possessions, dying alone with only one "little friend" left, his Uzi.

Comedian George Carlin once said, "We buy shit we don't need, with money we don't have, to impress people we don't like," and yet so many of us believe that this pattern of conspicuous consumption might make us feel good. Contrary to dorm room posters from the 1980s that read, "He who dies with the most toys wins," materialism actually can make people miserable, according to a George Mason University study.[7] **Being preoccupied by acquisition is associated with negative emotions and less gratitude, competence, and meaning, as well as being less connected with others. Research supports the conclusion that relentless acquisition seems to be a fast, flawless formula for *unhappiness.***

Even if you happen to be in dire financial straits, according to a London School of Economics study,[8] volunteering to serve others was associated with well-being and more happiness among those who gave their time to religious organizations. Maybe we can thank God for that. Low socioeconomic status *was* associated with poor health in volunteers and non-volunteers alike. However, low income was only associated with unhappiness among non-volunteers. High- and low-income volunteers were equally likely to be happy.

I wish everyone could experience being rich and famous, so they'd see it wasn't the answer to anything.

—Jim Carrey

CAN SPENDING ON OTHERS BUY HAPPINESS?

In terms of happiness, wealth comes in the quality and intimacy of our relationships. The way to nurture relationships—inside and outside your family—is by investing in others' happiness. Attention one-percenters: by investing in people, we don't mean putting them on the payroll and managing to remember the names of your staff's kids. We mean sincerely caring and connecting with friends, family, neighbors, by giving them your time and attention, in addition to money.

In 2008, *Science* published a landmark study[9] led, once again, by Elizabeth Dunn, Ph.D., co-author of *Happy Money: The Science of Happier Spending*, that sparked a lot of interest on the topic. How we spend our money may be at least as important as how much money we earn. The study found that spending more of one's income on others was associated with greater happiness. Further, it found that **participants randomly assigned to spend money on others experienced greater happiness than those randomized to spend money on themselves**.

In a 2012 follow-up study,[10] Dunn and colleagues Lara Aknin, Ph.D., and Michael Norton, Ph.D., asked participants to recall either making a purchase for themselves or for someone else, and then to report on how happy the purchase made them. After that, the participants were asked to choose how they would spend an imaginary windfall of cash. **The participants who'd recalled spending on someone else were much happier immediately after reflecting on that memory, compared to the group who thought of splurging on themselves.** The giving group were more likely to spend a sudden influx on others too, in the near future. The study shows two key points: (1) just the memory of spending money on others promotes happiness and (2) thinking about spending on others makes people feel so good they want to do it again, as soon as possible. The happiness of "prosocial spending" creates a feedback loop, a virtuous cycle, that keeps rolling. Helping brings happiness; happiness brings more help-ing. Live to Give superstar Paul McCartney (him again) sang, "My heart is like a wheel. Let me roll it to you," perfectly describing the yearning for transcendence, set to a catchy tune.

People are urged to "give till it hurts." But actually, giving doesn't hurt. Give till it helps.

Research shows that pleasure, "winning," collecting stuff, self-spending does *not* produce top-shelf happiness. *Giving* does that. Drs. Dunn, Aknin, and Norton widened their lens to analyze[11] surveys from all over the world, encompassing more than 100 countries and 200,000 people, and found that, **in every region on Earth, those who give do-nations to charity are happier than those who don't, regardless of in-come.** "This correlation wasn't trivial," said Dunn. "It looked like giving to charity made about the same difference for happiness as having *twice* as much income."[12] In fact, giving makes people feel wealthy. This is why one-percenters themselves get hooked on philanthropy. Giving is the only thing that makes them feel richer.

So, in the short term, to feel a happy dopamine hit to the brain *right now,* you could go to the store and splurge on something for yourself.

In the long term, to feel happier every time you think about it, sci-ence says you should go to a store and buy something for someone else. "How" you spend is independent of "how much" you spend. It doesn't matter how expensive the gift is. For an international study,[13] participants promised to either: (1) spend money on other people over a four-week period or (2) spend it on themselves for the same length of time. The first group was, in fact, more generous in general over that time period, and participants reported feeling happier than the second group. **In fMRI brain scans, researchers found that just the promise of being generous engaged the reward centers of the brain, regardless of the size of the gift.** The brain reacts to being generous the same way whether you intend to give someone a Lexus or a Matchbox car, as long as it is intended to be sincerely meaningful to the other person.

So it truly is the thought of giving that counts.

If you help someone else, you're less likely to feel guilty or regret-ful about the spending, which you might if you splurged on yourself. Guilt and regret are more relevant for some people than others based on psychological factors. For those who wind up regretting self-spending, the momentary dopa hit of the purchase is canceled out by guilt. (If that rings some bells for you, reread this paragraph before you hit that buy button on Amazon next time.) Guilt and regret are far less likely to happen if you give to someone else. In that case, you only feel good; so good, in fact, that you want to keep doing it. Not our opinion; it's what the science shows.

Giving—time or money—to others truly is *your* pleasure. We have a friend who loves to do things for her pals, like throw birthday parties and make crafty gifts, almost to the point of embarrassing the people who are on the receiving end. "When they say, 'You don't have to do that for me,' I tell them that I *want* to," she said. "It's my love language! When I throw a party for someone else, it makes me feel awesome." Doing things for others brings happiness in a purely biological sense by activating the reward/pleasure center of the brain.[14] Just watching someone else donate to charity can give you the same feel-good sensation as eating dessert. Maybe our friend throws all those birthday parties for the cake. Or maybe it's for the brain-on-cake feeling. Works either way.

GIVE EXPERIENCES, NOT STUFF

Another path to buying happiness is to spend your money on meaningful experiences. A pair of University of Texas–Austin studies[15] found that people derive greater life satisfaction from spending money on experiences (travel, meals out, tickets to concerts and theater) versus buying material goods (jewelry, furniture, gadgets, and clothes). While in the midst of either having a fun experience, making a material purchase, or not buying anything (the control group), participants were surveyed about their in-the-moment happiness. The group with the consistently highest happiness score were out in the world, sharing experiences with others.

What's the Live to Give link? The experience of, say, whitewater rafting isn't necessarily going to make you happy long term in and of itself. The positive emotion comes from sharing the experience with loved ones, bonding, triggering Fantastic Four hormones to flow through your brain like the rapids you navigate in that rubber raft. Any activity that strengthens and deepens relationships will, over time, produce more happiness—and health benefits—in your life.

We have a friend who invests in family bonding by paying for his entire family—his wife, kids, parents, siblings, nieces, nephews, in-laws—to go on all their vacations as a huge group. He's fortunate to be able to afford it, but as he says, "What's the money for, if not spending it on making memories with the people we care about the most?" When he talks about taking his parents and kids to Disney World for the first time and sharing the awe together, he gets a lump in his throat. "I loved it more than anyone because I got to watch the wonder on their faces," he said. "And every time I think about it, I burst with happiness all over again, like I'm seeing it for the first time. You don't get that kind of joy from a piece of furniture."

PLANTING A HAPPINESS GARDEN

Having positive emotions like happiness falls under the category of "psychological flourishing," the state of thriving in your relationships and feeling successful about who you are and how you function in the world. When we think of the word "flourishing," we picture a seed growing into a sturdy plant, stretching toward the sun, buds opening into colorful flowers, strong stalk swaying gently in the summer breeze, bees buzzing.

Contentment is okay. Contentment is being a frog on a log nearby. But what we really want is to *flourish*, to be dynamic, vibrant, growing, reaching upward, like that plant.

You will not flourish by focusing on your own happiness as a goal.

A study[16] by Sonja Lyubomirsky, Ph.D., and colleagues looked at the difference between self-oriented and other-oriented behaviors and their effect on mood and well-being. For six weeks, the researchers split their 473 participants into groups that performed acts of kindness either for others, the world, or themselves (a control group stayed neutral). The two types of **other-focused behaviors—kind acts for others and the world—both produced increases in "psychological flourishing"** (using a well-validated scale of measuring emotional and psychological effects and social well-being) and decreases in negative emotions. The self-focused and neutral behaviors didn't improve mood, increase positive emotions, or decrease negative ones. Those participants stayed the same, like a seedling that never takes off. Treating yourself will not make you a happier, more confident, successful person. But research shows that looking around for ways to help others is like fertilizer and direct sunlight for your emotional development.

An important aspect of emotional confidence and success is self-esteem. Ironically, you get more self-esteem by doing things that help other people. For a British study,[17] researchers recruited 719 participants and randomly assigned them one of two tasks, either taking compassionate action to serve others or focusing on themselves by writing about a childhood experience. Over six months' follow-up, those who took action to make someone else feel better showed big bumps in happiness and self-esteem. The other group got bupkis.

No one is going to say, "Don't be self-reflective" or "Don't write that memoir." If there is a memoir stuck inside you, it should probably come out. But bear in mind, as this study suggests, writing about your past won't necessarily change your present or future happiness. Taking action to help someone else does.

HAPPINESS FOR THE AGES

Getting old might not be so joyful in certain aspects, although, as previously discussed, you can mitigate the ravages of time through other-focused behaviors. You can also boost mood and happiness the same way. A Duke University study[18] of data from 689 older adult respondents to the national Social Networks in Adult Life survey found that providing social support—helping and caring—to friends and children is associated with well-being, even more than receiving it (unless from a spouse or sibling).

Re: spouse and sibling relationships. If you take every opportunity to help each other, you'd all reap the benefits physically, mentally, and emotionally and your relationship will be strengthened. Just pointing out the evidence. No guilt. Only science.

Here's a chicken-and-egg Big Question for you: *Which came first, happiness or success?*

Answer: *You're not happy because you're successful, you're successful because you're happy.*

This might go against the conventional wisdom about success. But, as we'll show you in the next chapter, it's possible that everything you've been taught about so-called success is actually wrong.

There are three ways to ultimate success:
The first way is to be kind. The second way is
to be kind. The third way is to be kind.

—Fred Rogers

Success Through Serving Others

We spend more of our waking hours at work than anywhere else. "As adults there is nothing that more preoccupies our lives. From the approximate ages of twenty-one to seventy—we will spend our lives working. We will not sleep as much, spend time with our families as much, eat as much or recreate and rest as much as we work," wrote Loyola University business school professor Al Gini in *The Journal of Business Ethics*.[1]

Unfortunately, during those forty-nine years of our working life, many of us are under constant stress. Are we working hard enough, pleasing the higher-ups, making enough money? Our American ideal is to strive, to reach for more. Nowadays, it's not good enough to have one job. You have to have a side hustle too. If you don't, you're missing out on the potential success and wealth that everyone else is raking in. Our culture dictates that if you're not perpetually "super busy," you're not working hard enough. And if you don't, say, take work emails over the weekend, you might look bad to the boss. So we work, work, work, knowing that, if we don't strive and drive until we're approaching burnout, someone else will gladly step into our job.

The culture of ambition and overwork is the driving force behind our current definition of economic "success." For many, it's all we know. But are we *happy* with our backs bent over the grindstone? Are we better at our jobs? We are, as a culture, living out the law of diminishing returns—the more work we do, the worse off we may be.

According to data from the Psychologically Healthy Workplace Program of the American Psychological Association (APA)[2]:

- Thirty-three percent of U.S. employees are chronically overworked.
- Twenty percent of employees report making serious mistakes.
- Eighty-three percent of employees show up for work even when sick due to a heavy workload and the perception that taking time off is "risky."

The impact of overwork on relationships—the crucial Live to Give factor that, long term, predicts happiness and well-being—is devastating. The scales of the work-life balance are tipped toward the wrong side. Per the same APA data set:

- Eighty-three percent of employees check their work email at least once a day while on vacation.
- Fifty-two percent of employees report that their jobs interfere with their personal/home life; 43 percent report that their families interfere with their job performance.
- Thirty-one percent of adults are stressed out from balancing family and work responsibilities.
- The conflict between work and family demands is associated with low life satisfaction and increased emotional distress.

We've been taught that, to be successful, we have to work ourselves to ashes and sleep when we're dead. (The irony: the chronic stress of intense self-focus may get you to your final rest much faster.) We've been conditioned to believe that we are in constant competition with our colleagues, and that bosses have to be tough to get the most out of us; corporations have to exclusively focus on the bottom line in order to grow.

None of that is actually true, according to the science of success. Crushing the competition to become the "winner" who takes it all might be the American definition of success, but egoist self-focus—as an individual and a company—is the antithesis of serving others and, therefore, extremely unhealthy and not as profitable as assumed.

True success in one's field means mastering the skills, the "science" of that profession. By developing those science skills, you will find engagement (flow) and fulfillment by applying them to serve others, including the people (your coworkers and managers) who you may spend more time with than your family. Striving for recognition and achievement—as opposed to engagement in the work or the meaning-fulness of using your skills to help others—is obviously self-focused. Although the research shows egoist strivers have a hard time getting to the top of the pyramid, if they defy the data and ascend only to look down on the people they trampled on their way up, it's unlikely they'll feel a sense of fulfillment or well-being.

> I know people who have a lot of money, and they get testi-monial dinners and they get hospital wings named after them. But the truth is that nobody in the world loves them. If you get to my age in life and nobody thinks well of you, I don't care how big your bank account is, your life is a disaster.
> —Warren Buffett

Often, "successful" people are actually miserable. The show *Succession*, about an insanely wealthy family that controls a media empire, dramatizes the trap of egoist success. Every member of the Roy clan is a back-stabbing, sniveling, loveless, self-hating person. "Success" without fulfillment isn't really success at all. If one is privileged with power and riches and doesn't use the "ink in the pen" to write a story of giving back by serving others, they have squandered their success. This causes a condition called "soul rot." Prognosis: poor. While the Roys in *Succession* are destroying each other for more power, nearly 46 percent of the world's population lives on less than $5.50 a day, according to the World Bank. In all of our striving to reach the next income threshold, the next promotion, we often forget to take perspective. You're prob-ably doing just fine where you are. And if you wonder why you're not achieving more or feel stuck in a rut, it might be due to not having an other-focused life. The data suggest that self-interest holds people back in their careers.

There is a huge *disadvantage* to stressing about your success goals. Shawn Achor, author of *The Happiness Advantage: How a Positive Brain Fuels Success at Work and Life,* said in his TED Talk[3] that we have it backward. We think success leads to happiness. But it's the other way around: happiness leads to success. According to his research, the external world (your awards, salary, job title) can only predict 10 percent of long-term happiness. Ninety percent of it comes from a positive outlook, like being optimistic and altruistic.

The equation "hard work + ruthlessness = more success" doesn't add up because, as Achor explained, every time you experience a win, your brain moves the goalposts. You're always upping the ante on what it means to be successful. You hit your sales target! Great! But now you have to set a new, bigger target to feel the same dopa hit of achievement. "If happiness is on the opposite side of success, your brain never gets there," said Achor. "We've pushed happiness over the cognitive horizon, as a society. And that's because we think we have to be successful, then we'll be happier."

When, in fact, if we're happy, we'll get the "happiness advantage" of a more highly efficient brain, increased energy and creativity, and reduced stress—the factors we need to be successful at work. Starting with happiness improves business outcomes. Achor's data show a 31 percent bump in productivity when the brain is positive rather than neutral or stressed. We agree with his finding that doctors are 19 percent faster and provide more accurate diagnoses with a positive mindset.

What all this has to do with Live to Give behaviors: we know that people are happier, and have more well-being and life satisfaction, when they are focused on others. So to become happy, and then successful, the science shows that serving others is the launch point for a brilliant career.

The world of the generous gets larger and larger; the world of the stingy gets smaller and smaller.

—Book of Proverbs

EARLY PREDICTORS OF SUCCESS

We love studies about kids. Adults have a lot of baggage and, as study participants, their personal histories can influence their responses. But kids are pure. Their behavior is more inherent than conditioned. A longitudinal Italian study[4] looked at the association between inherent kindness in third-graders and subsequent academic achievement. Researchers asked teachers and classmates to rate the students on their prosocial behaviors (cooperation, helping, giving, sharing, consoling) and antisocial behaviors (verbal and physical aggression, disruption, and selfishness). When they followed up five years later, the now-eighth-grade kids who'd previously rated high in giving behaviors on average did better academically and had more solid friendships compared to the antisocial kids. Specifically, they found that the **students' kindness for others in third grade explained 35 percent of the variance in academic achievement and 37 percent of the variance in social connections in eighth grade.** The study did not confirm that being a kind kid at eight means you'll get into Harvard at eighteen. Nor did it say that straight As in junior high guaranteed similar success in high school. But, being a kind, emotionally connected kid did predict good grades and having friends in early adolescence, supporting the conclusion that kindness leads to happiness, which then opens the door to success.

A longitudinal study[5] published in *JAMA Psychiatry* tracked 3,020 Canadian kindergarten children from 1980/81 to 2015 to see if their very early social development had any impact on their future income (the conventional measure of success) as thirty-three- to thirty-five-year-old adults. Initially, teachers rated the kids on their social behavior as well as attentiveness and anxiety. Fast-forward a few decades, the now-mid-thirties female participants were earning slightly less if they were inattentive kids. But the most striking findings were in the male participants. **Among males, after controlling for things like IQ and family background, a one standard deviation increase in kindness toward others at age six was independently associated with a 6 percent higher annual income at age thirty-three to thirty-five. If that association were to continue and compound over a career lifetime, it could be a lot of money.** Another study found that among kindergarteners from low socioeconomic neighborhoods, kindness predicted for better outcomes in education, employment, criminality, substance use, and mental health nineteen years later.[6]

"That is the ugliest f**king skirt I've ever seen."

—Regina George in *Mean Girls*

Tina Fey's 2004 film *Mean Girls* became a pop culture phenomenon because it challenged the idea that, to be popular (that is, accepted and revered), you have to be a Regina George/Queen Bee, secretly miserable while tormenting others with cruelty and intimidation. But if we really want our tweens and teenagers to be socially successful, we should teach them to prioritize kindness instead (and not to try to make "fetch" happen; *it's not going to*!). Giving behaviors, not intimidation, make a kid well liked. A University of California, Riverside longitudinal study[7] of nineteen classrooms of nine- to eleven-year-old students in Vancouver randomized the participants into groups. **One group was instructed to perform three acts of kindness per week for four weeks; the other group, the control, wasn't. The kind-acts group experienced significant increases in peer acceptance (popularity), compared to the control.** Increased social status was related to other benefits, like academic success and a reduced likelihood of being bullied. The perception that the nice kids are just low-hanging fruit for bullies to squash is not actually supported by the data.

And if we want our kids to be academically successful, we should teach them to prioritize helping others. Angela Duckworth, Ph.D., author of *Grit: The Power of Passion and Perseverance,* and colleagues randomized 1,982 public high schoolers[8] into one group who gave younger students an eight-minute dose of motivational advice—like how to stop procrastinating—or into a control group who didn't. The advice givers wound up getting better grades in math and other subjects during that academic quarter. If teens are given a position to support other people, they may feel good about themselves and do well socially and academically. While it may seem surprising that an eight-minute intervention boosted achievement over an entire academic quarter, this research suggests a valuable approach to improving academic performance: one that puts people in a position to *serve*.

All these studies, taken together, show how being other-focused as a kid—not for the wrong reasons like ego or guilt, but just because it makes them happy—can have long-term positive effects on relationships and future success.

NICE GUYS FINISH FIRST (EVENTUALLY)

Do you need to be a self-centered apex predator who eats underlings and colleagues for breakfast to get to the top? We know that being other-focused is a path to happiness, but does it doom you to the stagnation of middle management?

The stereotypical view of the person who rapidly ascends the corporate ladder or the entrepreneur who builds a wildly successful company is that they are an absolute predator. They will stop at nothing to destroy anyone or anything to achieve their goals. Many of us have a cartoon in our heads of an evil, devious, greedy villain like Charles Montgomery Burns from *The Simpsons,* muttering in a sinister voice while steepling his fingertips, "*Excellent, Smithers!* Release the hounds!" We have been conditioned to believe that we have to be selfish, combative, and manipulative—the three traits of a "disagreeable personality"—to rise. Although Mr. Burns types might stick out in your mind as prime examples that only jerks reach the top, workplace villains who get ahead are actually the exceptions rather than the rule.

There is no association between disagreeableness and gaining power in the professional realm, as we will show you in a bit. In fact, the people most likely to make it to the top of the success ladder are Live to Givers who demonstrate kindness, generosity, and compassion. It's not so hard to understand. If your colleagues like you, they'll be happy for your success. If they dislike you, they'll resent your rise, and plot to take you down.

Don't get us wrong: it's definitely possible to be a ruthless egomaniac and become the boss of everyone. But it will be tough. If you show up in our emergency department with arrows in your back, put there by everyone you've treated badly on your way up, you will get the medical attention you need. And we won't even say, "We told you so!" (Maybe.) Oh, let's just say it now. *We told you so.*

Every office (and *The Office*) has a Dwight lurking around, plotting power plays. As we already know from years of observing the power dynamics at Dunder Mifflin, a small paper company in Scranton, Pennsylvania, being out for yourself (or sucking up to the boss) will not help you get ahead or make you popular.

In a pair of longitudinal studies[9] from the Haas School of Business at the University of California–Berkeley, researchers looked at whether being aggressive, selfish, and manipulative actually help people attain power. Do jerks finish first? Researchers measured participants' "disagreeableness" (which they defined as aggressive, selfish, and manipulative behavior) before they entered the labor market. Fourteen or so years later, they followed up to see how their careers were going. Controlling for gender, ethnicity, and corporate culture, researchers found that **the subjects who'd originally scored high in disagreeableness did *not* advance up the ranks at work. The generous extroverts wound up getting promoted to positions of power.** Dominant, aggressive behavior might have reflected the participants' desire to grab power. But that was nullified by their lack of engagement with and generosity toward colleagues. What gets you the corner office is not aggressively fighting for it, but by engaging with the people in the office you spend so much time with. Send those birthday cards to coworkers. Share credit freely. Pitch in to help another team meet its deadlines even if you get none of the glory. If you ignore the niceties, don't be surprised if you wind up on your peers' enemies list. But if you are a Live to Giver, you'll generate peer support and their applause when you succeed. The choice is clear: a target on your back, or the wind at your back.

In 1958, social psychologist Edwin Hollander came up with the phrase "idiosyncrasy credits" to explain how nonconformists can still get ahead and be influential within a group.[10] It's an accumulation of goodwill based on the positive impression you make on others. If you are perceived by others as worthy, they will appreciate you, even if you rise above them or act differently from them.

In a corporate culture where there's an expectation that people are out for themselves, the most generous rack up idiosyncrasy credits that eventually help propel them to the top. Three experiments[11] from the University of Kent examined whether giving behaviors impacted one's status within a group. The first experiment, a "cooperation game," gave each participant a small amount of money to contribute to a shared fund. Then, the researchers said they'd double the fund amount and would split it evenly among the participants. If you gave all your money to the fund, the group would benefit. But if you held on to your own, you'd lower the group amount, and still get your portion of the divided kitty. You'd also be a self-dealing jerk, which some of the participants turned out to be. In the next experiment, the **participants had to break into teams and elect their leaders. Eighty-two percent of the time, they chose the people who were the most generous in the previous experiment to be team leaders. So the "chumps" who gave their money away were put in charge of the self-dealing jerks who didn't.** If people witness your acts of generosity, they will reward you by lifting you up in their esteem, and in your career.

Talented people make others jealous, and jealous people will try to take the gifted down a peg. But if the talented people are also givers, otherwise jealous people will like them, and even help them, as in, "You're special and you like me, so I must be special too." For a University of Minnesota study,[12] researchers investigated the relationship between cognitive ability (smarts) and victimization at work (harassment for being a smarty-pants). As predicted, the smarties were indeed victimized, as geeks and nerds have been by popular types for time immortal. However, the gifted types in the office who were disagreeable and standoffish tended to rub the rabble the wrong way and their victimization was increased. They might rise in power, but they were still mocked. The intellectually gifted who were agreeable and worked well in a team were given tons of idiosyncrasy credits and were much less likely to be made fun of.

So, right now, you might be thinking, *Being generous and agreeable is the way to get ahead! So I'm going to fetch coffee and write birthday cards for everyone at work, and watch my star rise!* Not so fast. The motivation behind giving behaviors matters. If you're only doing it to get ahead, you'll get nowhere.

Adam Grant has studied what motivates people to work at the

highest level, and it's not selfish dreams of glory. In one study,[13] Grant and team tested whether having an other-oriented task significance—for example, "Let's kick ass because we're doing it for a good cause!"—fired up employees and increased productivity. Task significance did increase job performance for university scholarship fundraisers at a call center when they interacted for just five minutes with someone who benefited from receiving the scholarship in question. Compared to a group of callers who read a letter from a beneficiary, the callers who interacted directly with a grateful human being were more persistent in getting money from potential donors, staying on the phone with them 142 percent longer and raising 171 percent more money. The other groups' performance was flat. Another experiment focused on swimming pool lifeguards. Those who read stories about other lifeguards saving lives had an increased perception of their social impact and worth to the community, which boosted their helping behaviors by more than 20 percent.[14] The callers and lifeguards weren't motivated by success, they were inspired by the benefit of the help they could provide. The science supports the notion that people who are motivated by significance, not success, are more successful.

GIVE MORE, MAKE MORE

Career advancement is one thing. But let's get to what many of us really care about: income. Does giving behavior increase your earning potential? It sounds counterintuitive. But the science shows there is a strong association between being a Live to Giver and making more money.

A recent study[15] set out to determine if cynical types (eye-rollers and side-eye-ers who assume the worst in people, are totally pessimistic, and don't trust anyone) were more likely to forgo valuable opportunities to work with others that are gladly accepted by their less cynical counterparts. The researchers gathered data from longitudinal surveys of a population of Americans' cynicism level (for example, did they think humans are, by nature, untrustworthy?) and then followed their incomes over time. **Researchers found that the participants who** said, essentially, "People suck!" had lower incomes than those who said, "People are awesome!" It's just a tiny leap of logic to assume that cynical people may not be enthusiastic givers. For one thing, they're obviously not giving their fellow humans the benefit of the doubt. The negative assumption, and correspondingly lower income, shows that you don't earn the big bucks by being a hater and a downer. We can assume that those who were eager to give the benefit of the doubt to others also had a more positive affect—that is, happiness—in addition to a higher income. Once again, happiness leads to success, not the other way around.

You might think that the opposite of giving money—holding on to it for yourself—would pay off, but a University of South Carolina study[16] blows up that theory. Like crime, selfishness does not pay. Drawing on cross-sectional and panel data sets, researchers found that people who give to and serve others tend to have both more children and more income than selfish people. As for why people persist in self-interest even though it hasn't worked out so well for them: the theory is, they have been conditioned to believe selfish people make more, despite personal experience to the contrary, so they're not going to change. You know that phrase "in for a penny, in for a pound," referring to British currency, about sticking with a plan, no matter what? If people are committed to selfishness, they're definitely in for a penny. But the pounds they long for might never materialize.

Economist Arthur C. Brooks, Ph.D., Harvard professor and former president of the American Enterprise Institute, analyzed data[17] from the 2000 Social Capital Community Benchmark Survey and found strong evidence that giving money away can make people more prosperous. As he said in *Y Magazine*, "Say you have two identical families—same religion, same race, same number of kids, same town, same level of education—everything's the same, except that one family gives $100 more to charity than the second family. Then the giving family will earn on average $375 more in income than the non-giving family—and that's statistically attributable to the gift."[18] He believes the formula for prosperity starts with happiness. Giving makes people happy, and happy people are eager to pitch in for the good of the team; they have lower stress and less burnout so they can be more productive; they have better health and can therefore show up for work more often and have the energy to do their jobs well. Therefore, they're more likely to be promoted and given raises. Giving can make you richer, in both a literal and a figurative sense.

One way to earn more is to negotiate for it. And, as you might expect by now, go-for-the-jugular negotiators who are only in it for themselves are less likely to get what they want in the end. **A Dutch meta-analysis[19] of twenty-eight studies found that negotiators who were less contentious and actively tried to solve problems for the other side of the table actually secured happy outcomes for both sides versus negotiators who refused to budge, as in, "My way or the highway."** Research shows that the best negotiators want to help the other party in addition to themselves, expanding the pie for a true win-win.

JUST BECAUSE YOU'RE IN THE DRIVER'S SEAT DOESN'T MEAN YOU HAVE TO RUN PEOPLE OVER

As we go through life, we hear many sayings about how to behave, from parents, mentors, and public figures. You can see how much we appreciate inspirational quotes from great thinkers from the way we've sprinkled them on these pages. Leadership seems to be one area in particular where you can apply the principles of those sayings, especially if they're about serving others.

One saying that has filtered in over the years is "People don't quit jobs, they quit bosses." Horrible Bosses are such a stereotype, and so reviled, that Jason Bateman made a movie about them—twice. Needless to say, tyrannical leaders are not focused on how they can best serve others. But did they start out as a disagreeable, high self-interested, low other-interested types, or did power transform them?

Rasmus Hougaard, author of *Compassionate Leadership: Doing Hard Things the Human Way*, co-wrote an article[20] in the *Harvard Business Review* about "hubris syndrome," a phenomenon originally described by English physician and parliamentarian David Owen.[21] Hubris syndrome is a mental disorder that occurs in people who have possessed power due to sustained overwhelming success. Spending so much time at the top, with all its pressures and responsibilities, can change people's ability to feel empathy and compassion. Wild success can rewire Big Shot brains to care less about the little people. Call it neural hardening. The only way to reverse it is to practice compassion or having the "intent to contribute to the happiness and well-being of others," wrote Hougaard. Habitual compassion is a countermeasure for hubris-related loss of empathy. Since empathy is an essential skill for a leader, proactive compassion allows a powerful person to reconnect to others and perform at his or her own job at a higher level.

"Never let them see you sweat" is an aphorism about making people think you're braver or more chill than you really are. People apply it at work to raise their competence profile. A more helpful saying for leaders would be "Never let them see you act like a jerk." According to a Western Washington University study,[22] **when both male and female leaders displayed "negative emotional tone"—anger or sadness—their underlings assessed the bosses as less effective. The drop in esteem was significant.** When the bosses expressed a neutral emotional display, there was no associated drop in employee's opinions of their competence. Interesting (sexist) finding: male bosses who displayed sadness had much lower effectiveness ratings, perhaps because, culturally, men's sadness is perceived as weak. Female bosses took a rating hit if they displayed sadness *or* anger. Unless women showed anything but positivity or neutrality, they lost some respect from their employees. It's a burden for male and female bosses to hide their real emotions at work. Expressing yourself negatively might feel cathartic, but it can have a bad effect on others. An other-focused approach would be to put the feelings of your staff first, and wait until after you leave the office to get angry and throw things and/or cry.

Another leadership aphorism we like is "Feedback is a gift." One of a boss's main responsibilities is to tell his or her employees what they're doing right (positive feedback as praise, reinforcement, and congratulations) as well as what they're doing wrong (corrective feedback as instruction, suggestions, and criticism). To teach, you have to correct, but it's not so easy to dole out negative comments. It can be embarrassing, awkward, and potentially emotional. People's feelings might get hurt. Jack Zenger and Joseph Folkman, CEO and president of Zenger/Folkman, a leadership development consultancy, surveyed nearly nine hundred people about whether they avoided (or preferred) to give (or receive) negative (or positive) feedback. **Fifty-seven percent said they preferred receiving corrective feedback; 72 percent believed their performance would improve if bosses gave them more of it. However, Zenger and Folkman also found that leaders avoided giving negative feedback like the plague.**[23] Leaders seem to equate giving criticism with being tortured themselves. But their staff wants to hear it.

In a study[24] of medical students, participants were broken into two groups. One group received specific, constructive criticism about how to tie surgical knots. The other group received only general praise from their educators. The students who received specific critique and suggestions for improvement bettered their performance and reported higher satisfaction in the experience. The students who were just praised? No performance improvement, flatlined satisfaction. As a patient, which student would you want sewing you up, the one who was actually taught, or the one who always got a pat on the shoulder?

People who aren't raging narcissists understand that unwarranted praise is empty and pointless. Still, a self-interested boss might shy away from criticizing to save him- or herself the discomfort of possibly making someone feel bad. An other-focused boss understands that feedback is a valuable gift they offer to their employees. By shining your light on them and offering an honest, timely, specific, well-explained evaluation of their work, they will be happier and more successful employees,[25] and you'll be a more effective leader. Also, when you praise, do it in public. Pride enhances performance.[26] When you criticize, do it in private. Humiliation serves no one.

This next saying comes from Mazz's mom: "Never ruin an apology with an excuse." When bosses or colleagues try to mitigate an "I'm sorry" with self-interest ("But it's not my fault"), the apology becomes meaningless and might cause resentment. The point of an apology is to make someone else feel better, not to defend yourself. Making excuses is all too common in toxic workplaces led by unforgiving bosses. Coworkers feel like they have no choice but to cover their own behinds to save their status within the organization. But even small children know that excuses are self-focused, and sincere apologies are other-focused. A British study[27] had 120 four- to nine-year-olds react to stories about people breaking the rules where the transgressor used an apology, gave an excuse, or offered no explanation at all. The kids thought that the transgressors should face the same consequences regardless, but they universally reacted far more positively to the apologizers. They rated a straight-up sincere apology as a more honest attempt to make amends with the aim of preserving social standing (as the scientists defined it, "prosocial motives"). Making an excuse was seen as immoral, and all about protecting yourself. Bosses and coworkers: if you screw up, saying you're sorry is how you serve others and earn idiosyncrasy credits to mitigate future mistakes.

Our colleague Tom Rebbecchi, M.D., an emergency physician at Cooper, always says, "You only have so many coins in your pocket." So if you spend your energy coins at the start of a busy emergency department shift by getting in an argument with another doctor or a nurse, you'll be so exhausted by the end, you'll have none left to do what you need to do. When a staffer comes to Mazz to complain about another colleague—busy doctors might get testy if they don't have time to help you—he asks, "So should we get them down here and unsheathe the sword? Do you want your pound of flesh? I'll take their head off for you, if that's what you want."

They look at Mazz like he's crazy and say, "Uh, no, that's not what I want. They're not so bad, just busy. It's okay. Forget it." All of a sudden, the complaining doctor is defending the person they were just mad at. Mazz steers them into empathy and connection, which serves everyone. The "I'll take their head!" ploy lowers the temperature in the room. By defusing a tense situation, leaders are being other-focused. By conserving staffers' energy through compassion—and dissuading them from wasting it on negative emotions like annoyance and anger—they can enhance job performance.

Case in point, the famous "Cookie Study"[28] by social psychologist Roy Baumeister, Ph.D. He and his team at Case Western Reserve University instructed their college student participants not to eat for three hours before coming to the lab for an experiment. The hungry participants were then randomly split into three groups: (1) those who were given a plate of chocolate chip cookies, which they were forbidden to eat, and a plate of radishes which they could nibble freely; (2) those who were given the same plates of cookies and radishes, but they were told to have at both of them as they wished; (3) the control group that wasn't given any food at all.

Next, all three groups were given geometric puzzles to solve. They didn't know at the time that the puzzles were unsolvable, a trick of social psychologists to test perseverance. The second group—those who were free to eat whatever they wanted, cookies and/or radishes—made on average 34.3 attempts over nearly nineteen minutes before they gave up. The control group made 32.8 attempts over nearly twenty-one minutes before they quit. The first group, who were allowed to eat radishes only? They made just 19.4 attempts and gave up in eight and a half minutes.

Why did the radish eaters give up more quickly? Their energy was so drained by the mental effort of not diving into that plate of cookies, they had nothing left to work on the unsolvable puzzle. The groups that didn't deplete their energy with restraint had more "coins in their pockets" to try to solve the puzzle.

As a leader, your job is to focus on keeping coins in your employees' pockets, and not cutting holes in those pockets with negativity. Happiness begets energy, begets high performance, begets pride, begets more happiness, begets success.

HOTNESS: A SUCCESS STORY

If culture were the guide, the Alpha Male archetype—big, brutish, competitive, ego-driven—is the most physically attractive to women. In movies, women swoon over emotionally distant, withholding, uncaring types who treat them badly. But do women in real life like what they see when a man acts like a selfish jerk?

Sara Konrath, Ph.D., and the University of Pennsylvania's Femida Handy, Ph.D., recently ran three studies[29] to find out if doing good increased physical attractiveness—what these researchers call the "good-looking giver effect." For the first study, 131 people interviewed three thousand senior citizens and rated them on physical attractiveness. Although the raters didn't know the seniors' giving behaviors at the time of rating their attractiveness (they were blinded to that data), seniors who volunteered to serve others were rated as more attractive. This association between giving behaviors and attractiveness remained consistent, even after adjusting the analysis for factors like age, marital status, and physical health.

The second study focused on teenagers and young adults. Subjects who were generous and volunteered to serve others as teenagers were rated as more attractive when they reached young adulthood. (Again, the raters of physical attractiveness knew nothing about the young adults' giving status years earlier.) What's more, when the study began, the teens who were rated most attractive tended to become more generous as they grew up.

The third study analyzed data from a very large fifty-four-year (1957 to 2011) longitudinal study conducted in Wisconsin. For the physical attractiveness piece, researchers went back in time to get more data—they pulled old (1957) yearbook photos from more than fourteen hundred of the original study subjects and rated their physical attractiveness as teenagers. The teens who were rated as more attractive in 1957 turned out to be most likely to donate money to worthy causes with up to forty years of follow-up data. But that's not all. Researchers also found that, as middle-aged adults, the subjects who were the most financially generous givers were also rated more physically attractive as they entered their Golden Years.

What on earth about being a giving person translates into attractiveness in the eye of the beholder, even if said beholder knows nothing about your giving behaviors?

Konrath and Handy considered a phenomenon called "the halo effect." Beauty itself causes others to attribute lovely types with

(Cont'd)

positive characteristics—intelligence, high moral standards, good social skills. Archetypically, as we've discussed, the villain is an ugly troll and the hero is an attractive prince or princess. Hence, attractive people get a big advantage in life. They earn more and have wider social circles, which might explain why they are givers (more money to give; more friends to give to). But their research mitigated the beauty bias by adjusting the analyses for income, gender, marital status, mental and physical well-being, and religious participation. So the givers didn't, in fact, donate to causes that serve others only because they were rich, healthy, and happy in life. In addition, the raters of physical attractiveness were blinded to the subjects' giving behaviors in all three studies, so that potential source of bias (knowing if they were Live to Givers when rating their attractiveness) was removed as well.

We can't help but think about David Brooks's observation, that Live to Givers radiate with an inner light that is plainly obvious to friends, strangers, and psychology research study attractiveness raters alike. Konrath and Handy drew a similar conclusion. **Giving behaviors are so beneficial to your physical, mental, and emotional health that the effects shine out of your fine eyes, glowing skin, and bright smile. They wrote, "Using the best available evidence, we find that it is indeed possible that doing good today may make you appear better-looking tomorrow."**

If you're single and swiping for a mate, up your giving game for a month, and retake your profile picture. It might net more winks, waves, and messages. Or, if you're looking for love the old-fashioned way, stop spending money on Botox and facials, and give it to a cause that serves others, and you might catch more eyes at parties and gatherings.

To quote the Greek poet Sappho, "He [or she] who is fair to look upon is good, and he [or she] who is good, will soon be fair also."

Conversely, to quote a friend of ours who works in the beauty business, "Nothing looks pretty on an ugly personality."

GOOD COMPANY

Not to overwhelm you with stats, but there are a ton of data that show that ethical companies that care about the well-being and advancement of their employees are more profitable than unethical ones that only care about profits and stock price. It only makes sense: employees that are supported by their organizations are more loyal, motivated, and productive, and that's a boon for the company's bottom line.

More from the APA's Psychologically Healthy Workplace Program report:

- "Presenteeism" (feeling pressure to show up despite an illness) is associated with seven and a half times the lost productivity of "absenteeism" (calling in sick).
- Employees stay with a company for these top five reasons: exciting and challenging work; opportunities for growth; high-quality co-workers; fair pay; and supportive management.
- Companies with high employee morale outperformed those in the same field with low employee morale almost 2.5 to 1.
- The valuation of high morale companies was 1.5 times higher than those of medium and low morale companies.
- Companies that support employees with extensive training outperform the market (86 percent higher returns) compared to companies that have low investment in employee training.
- High growth and profitability companies provide more employee growth and development opportunities, and have 20 percent higher engagement levels, compared to companies that leave employees out to dry.
- Companies with the most effective health and wellness programs achieved 20 percent more revenue per employee, had a 16 percent higher market value, and delivered 57 percent higher shareholder returns.

Both former U.S. presidents Ronald Reagan and Bill Clinton put the same sign on the Resolute desk that read: "There is no limit to the good you can do if you don't care who gets the credit." (Mazz and his co-CEO,

Kevin O'Dowd, have both put that sign on their desks too.) Workers in collaborative, inspiring environments don't care who gets the personal glory. They're not doing it for themselves alone. Just knowing that you were part of a team that helps each other for the greater good is its own reward.

Adam Grant has done extensive research that proves giving makes people happier, and happiness improves performance and success. He's also found that supportive other-focused environments fuel creativity and fire up intrinsic motivation (being productive because you care about what you're doing). Taking perspective by asking, "How does my work impact others?" encourages people to think bigger, to develop ideas that are both more creative and more useful.[30] And it's not about individual acclaim. It's about serving others because doing good feels meaningful and fulfilling.

A workplace environment that is kind, as opposed to ruthless, inspires workers to up their Live to Give game. For a University of Cambridge study,[31] 111 people in a corporate workplace were randomly assigned to be "givers," "receivers," and "controls." For four weeks, the givers performed five acts of kindness for a specific list of receivers. (The controls did nothing.) Although the receivers benefited in the short term (measured by workplace competence and autonomy) and the long term (measured in self-reported happiness), the givers' benefits were greater. **Two months post-study, givers were less depressed and more satisfied with their jobs and their lives. The true beauty of this experiment: it was found that the receivers were inspired by the givers' kind acts, and, over time, it increased their own giving by 278 percent compared to the control.** The participants started falling all over themselves to serve each other. If anything, they might have become competitively kind. Who wouldn't feel good about going to work in such an environment?

A Rutgers College of Nursing study[32] collected data on 686 registered nurses from eighty-two medical-surgical units in fourteen acute care hospitals in the United States over a period of eight months to calculate their number of medication errors per one thousand patients. Working in a supportive practice environment was associated with error interception—stopping errors before they happened. When nurses feel supported at work by colleagues, the culture, and management, they wound up making fewer mistakes and catching each other's errors, which can save lives.

Live to Give workplaces foster collaboration, and when people find it easy and appropriate to ask for help, they make fewer mistakes, which is obviously better for the company's profitability and reputation. Our colleague Dr. Tom Rebbecchi has another favorite saying in the emergency department, "Never carry a coffin alone." The idea being, if you work in a giving environment, there should be a low threshold to ask for help. That's what the phrase is meant to remind us. When you have a challenging case with a seriously ill patient, if more people weigh in, errors get caught and you wind up with better patient outcomes. And if bad outcomes do happen, at least you know that you have done all you could to avoid it, and the burden is not carried alone.

MORE EMPATHY, PLEASE!

We talked a bit about the intrinsic motivation of perspective taking. Here's a dose of perspective for you: a *Washington Post* analysis during the pandemic found that one in six Americans didn't have enough food to eat. One. In. Six. In the "richest" country in the world. Let that sink in. Meanwhile, the top tier of the one-percenters actually did better than ever during the pandemic.

It begs the question: Do we have the wrong system, the wrong "dream," in place? Scott Galloway doesn't think so. He believes we have the right system, just the wrong execution. In his latest book, *Post Corona: From Crisis to Opportunity,* Galloway called American capitalism "the greatest system of its kind, the greatest upward lubricant of the middle class in the history of civilization." But (and it's a big but) he added, "Capitalism fails unless it rests on a foundation of *empathy* for other people."

In capitalism, it's expected that corporations fail. Competition between companies spurs innovation and prosperity. That's how the system works. So we shouldn't have empathy for corporations, per Galloway. But we need to make sure that as a society we do not fail *people.* He said what is wrong with the current version of American capitalism is this: "We've decided to protect corporations, not people. Capitalism literally collapses on itself unless it rebuilds a foundation of empathy." To fix it, we need to take some of our incredible prosperity, and direct it toward helping people.

"If we don't grab each other's hand, if we don't show greater empathy, if we don't start protecting people, not corporations, capitalism implodes," wrote Galloway. "Capitalism is not an organic state. At its core, there must be empathy for others."

Infusing our lives with empathy is a Live to Give ninja move. As the research shows, we'll make more; be more creative, productive, and inventive; make fewer mistakes; befriend our colleagues; and impress our leaders if we shine our light on others rather than relentlessly climb the ladder of success for our own glory. In short, by serving others, we serve ourselves.

But success can't be your aim in serving others. It has to be a byproduct, a "side effect," an unintended consequence, or, sadly, you won't get all those benefits.

When it comes to reaping the health, happiness, and success benefits of serving others, motives matter. Which just so happens to be the title of the next chapter.

To give without any reward, or any notice,
has a special quality of its own.

—Anne Morrow Lindbergh

Motives Matter

Ample evidence shows that motivation for altruism impacts its effects.

People who are *truly* altruistic and other-focused reap the most benefits.

But people who serve others only (1) to make themselves look good, (2) because they were forced to, (3) to get something in return, or (4) to make themselves feel better get minimal benefits, if any.

Simply, being selfishly motivated for doing good is associated with doing worse.

To enjoy all the physical, mental, emotional, and professional benefits, you have to do good for *the right reason*. By "right," we don't mean the moral or ethical righteous reason. We're not even close to paragons of virtue. We don't hold ourselves up as ethicists or moralists (although Mazz does have a degree in bioethics). Fortunately, we're not coming at our conclusion from a moral and ethical perspective. We've drawn a scientific one. The best research out there tells us that altruism "works" to boost your own well-being only if you do it with **the genuine intention to help another human being.**

Just *doing* isn't enough. You have to do it with a mindset in which you actually care.

FAULTY MOTIVE #1: TO LOOK GOOD

"I gave a donation to _____ and I hope you will too."
#warmglow #dogood

You know the people who make splashy donations to charities, and then humblebrag about it on social media? Virtue signaling to promote an outward display of altruism might convince Instagram followers of your generosity, but it doesn't make you an other-focused person who's bursting at the seams with glorious health and wellness goodies. If anything, it cuts off altruistic behavior at the knees.

First of all, as a reason to donate, public recognition typically fails. For a recent University of Arizona and Vanderbilt University study,[1] researchers asked subjects to make a donation decision in two different contexts: privately or publicly. You might think that, given social pressure, people would give more if they were being observed by family and strangers alike. The opposite was true in both cases. **Being watched decreased the likelihood of giving more because the study participants didn't want the observers to think that the only reason they donated was to look good. It diluted the altruism "self-signal" and gave them pause. Making a private, anonymous decision to donate kept the motivation pure, and they gave more.** So if you want to get in the habit of giving, focus more on the giving itself than on the optics of people knowing that you are doing it.

A German study[2] upholds the recognition-stinginess connection. The only measurable effect of "image motivation" is that it leaves a bad taste in your mouth. It's only natural to want to show yourself in a positive, prosocial light. But the data support the idea that when this intrinsic motivation is met by public recognition, giving sometimes suffers.

What about extrinsic motivations, like being paid to, say, donate blood? Per a study by Dan Ariely, Ph.D., and colleagues at Duke University,[3] if subjects thought they were "doing good" in order to "do well" (monetizing prosocial choices), their self-image took a hit and decreased their motivation to continue. All of a sudden, it doesn't feel so great to drive around in a Prius, if you worry people assume you bought the car for the tax break and access to the HOV lane.

Serving others for personal glory glitches your giving incentives. It jams the altruism mechanism in your brain. So if you're only doing it for that purpose, it won't work nearly as well or maybe not at all. So forget the meaningless gesture of virtue signaling how generous you are. We're not saying you shouldn't donate to worthy causes. Of course, click hard and click often. But to get those benefits, you might have to give something more precious than money: time.

The Live to Give strategy: Give time. A longitudinal study randomly selected more than ten thousand high school grads in Wisconsin and followed them from 1957 to 2011. A fascinating analysis[4] of the data looked closely at different types of giving behaviors among approximately one-third of the original cohort. They found that **"time-giving" behaviors—volunteering, caregiving, lending emotional support to friends and family—were associated with lower mortality risk, but giving money was not.** Other research shows that time giving is likely to produce "warm glow" feelings. Just writing a check? It can leave you cold.[5]

FAULTY MOTIVE #2: BECAUSE YOU WERE FORCED

"They made me do it."

It's become a common practice for civic-minded educational and religious institutions to have community service expectations for students and flock. The idea is to instill in young people and devotees the goodness of volunteering to help others. If an institution claims to care about its community, it makes sense to expect the members to walk the walk. Mandatory volunteering—*a fun new oxymoron; you saw it here first! Aka, "voluntold"*—certainly benefits the good cause that's been bestowed this literal "workforce." But does the volunteer get anything out of it besides the satisfaction of fulfilling a requirement?

Promoting prosocial activity to adolescents can cause them to gain a healthy perspective about their own lives and it strengthens their ties to the community. For a randomized trial[6] of ninety-seven adolescents from fourteen to seventeen years old, researchers at UCLA split them into three groups with specific assignments to do three times a week: (1) perform kind acts for others, (2) perform kind acts for yourself, or (3) just keep a record of daily events (the control group). The researchers measured the kids' well-being every week for four weeks. At first, they found no difference between the three groups. But then the researchers dug deeper. At the beginning of the study, the subjects completed an altruism assessment like the one you took in chapter 4. The participants who scored high in altruistic attitudes reaped the benefits of lower stress and more positive affect when they were put in the kindness-to-others group, probably because it lined up with their intrinsic motive. Those not high on the altruism scale did not get a boost. This supports the conclusion that it is not just the activity, but the mindset and motives that matter.

But that study didn't test for *forced* kindness. Researchers at the University of Oregon published a study[7] in *Science* about the distinction between pure and forced giving. Nineteen subjects were studied with fMRI brain scans, and then researchers gave them $100 in an account. One group was given the opportunity to donate to a local food bank; another group was *forced* to do it as a kind of tax; the control group wasn't obliged to donate at all and could keep the money for themselves. The researchers found that mandatory giving did activate the brain's reward center and triggered a pleasurable "warm glow" feeling. But the results—degree of reward center activation and warm glow—were on a spectrum. **When the subjects gave the money voluntarily, their neural reward responses were significantly stronger and more of a predictor of future voluntary giving.** So you may get some warm glow embers from forced giving. But if you give voluntarily, of your own free will (the Live to Give motive), you'll get a full-fledged warm glow fire.

One thing young people and senior citizens have in common is that forcing them to do something they're not inclined to do on their own is not associated with a health benefit. In a longitudinal study[8] of 676 older Japanese adults, subjects were categorized into four groups: those who were currently "willing volunteers" (say, the cat lovers who spend Caturdays at an animal shelter holding kittens), "unwilling volunteers" (like a criminal who is sentenced to community service), "willing non-volunteers" (someone who likes the idea of serving others but is not doing anything about it), and "unwilling non-volunteers" (the person who wants nothing to do with serving others, and it shows).

The elderly subjects checked in over a three-year period about how well they got on with their basic activities of daily living. **Among the willing volunteers, only 6.6 percent of them experienced a decline in physical functioning, followed by 16.3 percent of the willing non-volunteers, 17.4 of the unwilling volunteers, and 21 percent of the unwilling non-volunteers. Independent of whether they volunteered or not, a major factor in all this was willingness.** The unwilling were more likely to experience a decline in functional status over the next three years. So selfless motive is not only important for your fulfillment, happiness, and well-being, it may also be important for your physical vitality.

Don't bother forcing kids to participate in mandatory gun-to-the-head giving or serving. They might get a hit of dopamine—a fleeting spark on the spectrum of giving—but it'll fade and it's hardly the incentive kids need to set up a lifelong habit of serving others.

The Live to Give strategy: Autonomous altruism. To *really* incentivize giving, parents, teachers, and religious leaders can encourage (but not force) kids to do it on their own. Self-determination is the key. According to a series of University of Rochester studies,[9] people feel "energized" by helping but only if it is autonomous, the givers' own idea. Not only does autonomous motivation provide more satisfaction and well-being for the giver compared to controlled/forced giving, it is better for the receiver as well. So if you *choose* to deliver meals for the elderly, you'll transfer the good vibes to them, delivering warm glow along with a hot dinner. And you'll feel the energizing effect every time you knock on their doors. Not only will you get and give self-esteem and well-being benefits from autonomous helping, but that kind of helping makes helpers *more effective* at helping, and inspires them to continue helping in the future.[10]

FAULTY MOTIVE #3: TO GET SOMETHING IN RETURN

"I'll scratch your back if you scratch mine."

The Reciprocity Motive, or give-to-get, can be a simple swap, an unforced transaction. For example, if you donate a new library to a college, perhaps your profligate child will get an acceptance letter to attend the school.

Another variation of give-to-get is what we call the Scrooge Motive. The Dickens character was terrified and ashamed after a night of visits from the ghosts of Christmas past, present, and future, and in his fear and self-disgust, he decided to donate a goose and pudding to his abused clerk's family. Although he might have discovered a grain of empathy in his stone-cold heart for the plight of ill and innocent Tiny Tim (*God bless us, every one*), Scrooge's motivation for his sudden spasm of giving was to save his own ass. He believed that if he didn't change he'd be dead in a year. Scrooge's turn-around was a great ending to the story, and it certainly helped Tiny Tim, but it was spurred on by a gloomy prediction about his untimely death. Would it actually have undone that fate?

Giving to help yourself does not necessarily hasten death, but giving for the benefit of others has been associated with longer life. Another study from Sara Konrath and colleagues[11] looked at the effects of motive for volunteering and the subjects' mortality risk over a four-year period. The subjects were, like Scrooge, of an age when death was not a vague future prospect. The researchers found that the **regular, frequent volunteers with other-focus had a lower risk of dropping dead than the subjects who volunteered for strategic reasons.** In fact, the give-to-get strategic helpers' who were trying to get something in return had the same mortality risk as the subjects who didn't volunteer at all.

Unless Scrooge's transformation to serving others was sustained and changed from panic-driven to kindness-driven, it would have no impact on the spirit's dire prediction. If his giving was a one-and-done, we'd know where to find him next Christmas.

It's all about making human connection. Caring is the ingredient that turns giving into the elixir of long life. The joy of giving has to be its own reward. If you give with the idea that it'll somehow improve your situation through reciprocity or reputation, you'll wind up sorely disappointed. British researchers conducted a meta-analysis[12] of thirty-six studies encompassing 1,150 subjects on the neuroscience of strategic versus altruistic giving. The fMRI brain scan results can't be fudged. When subjects gave strategically, specific brain regions and pathways were activated. When they gave selflessly, other, different regions and pathways were activated. So the images of the brain on altruistic decisions looked *nothing at all* like the brain on strategic ones. The decision to send a goose to an impoverished family might have the same outcome for the receiver. But the experience inside the giver's brain depends on intention. **A German/Swiss study[13] published in *Science* isolated the distinct neural pathways of empathy-based altruism versus reciprocity-based giving and found that predominantly selfish individuals show different brain responses than selfless subjects.** Because selfless giving and selfish giving have different patterns of brain activation, it helps explain why people can have different health and well-being outcomes. They are distinctly different phenomena, at least as far as your brain is concerned.

If you donate a library to Harvard to become known for having deep pockets, it's unlikely to change anyone's opinion about you. If you give a huge charitable donation to your boss's favorite cause to get a leg up with the boss, you might receive special notice, but it won't make you happier, more likeable among your colleagues, or more successful at your job. Serving others as a means to serving yourself is like running in place, furious activity that gets you nowhere.

I tell my students: Don't aim at success. The more you aim at it and make it a target, the more you are going to miss it. For success, like happiness, cannot be pursued. It must ensue. And it only does so as the unintended side effect of one's personal dedication to a cause greater than one's self.

—Viktor Frankl

The Live to Give strategy: Adopt a giving attitude. The positive outcomes of adopting a giving attitude are a pleasant (yet unintended) byproduct of serving others—like a side effect, but a welcome one. Adam Grant wrote in *Give and Take,* "Giving first is a promising path to succeeding later. But if you do it only to succeed, it probably won't work."

A study[14] from Case Western Reserve University looked at the contributing factors of "successful aging" among 585 senior citizen subjects and found that "altruistic attitudes"—wanting to volunteer and serve—made "unique contributions to the maintenance of life satisfaction, positive affect and other well-being outcomes." It's the attitude, not just the acts, that give life meaning, and keep people engaged and happy until the end. Focus only on the acts, and you'll get Scrooged.

No one hopes that they'll wind up grouchy and depressed, and look back on life with bitterness and regret. We all know people like that. And we all know their opposites, people of an advanced age who are joyful, satisfied, connected, purposeful, and full of vitality if not youth. Research supports the idea that a genuine Live to Give attitude is a means to that happy ending.

FAULTY MOTIVE #4: TO FEEL GOOD ABOUT YOURSELF

"Listening to other people's problems made me feel good about my own."

If your only motivation for listening to others' problems is to feel virtuous or superior, or to troll for gossip, the act of listening doesn't qualify as a beneficial other-focus behavior. And it might not even help the other person. Feeling like a taker doesn't sit well with most people. For a New York University study,[15] partners in eighty-five couples kept a diary of their mood and the flow of emotional support between them for four weeks. Being the receiver of support and not having an opportunity to give back was associated with a spike in bad mood for the receiver. Giving support without expectation of reciprocity had the opposite effect; it decreased bad mood for the giver. The condition that lowered negative mood for both was supportive equity, or each partner's giving and taking the same or a similar amount of support.

Along with reciprocity, an essential element for the giver and the receiver is empathy. You have to have awareness and understanding of others' plight for it to count as other-serving, and therefore ensure your benefits. Empathy leads to pure altruism.

Back to an interesting question we posed earlier: Does altruistic motive truly exist (or not)? In 1981, renowned social scientist C. Daniel Batson, Ph.D., published a study[16] that seems a bit sadistic. That's right: another *shocking* psych study.

Forty-four female college students were asked to watch another woman, Elaine, also an undergraduate at the college, but who was an actor within the experiment, receive a series of electric shocks. (But not really though. No actual shocks this time. Elaine was only acting like she'd been shocked. And the subjects didn't really witness her get jolts in real time as they were told, they watched a videotape.) The explanation for the shocks was to see how Elaine fared on task performance in adverse circumstances.

The subjects were divided into four groups of eleven each: (1) those who had things in common with Elaine and would be permitted to leave after watching her get two of ten shocks, (2) those who had nothing in common and could also leave early, (3) those who had things in common but had to stay for all ten shocks, and (4) those who had nothing in common and had to stay for all ten.

After watching Elaine receive two shocks—she was really hamming it up with facial contortions to feign pain—the observers were asked if they'd be willing to trade places with Elaine and take her remaining eight shocks.

Among the subjects who did not relate to Elaine personally, the key factor was their ease of escape from watching this horror show. Those who'd been told they could leave early didn't want to trade places with Elaine. They relieved themselves of the stress of witnessing her pain by saying, "I'm outta here!" **The ones who were required to watch all ten shocks did offer to trade places with her, but their motivation was egoistical. They thought it'd cost them less emotionally to take the shocks than watching another suffer.**

Doing something for someone else only because it relieves your stress or makes you feel good about yourself does not bring about big benefits.

The subjects who related to Elaine were more empathetic. They could put themselves in her shoes (empathy) and had a higher motivation to help her avoid pain. Regardless of the ease or difficulty of their escape, they offered to trade places with Elaine to relieve her distress, not just their own as witnesses. Through empathy, and the sacrifice that flowed from that, they would relieve their own stress.

There is a whole domain of philosophy around altruistic egoism, and the examination of whether or not altruism is really other-focused versus another mode of self-focus. In other words, can there really be such a thing as genuine other-focus because it always comes back to how it makes you feel and what you stand to gain?

Using this classic psychology experiment of Elaine and the electric shocks as an example, high empathy people would help regardless of whether escape was easy or hard. But if it was egoistic, the people with empathy should be more willing to help when escape was hard than when it was easy. The findings support the conclusion that true altruistic motive, driven by empathy, is a real thing.

The Live to Give strategy: Take action. Taking steps to relieve another's suffering is at the very heart of what it means to be compassionate. Empathy involves feeling and understanding others' pain. It comes at a cost. But compassion and active altruism bring rewards that can overcome the distress of empathy.

"Feeling their pain" doesn't mean it has to be painful for you. Engaging them with Live to Give behavior will light up the positive reward centers of your brain, so you'll feel good about helping.

Deep suffering is not essential though. You might look around at your life and the people in it, and think, *Yeah, we're good right now.* Rather than giving Elaine electric shocks, the researchers could have just made her late to catch a plane. If the subjects related to her and empathized with her problem, they probably would have stepped up to help, just as they did to end real (but actually fake) pain.

"I'M BEING ALTRUISTIC FOR ALL THE RIGHT REASONS, SO WHERE'S MY PAYOFF?"

We were talking about some research from Stanford University with a friend, and she completely disagreed with it. The study[17] focused on the distinction between lending emotional support versus instrumental support, and their impact on the giver's well-being. The findings were that emotional support predicted well-being in the provider; instrumental help (helpful acts or actions but not necessarily with any empathy or emotional attachment to the receiver of help) produced well-being for the provider, but only if it was combined with emotional support. In short, it's not enough to help someone. You also have to care about them to get warm glow for your efforts.

"Bullshit!" said our colorful friend. "Where's my warm glow?"

She described an encounter she'd had with her twenty-five-year-old daughter, someone she cares about deeply. "We were on the phone for two hours talking about her recent breakup. I gave her free-flowing support until I was blue in the face. By the time we hung up, I know she felt a lot better. And I felt *exhausted.* After that call, my being was far from 'well,'" she said.

Our friend made an **autonomous** choice to **give time,** assumed an **altruistic attitude,** and **took action** to help someone with genuine caring and empathy and zero expectation of reciprocity. She did everything correctly, and yet she was not feeling any Live to Give benefits.

What's going on here?

The key consideration is time horizon. Adam Grant studied[18] firefighters and rescue workers and the benefits of their service. Turns out, they do get an affective boost from working to save other people, but not in the heat of the moment. Only once they get home after work and can reflect back on the significance of the work they have done and the help provided does their mood go up. So our friend might've been drained by her conversation, but if she were to look back on it after some time has passed, she might experience positive feelings and reap some benefits.

Plus, the caring aspect does matter. We asked her to imagine having this same conversation about a sad breakup with, say, her daughter's friend, someone she doesn't have deep feelings for but whom she might feel obligated to talk to. Her instructional support would have been similar. But on the call with her daughter, she had an opportunity to express her love by talking her heartbroken child off a romantic ledge about a guy who wasn't worthy of her. (Sometimes altruism means listening to someone else's angst when you'd rather do anything else.) Providing that service might not result in an instantaneous gush of warm glow. Again, the positive benefits accumulate over time. But having deep human connection and intimacy, in this case with her child, can bring more life satisfaction and happiness in the long term.

Another benefit: while our friend was on this call to talk about her kid's problems, her own concerns disappeared. They melted away, at least temporarily. She wasn't thinking of her deadlines and work headaches. Even if empathizing is painful and heavy in the moment, if you care about the other person and engage them with compassion, you'll have protection from your own stress and anxiety. By turning your focus to somebody else, you'll feel lighter and easier and simpler.

Last, our friend and everyone else who is engaged in altruism needs to remember one essential point: **serving others isn't necessarily going to be easy work. It's going to be pretty hard. You might not perceive the rewards instantly.** But giving of your time and energy with real caring is worth it for the ultimate rewards of fulfillment, good health, success, and, in this case, a close, loving relationship with one of the most important people in her life.

THE ONLY MOTIVE THAT MATTERS: HELPING OTHER HUMANS

So let's talk about public health for a minute.

This next paragraph will bring up some bleak memories for so many, including us. Back in the first waves of the COVID-19 pandemic, thousands of patients came through our doors. Our ICU was packed with patients on ventilators. We lost a heartbreaking number to the virus.

Along with treating patients, we also educated people about interventions to avoid getting sick, such as mask wearing, hand washing, and social distancing.

We found that people were more motivated to abide by those preventative behaviors if they were pitched as a way to help others rather than help themselves. Researchers at Harvard affirmed this framing in a study of 6,850 survey respondents. They tested three approaches to messaging, emphasizing either personal protection, public health, or a combination of the two. All three were effective to some extent, but the public health motive (protecting others) was the most effective. The researchers wrote that "the perceived public threat of coronavirus was more strongly associated with prevention intentions than the perceived personal threat." So the prosocial motive was the best strategy to change behavior.[19] Not saying that it worked on everyone, of course. But when people came together to try to stop the virus, it caused another contagion that we could be proud of: feeling motivated to protect and serve one another.

But you don't have to choose between yourself and other people. We're not living out *The Hunger Games*. You just have to focus on serving others, sincerely and then Live to Give benefits will flow to you as a byproduct or unintended consequence. Just turn the spotlight of focus away from yourself and onto them. You don't even have to love the person, just as long as the spotlight is on them.

HOW TO SUMMON SINCERITY

The information in his book might seem like a cheat code for using the power of giving to get back all kinds of benefits and live a better life. However, the giving half of the equation is layered. You have to set out to give on your own, with genuine care about the people you help.

Perhaps some readers might be groaning about the added requirement of sincerity on top of everything else. It's not so hard to train yourself to care for real. Sincerity can be summoned, making the effort not seem so onerous.

This concept of "emotional labor" comes from service industries like luxury hotels and customer support call centers. We think of it as the work we all do to make others feel good. It is not a medical or health care thing, although it can be applied, like in a key paper from the University of Washington published in *JAMA*.[20] They asked how physicians can get to compassion and empathy when they do not necessarily feel it, like at the end of a really long and stressful day. They're not always going to feel like doing the compassionate thing. But if they can get there emotionally, by using emotional labor, then everyone will reap the benefits.

The authors identified two types of emotional labor. The first, *deep acting*, was defined as "generating empathy-consistent emotional and cognitive reactions before and during empathic interactions with the patient." You summon emotion and inhabit the role of caregiver fully, your own version of Daniel Day-Lewis–style method acting—but in this case, it's method caring. It's not faking. The emotion is real, but with intentionality exerted to get there. Just like a method actor does to get into their role and emotionally "become" their character.

The other kind of emotional labor was called *surface acting* and defined as "forging empathic behaviors toward the patient, absent of consistent emotional and cognitive reactions." In other words, faking.

The *JAMA* paper acknowledged that deep acting is "preferred" (of course), but when that's not possible—when emotion is tapped out or you just don't know someone well enough to conjure up real feelings—surface acting is considered better than nothing. Like learning a skill, empathy takes practice. A lot of practice. But just making the effort to engage with empathy makes doctors more effective healers and ups their professional satisfaction. And from that stronger footing, they have the emotional bandwidth to elevate surface acting to deep acting—which isn't really acting at all.

Anyone who has small children at home does this quite frequently. No matter how stressed, tired, overworked, or overwhelmed caring parents become, they usually try to summon up the necessary energy with their children. They offer a consistent message of love, understanding, and hope when speaking to them, especially when their kids are frightened or upset. People intentionally put on a different face with their children to connect with them in those moments. It's because parents take the responsibility of how their kids respond to their words and behaviors very seriously. Parents understand that their interactions with their kids make an imprint on them. The energy it takes for a parent to push worries—work stress, paying the bills, and so on—to the back of the mind in favor of a positive, nurturing message about why doing your homework or being kind to others is important sometimes requires emotional labor. It's not always easy if you're feeling completely stressed in the moment. But you do it anyway, because that's what parents do. It's love, not faking.

Around now, you might be thinking, even if you're motivated by the right reason and you understand how good serving others can be for your health and well-being, does the awareness of gain eliminate the beneficial effects? In other words, did you ruin all of the potential Live to Give benefits for yourself by reading the first ten chapters of this book?

Nope. Although it is true that motives need to be sincere in order for the benefits to be realized, if people are aware of the increase in health and happiness they will receive, research shows that the benefit will still be there.[21] So being aware does not ruin the benefit. But the motivation must be selfless, so that the health benefits are a byproduct rather than the motivation. If you believe that altruism is beneficial for your well-being, it will be.

So that's it. That's all we've got. The data curator has been ransacked, and now you have all the proof you need about the physical and mental health, happiness, and success benefits of serving others, and the best attitude and motivation it takes to reap them.

But exactly *how* does one become a Live to Giver? What are the actual steps, the prescription? Take two altruisms and call us in the morning?

We have seven specific and evidence-based treatments, with dose recommendations and guidelines to follow, coming right up, in Part III: The Prescription.

THE PRESCRIPTION

Seven Steps to Take Now

No act of kindness,
however small, is ever wasted.

—Aesop

Start Small

The Sixteen-Minute Prescription

There is an evidence-based prescription that moves the needle for you and anyone else. To fill the prescription for this wonder drug, you do *not* need to quit your job, move to a third world country and dig wells, become an inner-city math teacher, spend every weekend ladling soup for the homeless, or donate a massive chunk of your income to charity.

Total life upheaval is not necessary. There is no barrier to entry to become other-focused.

In fact, to become a Live to Giver, the change required is more mental than practical at first. Instead of just moving through your life, stuck within-ward, look around for opportunities in your life now to serve others. Once you start searching for them, opportunities will appear. In fact, they'll be everywhere, and will seem limitless. And if you start taking those opportunities to serve others, your Live to Give benefits will start accumulating immediately.

Simply make the decision to give, help, care, and connect *more,* and you could be happier, healthier, and more successful for it, no matter what you are currently experiencing. A study published in the *Journal of Organizational Behavior*[1] analyzed data for sixty-four participants who were going through rough midlife transitions. What allowed the participants to grow through things like career disruption, divorce, and death of a loved one was making that "personal paradigm shift" that we mentioned earlier—to be more positive, enthusiastic, and altruistic as they progressed through life. Not only did they survive a rocky period, their personal paradigm shift allowed them to flourish. The participants were all over fifty, proving it's never too late to get better at life, as long as you set the intention to change from Me-ness to We-ness. Making the switch is not hard, but you do have to be very intentional about it.

YEAH, BUT WHAT'S THE *REAL* TIME COMMITMENT?

Time is precious and limited. We completely get it. When we've talked to people about the Live to Give research in casual conversation, like at a party, they usually nod and agree with the principles. But then they often say, "I don't have the time right now to do it. Maybe later when I retire."

"No time" is a ready excuse that is actually not supported by the science. Perhaps you can't devote every Saturday to helping a neighbor or volunteering for a cause that serves others. But, then again, exactly how much time do you spend watching TV or scrolling through social media? Not to sound judge-y. The fact is, research indicates that claims of "time poverty" are typically overstated. That perception is actually a symptom of self-interest. A key Wharton School/University of Pennsylvania study[2] found that, **if you give time to other people—just a tiny bit is enough—your subjective sense of "time affluence" increases, meaning that you feel like you have an abundance of time and are not in a hurry.** The researchers randomized study subjects to four different uses of time: spending time helping others; spending time on oneself; wasting time; and gaining an unexpected windfall of free time. Of all four uses of time, only the people randomized to *giving time away* (helping others) felt like they had more of it. The research shows that there is something distinctive about giving time to help others that transforms how you feel about the time that you have. So giving time actually gives you time! And when you feel wealthy with minutes and hours, you're more likely to commit to future altruistic acts.

No matter how "super busy" you are, surely you have less than one minute to spare to shine your light on someone else. Researchers at Johns Hopkins conducted a study[3] to determine the effect of physician compassion on patient anxiety, information recall, treatment decisions, and assessment of their doctor. The participants—more than two hundred women, most of whom were breast cancer survivors—watched a video of an oncologist giving a standard consultation (information only) or a video of the oncologist speaking with "enhanced compassion," making supportive statements like "I want you to know that I am here with you," "We are here together, and we will go through this together," and "I will be with you each step along the way."

The participants who watched the enhanced compassion video rated the doctor as warmer and more caring, sensitive, and compassionate than those who watched the "standard" video. But that's not all. Using a well-validated scale, the researchers found that the compassion video group had a significant drop in anxiety compared to the control group. And here's the big reveal: the enhanced compassion protocol was only *forty seconds* long. In two-thirds of one minute, the cancer survivors were comforted and were measurably less anxious. The science supports the idea that, with hardly any time investment, doctors—anyone—can use compassion to make other people feel better, which in turn sets the mechanisms in motion to be healthier and feel better themselves.

The prescription is not just forty seconds of other-focus per day though. We have calculated the "dose" of altruism you need to get all the benefits of other-focus we've shown you so far. And if you've been paying attention, you already know what it is. The subtitle of this chapter is the Sixteen-Minute Prescription. Just sixteen minutes per day of kind acts, compassion, and selfless service for others can lead to a long life of health, wellness, happiness, and success.

How did we come up with that figure?

Adam Grant talks about the "100 Hour Rule"—that's the number of hours per year one needs to devote to altruism to get the benefits. That threshold holds up in scientific research from Japan,[4] Australia,[5] the UK,[6] and a study[7] (described in detail in chapter 6) by Eric Kim. In that longitudinal study of thirteen thousand U.S. adults, it was at least one hundred hours a year of volunteering that was linked with a reduced risk of death and physical functioning limitations, plus higher physical activity, positive affect, optimism, and purpose in life, and less depression and loneliness.

You usually do not take prescribed therapies once a year. Typically, you take your medicine every day. So we used a highly complex scientific device—a calculator—to determine your daily dose. One hundred hours equals 6,000 minutes. Divide that by 365 days (the total number in a year) to get 16.43 minutes per day. We rounded down, assuming that most people are generally other-focused for at least twenty-five seconds (.43 of one minute) per day already.

Just *sixteen minutes* per day of other-focus to reap enormous benefits for yourself and others. It's hardly anything.

Four Beatles songs.

A Three Stooges short.

A mile walk.

Half an episode of *Rick and Morty*.

The time it takes (one of us) to parallel park.

You don't have to set your stopwatch, but keep this number in mind. Some prefer to accumulate altruism in a few servings of kindness—like breakfast, lunch, and dinner—that add up to sixteen minutes per day. In *Give and Take*, Adam Grant wrote about "five-minute favors." Ideally, the favor will not be moving a piano, but, then again, we can all do just about anything for five minutes. And if you do small time-limited favors three times per day, that adds up to a lot of helping over time.

Some altruism opportunities might present themselves organically. If you want to go with the Live to Give flow, just wait for them. Others might prefer to plan their sixteen minutes. Also, it's sixteen minutes *on average* every day. So you may want to slot every Saturday morning as "giving time" and schedule a two-hour stint to teach English, sort at the Salvation Army, or visit a sick relative, for example. Or maybe you are just scanning every person you come upon for opportunities.

Mixing it up works too. We love medical analogies, so small daily acts of kindness are like taking your blood pressure medication every morning, health maintenance and prevention stuff. But then you push yourself to do more every so often, like a weekly long run, the equivalent of weekend volunteering in a service project. And then, once every five years, you do a major push, like signing up to be the class parent or organizing a major fundraising drive for a good cause and consider it to be your compassion colonoscopy.

Serving others for sixteen minutes doesn't give you license to be a self-centered jerk for the other 1,424 minutes per day. That said, you don't have to be a saint 24/7 either. That wouldn't be possible for the vast majority of us. We're human, after all. But if we can consciously dig deep to be kinder and more compassionate and carve out small chunks in our day to do it, we can move mountains.

OKAY, THEN, BUT WHAT ABOUT MONEY?

When we talk to recent college graduates about giving and helping others, they often say, "I'm thousands in debt with student loans. I don't have any money to give. When I make more money, I'll give to charity then." As we've shared previously, **research supports the idea that by giving money away, you may set yourself up to earn more and climb the ladder of success** so that you'll actually be able to pay off your loans more quickly. It can improve the quality of your life profoundly, so you don't feel as depressed about your loans. Full disclosure, one of us finished paying off all of his medical school loans a few years back and the joy of giving more money to good causes has mitigated the resentment of so many years paying interest to lenders. "I'm broke" can be an excuse. You don't have to be wealthy to be a Live to Giver. We've already presented evidence that people with low socioeconomic status can realize the benefits of generosity, even if they give a tiny amount of their time, talent, or treasure.

Being generous makes people happier than self-indulgence,[8] which is something to think about when you buy yourself an $8 macchiato. If you hesitate to donate because of a mental block you've constructed in your own mind about what you can afford, you can induce yourself to tear down that wall with reframing. Robert B. Cialdini, Ph.D., the OG researcher on the science of influence, author of the bestselling book *Influence: The Psychology of Persuasion,* ran some experiments[9] in the 1970s at Arizona State University about using certain language when asking for money. One hundred sixty-five participants tested the effectiveness of different techniques when asking strangers to give in the context of a door-to-door charity drive. They found that people were more likely to give if the participants "legitimized" instead of "requested" small donations. Saying, "I'll take even a penny" led people to decline the ask. But adding the sentence, "Every penny counts," induced people to give more often. The size of the donation didn't change; the willingness to make it did.

Practice the science of influence on yourself. By legitimizing small donations in your own mind, your giving is likely to increase. A small amount *can* be a big deal, especially if sustained over time. A small offering or act of kindness is a first step. And once you start, given the huge benefits for yourself, you won't want to stop.

"WHO?" MATTERS MORE THAN "HOW MUCH?"

The happiness research dream team, Drs. Dunn, Aknin, and Norton from the University of British Columbia and Harvard Business School, studied[10] the happiness effects of spending money on people with whom you have either strong or weak social ties. Since a key to good health and happiness is satisfying relationships, it would be useful to know if spending money on family, friends, and acquaintances made a difference, regardless of how deep the connection.

The eighty university student participants were randomly assigned to one of two different spending recall conditions: (1) to remember, in detail, a time they spent approximately $20 on someone they considered to be a strong tie, like a good friend, close family member, or romantic partner, and (2) to remember, in detail, a time they spent the same amount on a weak tie, like an acquaintance, co-worker, classmate, or the friend of a friend. After recalling that moment of generosity, the participants reported their happiness level on a standard scale.

As predicted, **the memory of spending on a strong social tie was associated with significantly higher levels of happiness than doing so for a weak social tie, no matter how long ago the spending took place. The more intimate the connection, the happier they were to** make the small sacrifice. As the authors wrote, "To reap the greatest emotional reward from spending on someone else, one should direct their purchases to close others." Positive feelings that arise from giving to strong social ties reinforces the participants' giving behavior. If it feels good to give, you're more likely to do it, again and again.

The lesson here isn't to be stingy with spending on acquaintances or helping strangers. Not at all. Spending money on weak ties generated feelings of happiness as well, just not quite as strong as spending on strong ties. Besides, you never know if the kind act of buying a casual acquaintance a macchiato could be the beginning of a beautiful (and strong) future friendship.

SO WHERE TO BEGIN?

Start where you live. Literally. In your own house and/or workplace. Helping your family, roommates, and best friends (strong social ties) can be just as powerful as serving in a remote village in a poor country. Volunteer to do the dishes or take out the garbage. Paying a compliment actually costs you nothing. No "paying" involved. All you have to do to kickstart Live to Give behaviors is to express appreciation and help the people you love most.

A study from Cal Berkeley's Dacher Keltner and colleagues[11] looked at the intrinsic rewards of making small sacrifices for romantic partners without any strings attached, what they termed "communal strength." **Sixty-nine couples participated in a two-week experiment of doing nice things for each other every day.** Little things, like putting the phone away and engaging in meaningful conversation, making dinner without having to be asked, giving him or her your undivided attention and support. **The findings were as clear as they were predictable: communal strength was associated with positive feelings during the "sacrifice," partners feeling appreciated, and deeper relationship satisfaction all day long.**

A study[12] from Utah State University looked at the "relationship maintenance behavior" data from a national survey of 1,365 married couples, and found that small kind acts, displays of respect and affection, and the willingness to forgive a partner's faults and failings were associated with more marital satisfaction, fewer fights, and a decreased perceived likelihood of future divorce. A little Live to Give goes a long way.

Happy relationships mean less stress. Less stress can mean longer life. So if you want to live longer, improve the quality of your marriage through small kind acts immediately. A longitudinal study[13] analyzed data for 4,374 elderly couples over eight years. After controlling for household income, baseline health, and other factors, researchers found that **one level higher in the life satisfaction of one's spouse was associated with a 13 percent drop in mortality risk.** Based on these findings, the phrase "happy spouse, happy life" could be edited to read, "happy spouse, happier—and longer—life."

Another angle on doing it "where you live" is using your natural skill set to serve others. Do what you do best. By serving in a way that feels natural and right for you, you can achieve "flow" and engagement while serving, which is twice the bang for your (donated) buck.

For example, we are physician leaders and researchers. We don't abandon our day jobs to be Live to Givers; we leverage those skills to help others by staying in that strength. For example, since Steve is an intensive care specialist, medical missions to the poorest areas of the globe may not be the most effective use of his skills if they have few intensive care units there. But he can and does leverage his hard-won research skills to systematically analyze the beneficial effects of altruism, and uses his communication chops to speak to groups and spread the Live to Give message to help people improve their lives.

Mazz uses his platform as an occasional radio and TV personality as well as his role as a CEO at a major academic health care system to raise money and share information about the benefits of compassion and altruism. Mazz and his co-CEO, Kevin O'Dowd, try to serve up humor, warmness, and positivity—important tools in leaders' skill sets—in their interactions with the staff and faculty at Cooper to create a more positive workplace.

What skill can you leverage to do good? Are you a born salesperson?

Then you can probably fundraise. Are you a gifted teacher? Then you can mentor or tutor young minds. Figure out your "one thing I can do" (the "talent" part of the "time, talent, and treasure" giving triad) and use it, stick with it, and watch in awe as your impact is fully realized for others (and yourself). An important part of your "talent" may actually be your *influence*, and leveraging whatever scope of influence you have in your corner of the world to make meaningful differences for others—and encouraging those around you to do the same.

How do I know who I am until I see what I do?

—E.M. Forster

A SMALL STEP FOR HUMANKIND

Ultimately, being a Live to Giver comes down to making a decision to give. Help. Care. Connect. Make that decision, and repeat it often, every day.

Start small. If you were going to, say, launch an exercise routine, you wouldn't go from couch potato to marathoner overnight. You'd begin your first day of training by walking around the block a few times. If you were to implement a healthy eating plan, it won't stick if you go from cheeseburgers and beer to a full-on vegan diet and kombucha overnight. It'd be wiser to cut back on fried foods and alcohol and gradually make healthier choices until that becomes your default setting.

It's the same with becoming a Live to Giver. Every kind act, generous donation, and mindful moment of focusing on someone else adds up. And before you know it, you'll consistently hit sixteen minutes per day, and then exceed it.

Start with as much or as little as you can handle, as long as you *start doing* it to make giving and helping your new default setting. Cribbing from James Clear, author of the bestselling book *Atomic Habits: An Easy & Proven Way to Build Good Habits & Break Bad Ones,* to establish the habit of serving others:

- **Start incredibly small.** At home, with people you love, with just tiny kind gestures.
- **Chunk it up.** Divide your one hundred hours per year into sixteen minutes per day or into bite-size portions, like five-minute favors.
- **Increase gradually, granularly.** Work up to sixteen minutes per day; slowly increase your "costly giving" so it never feels like much of a sacrifice at all.
- **Be consistent.** If you miss a day of serving others, forgive yourself and start (small) again tomorrow.

Sooner than you might think, altruism will become a habit, like drinking coffee in the morning or locking the doors before bed. You won't feel right without it.

Consistent giving eventually becomes integrated into your *identity*. Even if you join a helping organization for selfish reasons, like advancing your own career, over time, you will begin to see yourself as a giver because it's what you do. Over time, what you do becomes *who you are*, authentically.

Just setting the intention to serve others is not going to cut it. James Clear draws the distinction between "motion" and "action." Motion is a pre-action phase, when you're planning to do a thing. Ineffective people often can't get out of the motion trap (that is, they're all talk, no action). For example, the "motion" of writing a book is to get the big idea, do a little research, and talk about it a lot. Motion is important, necessary, and useful. But unless you take "action," motion isn't getting you where you want to go.

The "action" of writing a book is to sit your butt in the chair, put in the time to do rigorous research, type sentences into Microsoft Word every day (or every night and weekend), until the pages are filled, and the book is finished. Action is whatever behavior will get you to the outcome you want. If the outcome you desire is to be a Live to Giver, the motion component is reading this book, making the personal paradigm shift to look for and seek out opportunities to serve others in your everyday life, figuring out your skill to leverage, and deciding who you want to start serving. The action component is the actual *doing*—doing the helping, giving, caring, and connecting with sincerity—at least sixteen minutes (on average) every day.

Clear suggests two strategies to shift from motion to action: (1) picking a start date for action to begin, as in, "This Monday, I will do kind acts for my partner," and mark it on your calendar, and (2) scheduling repeated action, as in, "Every night at 9:00 p.m., I will take a walk with my partner and engage in meaningful conversation for sixteen minutes [or some combination of acts of giving to hit that daily average]." Research from the University of Oxford indicates that **just *seven days* of small acts of kindness can actually boost happiness in measurable ways,** so if you stick with it, the happiness effects may start to kick in by the end of the week![14]

A SMILE CAN SAVE A LIFE

In his book *Why People Die by Suicide,*[15] renowned psychologist and suicide expert Thomas Joiner from Florida State University quoted from one man's suicide note: "'I'm going to walk to the bridge. If one person smiles at me on the way, I will not jump.'"

One smile was all it would have taken to change a terrible outcome for that man. Talk about a small act of kindness. None of the people he passed on his fateful walk had any idea what kind of pain he was carrying around. From their vantage point, he probably looked like anybody else. Perhaps if he had been lucky enough to pass a Live to Giver on his way to the bridge who took a few seconds to smile at him, he wouldn't have ended his life that day.

Transmitting little messages of hope to people we know and love, as well as complete strangers, can make a huge impact, although we might never know it. A smile, unexpected gift, encouraging word, or sympathetic ear at exactly the right time can change someone's outlook and outcome for the better, and perhaps forever. The data show that spreading little messages of hope for sixteen minutes per day will make all the difference in the world *for you,* as well as whomever receives it.

Figuratively, we all live next to a bridge. We're all walking by people who are just hanging on by a thread. A self-focused person might not notice at all. Or, if they did see a gloomy man walking toward them, they might cross the street to avoid the dark cloud over his head. An other-focused person would see the dark cloud and recognize it as an opportunity to bring a little sunshine (and hopefulness) into someone's life with the smallest of gestures, even just a kind smile.

The Live to Give prescription for starting small: The "Daily Sixteen"—acknowledge that you can do just about anything for sixteen minutes on average per day, so serving others for that long isn't too big of an ask. The more time you give, the more time you will feel like you have, so don't bother with the time poverty excuse.

By making the personal paradigm shift to other-focus, you can change the trajectory of another person's day. By being a Live to Giver and accumulating moments of giving and helping, you can lift your own dark cloud and change the trajectory of your day as well. You might even wind up saving a *life*—your own.

Gratitude is not only the greatest of virtues,
but the parent of all others.

—Cicero

Be Thankful

Unless you have been living under a rock for the last decade like Patrick the Starfish on *SpongeBob SquarePants,* you must have heard that having an attitude of gratitude can increase your well-being and happiness. We scoured PubMed for proof of this claim and found approximately five zillion studies to confirm it. Hence, mindful types should continue their gratitude habits—not just giving thanks before breaking bread, or common courtesies of saying "thank you" whenever someone does something helpful, but incorporating gratitude into their way of life as an intentional practice.

But we have a different vantage point on gratitude.

Lots of research shows that a grateful disposition is good for you in general, but we believe much of the benefit from gratitude comes from driving you to be a Live to Giver. This chapter will share evidence specifically for that, which tells you why being grateful is part of the wonder drug prescription.

AN ATTITUDE OF GRATITUDE

A University of Nottingham study led by researcher Robin Locksley looked at whether stealing from the rich to give to the poor is prosocial or criminal behavior. They found that the practice is indeed prosocial, if the rich people in question are selfish, greedy bastards who imprison fair maidens named Marian.

A *different* team from the University of Nottingham (not known for wearing tights) did a meta-analysis[1] synthesizing all of the data from the scientific literature—ninety-one studies with 18,342 participants in all—to test the association between gratitude and prosocial (giving, helping) behaviors. And they most certainly did find an association; that is, gratitude motivates service to others. But! Not all types of gratitude give you the same altruistic motivation.

When gratitude was directed at other people (relational) and/or passing back and forth between people, they were highly motivated to continue altruistic behaviors that would lead to more interpersonal gratitude.

When gratitude was generalized, a free-floating sense of appreciation for all the good stuff in your life or thankfulness for just being alive, people got a lift in well-being, but they were *not* more motivated to do kind acts for others. In summary, the research supports the conclusion that *relational* gratitude—thankfulness for a specific person (or persons)—beats generalized gratitude for turning you into a Live to Giver.

THANK IT FORWARD

Feeling and expressing gratitude is a great way to resonate with the other-focus frequency. Once you start feeling and expressing "thanks," the Live to Give signal and the message it transmits—serve others and you'll be happy!—get stronger. When your brain is tuned in to the gratitude station, you're more likely to give and help others.

A University of Oregon/Harvard University study[2] looked at the neuroscience of gratitude as an altruism motivator. In a double-blind study, the researchers randomly assigned young adult female participants to keep either a gratitude journal or a neutral journal (the control) for three weeks. They studied their brains with an fMRI scanner before and after the journaling period. Compared to the control group, **the grateful scribblers increased their "neural pure altruism" response in the**

brain's reward center, indicating that practicing gratitude changed their brain activity to make them feel even better about doing selfless, kind acts for others.

David DeSteno, Ph.D., of Northeastern University, has done extensive research on gratitude's effects on altruistic behaviors and relationships. He and his team tested this by inducing gratitude in participants in a series of laboratory experiments. How did they "induce" gratitude? By randomizing participants to an "emotion manipulation" condition versus control (no manipulation). The emotion manipulation was an elaborate sham involving—you guessed it—a confederate (actor). The confederate pretended to go out of their way to be especially helpful in fixing a (fake) malfunction of the participant's computer just before beginning the experiments. In all of their experiments, the researchers found that, compared to participants in the control groups, those who were helped by the confederate felt more grateful during the experiment (measured with a validated scale, to show that the gratitude induction did in fact work in making participants more grateful).

Using this methodology, DeSteno and his team found that being grateful facilitated and strengthened existing social affiliation (closeness), and that, in turn, increased giving behaviors, which build and strengthen relationships.[3] They found that **gratitude, as an affective state, strengthens relationships more than mere reciprocity (repaying kind acts), and generates a desire to affiliate with (spend more time with) those we feel grateful for, even when costly.** They also found that the affective state of gratitude is a more potent stimulus of helping behaviors than a general positive affective state (that is, happiness) or simple awareness of reciprocity norms ("You helped me so I will help you"). This finding held up even for giving help to strangers and when helping was costly to the helper.[4] In another experiment testing how gratitude impacts monetary giving, DeSteno and colleagues found that, compared to participants in the control group, the more grateful group gave about 25 percent more of their money to others (including strangers), even at a cost to their own gain.[5]

So when people feel grateful, whether they reach that affective state on their own or they are manipulated by actors in a laboratory experiment, it helps them be more other-focused and take action through giving to others. Taken together, this line of research supports the idea that gratitude can be a powerful motivator for becoming a better Live to Giver.

THANK BACK

Old people imparting their wisdom on the young is a giving behavior called "generativity," and it's been associated with greater life satisfaction and well-being for senior citizens. Gratitude in young people motivates them to do more for their communities, a phenomenon called "upstream generativity" that offers the same benefits for junior citizens.

A longitudinal study[6] from the University of California–Davis's Robert Emmons, Ph.D., and colleagues found that feeling gratitude predicted a desire in kids to get more involved in their neighborhood, community, and the world. Researchers first measured their seven hundred middle school participants' gratitude, prosocial behavior, life satisfaction, and "social integration" (how motivated they were to use their skills to help others and connect to something bigger than themselves) and followed up regularly for six months.

The adolescents who were most grateful at the study's onset were more likely to give back to their communities via serving others. Gratitude is the ignition that starts the Live to Give bus. And once that bus gets moving, and kids become more involved in doing good on a macro level, the bus *keeps* rolling along in a virtuous cycle. To inspire a kid to get out of his or her head, and to look around at what can be done to help the world at large—even if it's just in their own patch—teaching them the importance of gratitude is a great place to begin.

SINCERELY, YOURS

Authentic Happiness author Martin Seligman came up with a practice called "gratitude visits." How it works: think of someone from your past for whom you didn't express sufficient gratitude way back when, and then pay them a visit to express it fully now. He's found that it increases happiness and well-being for both the giver and receiver. If you can't afford a plane ticket to see your ninth-grade English teacher who retired in the Bahamas, you can always do the economy version of the gratitude visit, and just write a letter.

The very idea of paying a "gratitude visit" might make you a bit queasy. Like, how awkward would it be to knock on someone's door and say, "It really meant a lot when you stood up for me on the playground thirty years ago. . . ." It'd be super embarrassing for both of you, if you show up out of the blue and bleed emotion all over them. No one wants that, right? That fear is a version of "ego bias," the belief that your own opinions about what others may or may not think about you is correct. Naturally, an ego bias is self-focused and therefore not a Live to Give mindset, and, importantly, science shows it's usually *wrong*.

A study from the University of Chicago's Nicholas Epley, Ph.D.,[7] tasked participants with writing gratitude letters and asked them to predict how surprised, happy, or awkward the receiver would feel. Then the researchers checked in with those recipients and asked them how they *actually* felt. What the researchers found is that the letter writers underestimated the surprise and happiness it would bring to recipients of the letters, and way overestimated how awkward the recipients would feel about it. In fact, the recipients typically felt no awkwardness or embarrassment at all. Epley concluded that when we consistently downplay the effect that gratitude expressions can have on others' happiness, and consistently overhype the notion of embarrassment among receivers of gratitude, it can keep people from doing and saying kind things that would increase their own—and others'—well-being. It causes us to underutilize the power of gratitude. So here's some evidence-based advice: get over yourself (and the awkwardness you erroneously associate with heartfelt expressions of gratitude) and start harnessing the power of "I appreciate you." In fact, the science behind gratitude as a means to becoming the best Live to Giver you can be is so robust that we are prescribing it for you.

An example: when Mazz and the other senior leaders at Cooper meet, one of the things they regularly do is select people within the organization (not just clinical people like nurses and doctors, but those in supporting roles—for example, registrars, security, food service, environmental services, maintenance) to single out for their fine efforts. As a gratitude practice, Mazz and anyone at the vice president level and above write thank-you notes to those people who deserve special appreciation. The notes aren't long or gushy missives. They usually just say something like, "Thank you so much for doing such a great job on that project," or "You showed incredible care with that patient, thanks." When Mazz first started doing this, he'd write letters on actual paper, address them to the recipient's home, and put them in the mail, as did other leaders in the organization. This relational gratitude giving was one of his favorite parts of his job.

On occasion, Mazz received a thank-you letter too, sent to his house. His wife, Joanne, found one in the pile one day, and asked, "What's this?"

He explained the new practice of sending the gratitude notes.

"That's stupid," she said. "No one cares about that." (An opinion that we now know is not evidence-based, by the way.)

More notes kept coming, sometimes one or two a week. After a month or so, Joanne, a cardiologist at Cooper, said, "Do you think anyone is going to send me a note? I hope I get one."

Mazz said, "I thought they were stupid."

She told him to shut up, and he dutifully complied. Soon after, she did receive one, and it didn't feel corny or awkward at all. She was really happy about it. Mazz buttoned his lip and didn't say, "I told you so," a wise display of "relationship maintenance behavior" that served them both. To be fair, the overwhelming majority of the time it is Joanne who has reason to say "I told you so" and she is even better at not actually saying it.

The Live to Give prescription for gratitude: As doctors, we advise you to intentionally write at least one sincere thank-you note (or email) per week and send it to someone who really deserves it. Although we are prescribing this behavior, it should be of your own volition, not mandated. As we've already shown, if the motivation isn't autonomous, you won't get the giving benefits. When we say "one per week" we don't mean "just once and then forget about it." You have to build gratitude into your daily practice and make it a habit, like taking your medicine every day, to see significant change.

This practice forces you to reflect consciously about the feelings behind the words. The words themselves could be identical whether you reflect on the emotion or not. But if you feel the gratitude and are motivated to serve others even more, Fantastic Four hormones will be released, and you start getting all the benefits immediately. If it takes five minutes to compose a message (and reflect on it), you're nearly a third of the way to reaching your Daily Sixteen.

It doesn't have to be fancy and it doesn't have to be handwritten. "Dear _____, I had to let you know how much I appreciate you and what you've done [*add details*]. Thank you." If the sentiment is genuine and comes from the heart, the specific words don't really matter.

Finally, we'd like to take this opportunity to say "Thank you, readers" for getting this far in the book, and for tolerating all of our pop-culture references. In this respect, we can't help ourselves.

The meaning of life is to find your gift.
The purpose of life is to give it away.

—Pablo Picasso

Be Purposeful

We've talked about purpose in a couple of different contexts so far.

First, we declared that "passion is not purpose," to try to convince you that the path toward fulfillment and success lies in pursuits that serve other people, as opposed to paths that indulge your deep, abiding love for music and/or motocross.

We also talked about the specific health benefits of having purpose in life, of being part of something larger than yourself that can make a difference for others. Life purpose can be defined as "a damn good reason to get out of bed every morning," and if it's other-focused, science shows that you may be more likely to live longer, have a healthy heart, avoid fatal disease, have lower stress, sleep better, and become more successful, among other benefits.

In this chapter, we're writing you a *purpose prescription*.

How does one become purposeful? How do you make the changes in your everyday life to focus on others? Do you need special glasses? An electronic device that buzzes every time you use self-absorbed language ("I", "me," or "mine") to remind you to say "you" and "we" instead? That would be a super-cool gizmo to have, actually, and maybe it could even *save lives*. Better than a pacemaker! Sadly, it does not yet exist.

The evidence-based way to fulfillment isn't chasing passions or

dreams. **It's finding the greatest** *need* **that you possibly can and then filling that need (in service to others).**

By now, you've learned to intentionally and actively shine your light outward. To be purposeful, do a little bit extra. Hunt around for ways to help. Ask the right questions. Seek information from people to detect when you can make a difference for them and how to serve them to improve their lives—and in so doing, make a profound impact on your own health, happiness, and success.

ASK

According to what we have learned over the entire history of neuroscience, humans are not mind readers. (We can be mind melders though; see page 91.) Intuitive people can sense how others are feeling. That skill is called "empathic accuracy"—but unless we ask others for information about what they are thinking, we may never really know. By failing to ask, we miss opportunities to serve.

In an eye-opening study[1] from the University of Colorado School of Medicine, researchers distributed cards to patients receiving care in the emergency department (ED) asking, "What worries you the most?" The patients wrote in their answers. Then the researchers compared the patients' greatest worries to what was listed as their chief complaint (the symptom or condition that caused them to show up, such as a stomachache or twisted ankle) on their medical chart according to the ED triage nurse. **Patients' most pressing worries were often unrelated to what brought them to the ED in the first place. In fact, patients' main worries only matched their chief complaint** *26 percent* **of the time.** For example, a forty-five-year-old man had a chief complaint of chest pain per his medical chart, but his greatest worry was actually, as he wrote, "Dying too young to see my kids grow up. I've got trouble with my heart because of the drugs. I don't want to be here again, but I can't stay away." A twenty-seven-year-old pregnant woman came in with vaginal bleeding, but her greatest worry was depression. She wrote, "I don't want to go into depression again. A miscarriage is hard." If the patients aren't asked about their worries, which is different than what brought them in, their underlying condition (like addiction) or a grave danger (depression) could have gone undetected and never acknowledged, let alone addressed.

Obviously, doctors need to ask patients about their concerns along with their symptoms to give them the highest-quality, patient-centered care. We initially covered this study in *Compassionomics* and made a point ever after of asking our patients and their families, "What worries you the most?" and have been blown away by what is really front-of-mind for them. We may have had no idea how they were suffering on the inside and how we could help otherwise.

What if we all got in the habit of asking those around us, "What worries you the most?" We may be shocked by what we learn, but it would bring new opportunities for impact that we would never otherwise know. Asking specifically about worries provokes a raw, revealing response that will help you find a need and fill it (which is your Live to Give purpose). Asking the perfunctory question, "How are you?" often serves no one. In our experience, even if patients are miserable down deep inside and someone asks them, "How are you?" they often give the rote reply, "fine" or "good," even when it's not true. Why? Because it was the wrong question to ask at that time.

Hans Selye, aka Dr. Stress, found that the questions "Do you need help?" or "Is there anything I can do?" registers in the askee's ears as an invitation to say the equivalent of "No, thanks, I'm good." Instead, ask a question that can't be replied to with a "yes" or "no" answer, such as Dr. Selye's suggested "What can I do to be helpful to you today?" We also like "What can I do to make your day a little better?" The question suggests to the other person that we really want to know how we can help and prompts an honest response. Then, when you get an answer, do what you can to respond to that need.

Start small by asking the right questions to the people in your orbit and it'll eventually become habitual, the way you automatically interact with people. A tiny example: when Steve asks his wife, Tamara, "How are you?" he gets nothing actionable. But when he asks, "How can I make your day better?" she can always come up with something, like pick up their daughter and a gallon of milk. When he arrives at home with his daughter and the groceries, he feels a bit helpful and gets a jolt of just enough serotonin to carry over till the next day.

We've found that some of our most rewarding experiences as leaders (Mazz as CEO and Steve as a department chair) are when we've observed a colleague's struggle, invited them to come to our respective offices, and closed the door for privacy. Usually, when people are called into the boss's office, they're on guard, expecting to be reprimanded and put on notice. But we don't accuse or criticize. We shine our light on them and say, "I'm worried about you and I want to know what I can do for you. What can I do to help you?"

An unexpected lesson of leadership: you have no idea what kind of pain people are carrying around. Until you care enough to ask, that is. People can be so taken aback by the demonstration of compassion and the purposeful offer to help that they immediately burst into tears. At the very least, they unburden the struggle they've tried to hide, that their home life is falling apart, they just received a bad diagnosis, or that they feel totally overwhelmed. Once the truth comes out, we do what we can. If you ask the hard question, you have to be prepared to respond, even if you don't or can't fix a colleague's problems.

In one instance, a colleague revealed that she was just diagnosed with a very serious progressive debilitating illness. The way to serve her needs was to let her talk about how she was coping, check in regularly to see if she needed anything, and go to great lengths to protect her confidentiality (she didn't want anyone to know she was sick). After a couple of years, when she was no longer able to do her job to the high standards she always set for herself because of the effects of the illness, one of us helped her exit from the organization on her own terms and, most important to her, preserve her dignity. That experience over time forged a new bond and special relationship that lasts even to this day.

"Asking and answering" isn't appropriate in all situations though. In the ICU, Steve's domain, it's common that there are no words to make patients or their family feel better, like when they get the news of a grave prognosis for which there is no treatment. In that moment, the best way to serve others can be to just sit with them in their suffering, and keep your mouth closed—"show up and shut up." Resist the urge to fill the silence. Giving silence in the service of others is a way to say without speaking, "I can't change the circumstances, but I care. I'm here, and I am not going anywhere."

Asking the right questions sometimes takes a little courage. By asking someone to open up, you are committing to help them, and that can seem scary. The fear of not being prepared or capable of helping can be a big deterrent for people even asking what's wrong; they think they need to be a "fixer." But you don't always need to have solutions or fix anything. Just being present is meaningful help. Just showing up for somebody or offering to take their call when they need to talk. That's purposeful in and of itself. Sometimes you can be purposeful just by being in the room, showing people that they are not alone.

Don't let fear stop you from asking. If you never ask, you have no idea what Live to Give opportunities you're missing. Glossing over people's feelings and concerns with superficial asks—"You good? Great!"—only shows others that you can't be bothered.

Be kind, for everyone you meet is fighting a hard battle.

—Ian Maclaren

THE TEN-FIVE RULE

When Mazz was an undergraduate at Washington and Lee University (go, Generals!), he learned about the "Speaking Tradition" of the school, which was to always say hello when you pass by someone. It was later adapted into the Ten-Five Rule, and Mazz practices it to this day. Following it is a simple way to stay other-focused and maybe even detect who might be in need of help.

Be attentive! Look for opportunities to ask or help.

The rule is:

If you walk within ten feet of someone, acknowledge them with a nod or a smile.

If you walk within five feet of someone, say something, like "Hello" or "Nice day."

This is how your radar can be up for Live to Give opportunities, in contrast to what so many of us do now, head down, face in our phones, texting and walking, missing the cues of who might be in need of help today. Help rack up your Daily Sixteen minutes of other-focus by practicing the Ten-Five Rule. An evening stroll through the neighborhood could push you over the top.

TAKE RESPONSIBILITY FOR OTHERS

Austrian psychologist, neurologist, Holocaust survivor, and author Viktor Frankl wrote in *Man's Search for Meaning* about his experience in Nazi concentration camps during World War II. He found that the prisoners who broke down and died the most quickly had few commitments in their lives outside the camps. The ones who survived had something to live for, a commitment, a purpose, outside the camp that gave them the strength and wherewithal to keep going.

As he described, asking, "What makes me happy?" does nothing for you. It focuses your thoughts on how life has not met your expectations. But asking, "What is life asking of me?" erases want and desire—and dissatisfaction—and focuses your mind on your "why." Having a purpose saved lives and minds in some of the most horrific circumstances that history has ever seen. Frankl wrote, "A man who becomes conscious of the responsibility he bears toward a human being who affectionately waits for him, or to an unfinished work, will never be able to throw away his life. He knows the 'why' for his existence and will be able to bear almost any 'how.'" Frankl's observations keyed in on what is now supported by robust research.

Purpose is taking on the responsibility of serving others, to do what we can for each other. We owe it to our fellow humans to be there in times of suffering. When we're not, it's shocking to behold. During a rash of anti-Asian violence in New York in 2021, city residents were aghast to see a CCTV video of a middle-aged man brutally attacking an elderly Asian woman in broad daylight in front of a Times Square hotel while yelling racial slurs. The assault was awful enough, but what really disgusted viewers was the three men inside the hotel who watched it and did nothing—other than shut the door. It goes against our human nature not to help and serve others, and when we see an example of blatant disregard, we recoil. New Yorkers of every stripe had to ask themselves, "Would I have intervened or at least rushed to help the woman on the ground after the violent maniac was gone?"

A famous study[2] conducted by renowned Princeton University psychologists John Darley and C. Daniel Batson used students at Princeton Theological Seminary (that is, pastors in training). They randomly assigned the seminarians to either an intervention arm, in which they read a Bible passage on the parable of the Good Samaritan (a message of compassionate helping for a stranger who'd been beaten and left on the side of the road), or a control arm that read a passage about ministry in general. After reading the passages, the seminarians were instructed to walk to another building on campus to give a brief talk on the passage they just read. But there was a second aspect of randomization—"the hurry condition." Randomly, half of each group were told to get a move on because they were late to give their talk versus others who were told they had time to spare. (Note: none of them were actually late for anything; they were just made to think they were.) They knew where they were going on campus and how long it takes to get there. So with the two randomly assigned conditions, there were four groups of participants: (1) Good Samaritans in a hurry, (2) Good Samaritans in no hurry, (3) control group in a hurry, and (4) control group not in a hurry. The participants were also measured on factors like their "religiosity"—that is, how religious they were.

On their way to the other building to give their talk, they encountered a stranger in need: disheveled, lying in an alley, moaning, obviously in distress like someone had just beaten the crap out of him. Of course, the "victim" slumped over on the ground was a confederate who was part of the experiment.

Would the students stop to help, or ignore the victim in their path? Overall, 40 percent (sixteen of the students) gave direct or indirect help, which means that the other 60 percent of the pastors in training blew right by the victim without a backward glance. Religiosity did not pre-

dict whether students stopped to help, but if they did stop, the especially pious seminarians had a higher "helping rating," meaning they
did more than offer indirect help (telling another person, "Some guy
is groaning in the alley back there"), or asking, "Are you okay?" The
highest-rated helpers stayed with the man and insisted on helping him
to an infirmary for medical attention.

**The researchers found that the main predictor of providing help
was whether or not people thought they were in a hurry. In fact,
some of them literally stepped over the victim in their rush. Sixty-
three percent of the seminarians who were *not* in a hurry stopped
and gave meaningful help; only 10 percent of those racing to get to
their appointment did.** Some of the "in a hurry" students acknowledged in a post-experiment interview that they saw the victim crumpled
in the alley but, so focused on their own agenda, they didn't perceive his
need for help. Others felt anxious about seeing a man in his condition
and were so unnerved they intentionally ignored his need.

Even if the students were in a hurry to give a lecture about the Good
Samaritan, the righteousness of stopping to help someone groaning on
the ground in distress, the majority did the opposite. Reading the parable of the Good Samaritan right before the encounter did *not* predict
helping. This leads us to conclude that Drs. Darley and Batson had a
sharp sense of humor. They concluded, "Ethics becomes a luxury as the
speed of our daily lives increases. . . . Conflict, rather than callousness,
can explain their failure to stop."

The conflict in question is between relentless self-focus versus other-
focus. If we are so self-focused in our hurried, super-busy lives that we
avoid helping someone clearly in need or don't even see them, we have
failed at our human responsibility to each other, even if helping is consistent with our values. If we assume the purpose of other-focus is to not
only see the groaning victim, but to rush toward them and help, we are
actively fulfilling our purpose to each other and can benefit *measurably*
for our effort. Who do you want to be? The one who steps over/around
(doesn't see) or the one who helps?

Our medical school, Cooper Medical School of Rowan University (CMSRU), is known for "service learning." In addition to the

conventional medical school curriculum, it is also an expectation of our students that they will serve the Camden, New Jersey, community (one of the poorest cities in America by median household income) in some meaningful way. It's one of the things our school is known for, so students who choose to attend CMSRU know that service is a key part of the experience here. Some students do after-school tutoring for Camden elementary kids. Some students provide socks, water, and referrals to free clinics for homeless people in a program called "Street Medicine." Some students plant gardens to grow nutritious food in "food deserts" in Camden. It is such a success that CMSRU received the prestigious Spencer Foreman Award for Outstanding Community Engagement from the Association of American Medical Colleges (AAMC). The ethos of CMSRU—built upon its commitment to serving the Camden community—gives its students a special Live to Give experience throughout medical school, and that is one of the reasons our students love our school so much and feel so connected to it.

TAKE RESPONSIBILITY FOR YOURSELF

At Cooper, two very special primary care physicians have witnessed firsthand the power that purpose in life can have in achieving health outcomes among the most challenging patients. Alexandra Lane, M.D., and Jennifer Abraczinskas, M.D., practice in what we call the "Ambulatory Intensive Care Unit" (ICU): an outpatient clinic that specializes in the care of patients with the most complex care needs. Sometimes health care providers callously refer to these patients as "frequent fliers," because of the frequency with which they are admitted to the hospital. Along with their severe chronic physical health (and sometimes mental health) conditions, they commonly have very complex socioeconomic factors like poverty and a lack of social support that complicate their health care.

This medical specialty is one of the toughest. Nevertheless, for Drs. Lane and Abraczinskas, caring for patients with the greatest, most complex needs has become a calling, and it has given them a great sense of purpose. They are deeply passionate about what they do, as evidenced by their amazing results for some of their patients: better health, better quality of life, fewer hospital admissions, and lower costs among patients they care for with this intensive strategy.

There are many intricate aspects of their practice that contribute to their patients' health outcomes, and after building long-term relationships with patients they have found that having *purpose in life* is one of the best motivators for better health. The docs have observed that the high-needs patients that are most likely to improve have something that gives their lives meaning. If the docs can help their patients connect to that purpose and align their health goals to their values, the results can be truly remarkable.

One example is a middle-aged patient who we will call Robert. As Robert approached his fifties, his health started to fade and he visited the emergency department at least once a month and often needed admission to the hospital. He had severely high blood pressure, heart disease, active substance use disorder, and depression that was made worse by the violence he encountered as a child. He was the caretaker for his aging mother, who, like Robert, lived in poverty. He also had an eye condition that required him to wear sunglasses indoors, which, although fine for movie stars, made Robert less approachable and contributed to his isolation and depression. Robert felt his life was spiraling out of control, and was left wondering if his next trip to the hospital would be his last.

Thankfully, he was referred to Drs. Lane and Abraczinskas. As per their Live to Give approach to caring for patients, they used compassion to look beyond his extensive medical history to see the person who desperately needed help. They set out to uncover the root causes of his years of uncontrolled disease and substance use, and to partner with him in defining his purpose in life. At that point, he didn't have any.

After gaining Robert's trust over time, he shared more of his life story with the doctors. They were encouraged to see that as his health improved, Robert became more connected to his community, offering a helping hand to those in need. Seeing this, Drs. Lane and Abraczinskas encouraged him to continue to *serve*. They were so inspired by his progress that they developed a new program, with input from Robert, on connecting high-needs patients with their life's purpose as a way to change their health.

This new beginning proved to be nothing short of miraculous for Robert. He became active in service to his church community, many of whom were suffering from poverty, substance use disorder, and complex chronic health conditions themselves. He found this work to be so rewarding and energizing that serving others in his church "family" became Robert's newfound purpose in life. This also provided a way for him to engage in his spiritual side, something he felt he had lost touch with years ago.

As a result, Robert became newly motivated to take the best possible care of himself. He knew that the only way that he could effectively serve and have the biggest impact on others was to take control of his own health. For the first time, he completely stopped using drugs. With a clear head, he was able to strictly adhere to his prescribed medication regimen. He never missed a dose. He felt well enough to keep all of his appointments with mental health professionals. He was finally able to have the eye procedure that he needed, so that he no longer needed to wear dark glasses all the time. And although he had ups and downs, having purpose in life made him feel like a new person! Robert became a shining example for all those around him who were struggling and needed help.

Robert still has chronic health conditions, but since rededicating his life to serving others his overnight admissions to the hospital have reduced dramatically. His health—and his whole life—have made a complete 180-degree turn.

When we commit to filling our own needs with purpose, we can influence and motivate others to do the same. Purpose is the push that gets a virtuous cycle rolling.

Many persons have a wrong idea of what constitutes true happiness. It is not attained through self-gratification but through fidelity to a worthy purpose.

—Helen Keller

EYES WIDE OPEN

We are constantly inspired by the uplifting actions taken by everyday people who purposefully help others and, in so doing, improve their own well-being. Research has found that even small kind acts enhance one's sense of meaning in one's life.[3] All it takes to find purpose opportunities is to pay attention to what's going on. And if there is personal or communal outcry for help, give your time, talent, or treasure to fill that need, and your heart will grow ten sizes.

In the early days of the COVID-19 vaccination rollout, shot availability was scarce and in high demand. It was nearly impossible to secure an appointment. It was especially hard for non-tech-savvy older people who couldn't navigate various states' vax finder online portals. Grassroots volunteers nationwide saw the need to help the elderly—those most in need of a vaccine—to get their shots. An article in *Scientific American*[4] by Marla Broadfoot reported on teenage cousins from Kentucky who set up a Facebook page to walk seven hundred seniors through the verification process and help them book their appointments. A group of teachers from Maryland used social media to find Spanish-speaking seniors in need of aid and scrolled through dozens of vaccine finder sites to slot in more than four hundred names that they'd collected. A Google engineer recognized how bewildering it was for regular people to find a place to get a shot, and, with the help of two hundred volunteers, created a website that tracked every available appointment in the entire state of California and served tens of thousands per day. The site founder, Manish Goregaokar, told Broadfoot, "This may be the most impactful thing I ever do. I've done other volunteering, but this directly translates to lives saved. It's humbling and scary to be in that position."

These people had their eyes wide open and were rewarded for their volunteering to serve the needs of others with an experience that they will remember forever, and continue to benefit from for the rest of their lives. It'll inspire them to do more, feel continued uplift, that will motivate and inspire others to find ways they can help. We should all be on the lookout for ways to do what we can, and consider every opportunity to be purposeful and serve others as a gift we give ourselves.

The Live to Give prescription for being purposeful: As we've been saying all along, get out of your own head. Stop rushing through life in pursuit of acclaim and success, and open your eyes to the big world we all live in. People right in your path need your help, and it doesn't take much to serve them. But to do that, and reap the benefits of giving, you have to see them, and make that quantum leap of courage to ask and then help.

Here's our adaptation of the Peter Parker Principle: with great *purpose* comes great responsibility. But in taking on that responsibility, we have great power. Enough to change our own worlds, and the entire world. It really is as simple yet profound as that.

In order to empathize with someone's experience,
you must be willing to believe them as they see it,
and not how you imagine their experience to be.

—Brené Brown

Find Common Ground

You probably knew this chapter was coming. Previously, we've provided the evidence that the assumptions we make about other people (for example, underestimating their altruism and other-focus) is often wrong and perhaps even hindering our own health and happiness. And now we're writing an official Live to Give prescription to do the one thing that seems to be more and more challenging in our hyperpolarized culture: have empathy for others and seek to find common ground with the people you disagree with wholeheartedly.

They say that the biggest thing that killed civility in Washington, D.C., was the jet engine. Politicians used to stick around on weekends and intermingle. But for the last half century, they've been flying home instead, and if they do hang out in D.C., it's inside their own factions. It'd be a lot harder to bash each other on cable news if they actually broke bread together or saw each other at Sunday services. These days, politicians are shamed by their own side for having a meal with a colleague from the other side. Compromise is thought of as weakness, or worse yet, surrender.

The rise of internet algorithms have driven us further into our bubbles. If you haven't already, watch *The Social Dilemma*, a documentary on Netflix that explains how artificial intelligence (AI) tracks everything we read, post, and search, in order to figure out exactly what products to sell to us. A side effect of AI data collection is that it's become much bigger than targeted advertising for shoes and vacations. Every link that appears in your various newsfeeds has been matched with your established ideology. You are unlikely to see articles that don't line up with your belief system. We are being systematically separated into factions based on algorithms, and the more you embrace one type of worldview, the more extreme the messaging to affirm it. Our bubbles are really more like balloons. After all, a bubble is transparent. You can see through it.

Both of us make a point of reading news from a variety of perspectives. Mazz does a fair amount of media appearances, but sometimes his "big tent" perspective makes him an unattractive guest for news shows. Television producers on more than one network have refused to book him on commentary shows unless he promised to bash a specific person in a specific way. When he said, "My take is more nuanced than that," one producer hung up on him. Once, he was recruited to be a regular guest on a show on a news network that was seeking people in the middle, ideologically. But the show was scrapped because they couldn't find enough regular guests who weren't extreme in one direction or the other. Nuance doesn't get ratings. When he does appear on radio and TV and expresses views based on science and that present all sides of an issue, he'll receive dozens of emails from conservative viewers to say he's a shill for the left. At the same time, just as many liberals will write to condemn his conservative views. They all listened to the same exact content, but they heard whatever they wanted to hear (or whatever their ears were primed to hear). It's become harder to find empathy or even attempt to shine one's light on people from the "other" side. In political discourse, who bothers to pretend to try to understand where others are coming from? Both halves of the country think the other half is totally crazy. If you take the position that you can't talk to crazy, you shut yourself out from a whole lot of people.

The Live to Give prescription for empathy is to assume that different people from different backgrounds or ideologies are not immoral or crazy, and to further assume that they have good intent. Just start there. You might not agree with them. That's okay! But try to go into every interaction believing that the other side doesn't advocate for atrocities against humanity or hate America.

It might be a Grand Canyon–spanning leap of faith for many of us. A 2017 study[1] from Louisiana State University and the University of Maryland looked at the rise of our toxic political divide in a paper titled "Lethal Mass Partisanship." Political scientists Nathan P. Kalmoe and Lilliana Mason polled one thousand Americans and found that **40 percent of Republicans and 40 percent of Democrats defined the opposing party as "downright evil." Twenty percent agreed that members of the other side "lack the traits to be considered fully human—they behave like animals" and believed that the country would be better off if giant swaths of them spontaneously died. Five to 15 percent of each party said they'd endorse acts of violence against their opposites!**

It might seem like we've always been as divided as we are now, but the science shows that our demonization of the opposing party has gotten worse over time. Lynn Vavreck, Ph.D., professor of political science at UCLA, wrote an article[2] in the *New York Times* titled "A Measure of Identity: Are You Wedded to Your Party?" that looked at the findings from Gallup Organization polling about interparty marriage over the years. In 1958, a random sample of Americans were asked what kind of person they hoped their child would marry. Regarding political party affiliation, the vast majority said they didn't care either way. They'd be fine if their kids brought home a Democrat or a Republican. A week before the 2016 presidential election, Vavreck polled a representative sample of people with a version of that same question and found that the numbers had changed *a lot.* The majority of respondents cared deeply about the politics of their future son- or daughter-in-law. As for those with a strong political affiliation, roughly two-thirds want their children to marry someone with their own views, and 40 percent of parents would have a negative reaction to interparty marriage, as opposed to only 5 percent just a few decades ago.

In order to find common ground, the first step is to acknowledge that it even exists. Logically, we can all agree that not *every* Republican is an immoral racist and not *every* Democrat is a tax-loving spender who hates America, right?

WE *DO* HAVE THINGS IN COMMON

We love our children.

We go "ooh" and "ahh" at fireworks.

We're humbled by a dramatic sunset.

We cry when a loved one dies.

We vow that, tomorrow, we won't procrastinate.

And that we'll start eating better and exercising next week.

No matter our obvious differences, at the very least we are all human. If we can't even see the basic humanity in someone we disagree with, then we, as a country, will not be able to solve problems or achieve to our potential.

In medicine, empathy is a vital clinical competency—an emotional bridge that drives compassionate care for patients. Without empathy, there can be no compassionate action, because the opportunity to take action to alleviate another's pain or suffering would be undetected and missed entirely. Thus, empathy is a necessary antecedent for compassion.

But there is also a necessary antecedent for empathy: fully seeing another's humanity. Without that, empathy fails, and thus compassion fails as well.

Discrimination, racism, hate crimes, and genocide are examples of failing to see our shared humanity. When you watch Holocaust footage of concentration camps in Germany, you see the failure of those running the camps to see the humanity in the Jewish lives that are before them.

When we witness the brutal data on health disparities (like coronavirus fatality rates in non-white and low socioeconomic status populations), we witness the effects of a failure to fully see the humanity of disadvantaged people. Failing to do so brings an absence of empathy and a void of compassion.

As physicians, we see patients in health disparity populations who feel the effects of a systemic lack of empathy and compassion routinely. At a systems level, all health and health care disparities are likely rooted in a societal lack of empathy and compassion for disadvantaged people. You may have heard about a "compassion gap," that some health care providers treat certain people differently based on race. For example, research shows that in the treatment of patients with painful conditions, doctors sometimes give less pain medication to Black patients compared to others due to unconscious bias. Unconscious bias is a real problem in medicine, and we have to confront it head-on in order to change it.

Our research group at Cooper has begun to study clinician compassion from the patient perspective. Ultimately, we aim to develop interventions to close compassion gaps by raising compassion for disadvantaged patients and improving their care.

No matter your views on social justice, we can all agree that all patients deserve quality health care. Whether or not you believe climate change is manmade, we can agree clear air is good and wildfires and floods are bad. Whether you believe in capitalism or socialism, we can agree that massive unemployment takes a toll on people and the economy.

The questions we need to ask each other are *not* "Which side are you on?," "Are you for or against?," "Pork roll or Taylor ham?," "Stones or Beatles?"

Spoiler alert for Warner Bros.'s *Godzilla v. Kong*: If Godzilla and King Kong can make friends, so can Democrats and Republicans.

Live to Givers are always thinking of how they can help alleviate inequity and injustice, at least to some extent. The best question to keep in mind is, simply, "What can I do to help make things better for my neighbor, for the world, today?"

We don't have to work hard to look for the opportunities. Just keep your eyes open and be open to responding when they appear. In a recent study[3] of 246 adults (representative sample of the general population), **researchers at the University of Toronto found that, on average, *nine* unique opportunities to empathize with others arose daily** for participants, usually for those who are close by (that is, those we routinely encounter in everyday life). Importantly, and not surprisingly based on the happiness research you read about earlier in the book, they found that empathy in daily life was associated with increased well-being.

THE HOME TEAM

We live between New York City and Philadelphia, between Giants and Eagles country. In case you aren't aware, the Giants and the Eagles football teams are bitter rivals. For every person we know who says, "My two favorite teams are the Eagles and whoever is playing the Giants," there is someone who says the opposite. It'd be easier for us if all our friends could come together in their shared love of the game instead of despising each other for rooting for a different color jersey.

How far does that enmity go? Can fervent team allegiance turn you into a bad citizen?

Professor Mark Levine at Lancaster University in England (the same researcher who revisited witness testimonies in the Kitty Genovese case), ran a pair of experiments[4] about "social category membership" and helping behavior. But since this is the U.K. we're talking about, the participants were fans of the other kind of football (soccer), namely, Manchester United. First, the forty-five college-age male participants completed questionnaires about how devoted they were to "Man U," which was a research trick of reinforcing and revving up their allegiance to the team. Next, they were told that part two of the experiment was watching a movie about soccer at a second location. They were given directions to a screening room in the building next door.

Along the way, a man (really, another confederate [actor] who was in on the study) ran by, slipped, fell down, grabbed his ankle, and screamed in agony.

Sometimes, the fall guy wore a Man U shirt. Other times, he wore the shirt of Man U's bitter rival team: Liverpool. (For the control group, the fall guy wore a non-soccer, neutral shirt.)

Hidden observers watched and rated the participants on a five-point helping scale, from not even noticing the fallen jogger to escorting him to get medical attention. **Ninety-four percent of the time, the soccer fans helped someone in their "in-group," the fall guy in a Man U shirt. Only 30 percent of the time did they help the** "out-group" man in a Liverpool shirt or a neutral shirt. They just left him groaning on the side of the road. Some participants *didn't even notice* the Liverpool shirt guy at all.

In experiment number two, Levin and team did the whole thing over again with thirty-two young male participants. This time, the priming initial questionnaire focused on love of soccer ("the beautiful game"), not love for Man U specifically. With that change, around 80 percent of Man U fans helped the slip-and-fall-er in a Man U shirt, slightly less than when they were primed with team allegiance. Seventy percent helped the Liverpool shirt guy, a 40 percent *increase* in helping behavior compared to the previous experiment. The reasoning was, he was now "in-group" as a fellow soccer fan. The neutral shirt guy was left to his lonesome; only 22 percent of Man U fans bothered with him, an out-group-er as a non-soccer fan. Overall, the number of participants who didn't even notice the slip-and-fall victim went down as well.

Lesson learned: if we expand our view about who is in our in-group by finding common ground, we increase empathy and compassionate action for more people. Naturally, we are not holding our breath for Eagles and Giants fans to agree on this.

EMPATHY NUDGES

To increase empathy, you can nudge yourself in a compassionate direction with the power of imagination.

Imagine how someone else feels. Imagine what their life is really like. What circumstances have they faced that made them the person they are? This is not so much a protective, selfish thought process, as in, "There by the grace of God go I." It's a practice called "perspective giving," or shifting your point of view out of your own head and life circumstances, and for just a few minutes, to get into someone else's.

Back in the 1980s and '90s, AIDS patients were commonly stigmatized for having contracted the disease. The group-think placed blame on the patients' own behavior that might have increased their risk. If they brought the disease on themselves, some people reckoned, why empathize with them? If you didn't know anyone who had AIDS, the statistics about the epidemic might not have made an emotional dent. They were numbers about strangers, not individuals you cared about. Of note: the disease is viewed very differently today, and incidentally, the groups with some of the highest rates of new HIV cases are the elderly, heterosexuals, and non–drug users.

C. Daniel Batson, he of the Elaine shocks and the Good Samaritan experiment, put together a study[5] in the late '90s to test whether empathy could be manipulated, depending on framing.

First, the participants were told that they were going to hear a recording of "Julie," a young woman, talking about her experience as an AIDS patient. One group was given a "low-empathy condition" and told to listen objectively to Julie's story and to try not to get caught up in her emotion. Another group was given a "high empathy condition" and instructed to try to imagine how she feels about what she's going through. Those groups were then split again: some participants heard Julie explain that she got AIDS from a blood transfusion after her car was hit by a drunk driver. Another group heard her explain that she had a wild summer during college and slept around a lot and caught the virus that way.

The factor that determined the participants' empathy turned out *not* to be whether Julie had responsibility through risky behavior. What increased empathy—for Julie and all AIDS patients—was the manipulation of encouraging the listeners to imagine how Julie felt about what she was going through. As for the purposefully objective listeners who were instructed not to imagine how Julie felt, their empathy didn't budge a hair.

When engaging people with ideologies that are different from ours, we strongly believe that we all can make a smidge more of an effort to see the other person's take, or at least be respectful about them having differing views. You don't have to nudge your own empathy so far that you agree with them. But if you can shift your POV to imagine where they're coming from, you might form a bond of mutual respect, which is a good place to find common ground.

Early on in the COVID-19 vaccination program at Cooper, Mazz approached a group of about twenty staffers to talk about the benefits of getting the shot. One was a twenty-five-year-old male conspiracy theorist who believed that the vaccines were a way to implant tracking devices into people's bodies, and that the COVID-19 disease is actually caused by 5G towers, and so on. Others in the group just tittered at him.

Mazz knew there was nothing to gain by showing blatant disregard to a member of his staff, and vaccine-shaming would never be effective in changing people's minds, so he didn't roll his eyes or say, "Take off the tinfoil hat, buddy." Mazz spoke to him as if he were counseling a patient of his by presenting the available science on the vaccines and engaging him as an equal. At the end of the discussion, he told Mazz, "I know these other people were laughing at me, and I appreciate how you're talking to me. You moved me closer to the fence than anyone else has." He still wasn't going to get a shot, but he agreed that he wouldn't try to convince anyone else not to.

The fact that Mazz could move him even a little bit was a victory. But the real win had nothing to do with the conspiracy guy. It was demonstrating to the other people in the room how you can respectfully disagree and use empathy to walk someone closer toward a common goal. Laughing at someone's ideas, however wacky they might seem to you, further entrenches people in their foxholes.

The benefit of this approach is twofold. First, you can only change someone's mind if they are at the table talking with you. So with respectfulness, you might help change someone's openness to your opinion. Second, and in some ways better yet, they may change *your* mind and you will conclude you were wrong about something. The moment you agree you are wrong, you have become more right. Ultimately, knowing you are wrong makes you less wrong! Right?

ALL-OR-NOTHING BURGERS

One of Mazz's favorite analogies has to do with hamburgers. If you had a delicious juicy hamburger and a fly briefly landed on it, would you throw out the entire burger, or just cut off that one part? Most of us would remove the tainted part and savor the rest. Some (one of us) would eat the whole thing anyway. Hardly anyone in our highly unscientific polling of friends and colleagues would trash an entire meal because of a tiny, microscopic contamination.

People are like hamburgers. Do you reject a whole person because one belief of theirs doesn't pass your purity test? If you *really* believed that, you'd have to block and/or cancel every person you know. Perhaps it's possible to put aside that one conflict and judge people on what you respect and appreciate about them instead. If you can do that, you might find that you have tons in common and actually like them. You might even enjoy grabbing a burger together. But if they put mustard on their hamburger—or God forbid, a *sunny-side-up egg*—they are evil, and you would be justified in not having any empathy for them at all.

GET IN WITH THE OUT-GROUP

As previously mentioned, "in-group" is the term used by psychologists to define people in your bubble. "Out-group" is a term that refers to those you don't personally relate to, agree with, or know: the "other." In *The War for Kindness,* Jamil Zaki, Ph.D., explored the dangers of being too insulated in one's in-group, and how social isolation as such can lead to intolerance, prejudice, and hatred of anyone in an out-group. For example, a neo-Nazi who has never met or interacted with someone who is Jewish may have no reason to doubt or challenge his hatred of *all* Jewish people. Zaki wrote, "Hatred buries empathy but it does not kill it." The more people can get to know "outsiders," the less they will hate (and fear) them.

American psychologist Gordon W. Allport, Ph.D., wrote in his 1979 book *The Nature of Prejudice* that one solution to bigotry is acquaintance. When people meet and get to know each other, they realize that they share a common humanity. Allport came up with the concept of "contact therapy," theorizing that it's not enough to *see* out-groups, as any city dweller would just walking down the street. You have to *talk* to them, get to know them, and explore what you have in common. "The more time someone spends with outsiders, the less prejudice they express. Contact warms sentiments toward many types of outsiders," wrote Zaki.

Get out of your own head, venture forth into other social circles, and make contact with people you wouldn't ordinarily get to know. Mark Twain once said, "Travel is fatal to prejudice, bigotry, and narrow-mindedness, and many of our people need it sorely on these accounts. Broad, wholesome, charitable views of men and things cannot be acquired by vegetating in one little corner of the earth all one's lifetime." "Travel" in this sense doesn't have to mean getting on an airplane and going to foreign lands. It might mean just going up to someone in your office, school, or neighborhood who comes from a different background and engaging them in conversation. Zaki told the story of an American neo-Nazi who went back to college and worked closely with a professor who he came to greatly admire and respect. One day, he confessed to his professor that he was a longtime anti-Semite. The professor smiled and revealed that he was Jewish. Did the student's admiration for his professor suddenly disappear? No. His prejudice did.

Researchers from Singapore ran a series of studies[6] to test the hypothesis that if people lived in diverse neighborhoods, their sense of identity would broaden to be more inclusive and helpful to all types of people. They found an association between living in racially diverse metropolitan areas and promoting prosocial behaviors on Twitter, being helpful to strangers, and identifying with all humanity (looking at people as people, not members of a group). They also found that **in the aftermath of the 2013 Boston Marathon bombings, people from diverse neighborhoods were more likely to spontaneously offer help to people who'd been stranded in the confusion after the terrorist act.** In a final experiment, just asking people to *imagine* living in a diverse community made them more likely to be willing to help others in need, to take on the identity of being an inclusive, helpful person.

Another approach to combating in-group favoritism is to expand your definition of who is in your in-group. If you widen the lens of who you consider to be "one of us," you're more likely to empathize and help a wider range of people, like embracing all soccer fans instead of just people who root for your team.

To increase empathy and our Live to Give benefits, we need to do whatever we can to put more people into the in-group column in our minds. Because if we view others as our enemy, our brains can actually make us feel good when we see them in pain, and *schadenfreude* (taking pleasure in others' misfortune) is harmful to us all.

A University of Zurich study[7] looked at the brain mechanisms of what prompts someone to help a member of one's in-group or out-group. As per usual, in re-creating real-world circumstances (not), electrical shocks were involved. **Soccer fan participants were asked to watch a fan of their favorite team (an in-group) or a fan of a rival team (an out-group) get shocked via electrodes attached to the back of their heads.** The participants were given the option of choosing to help the in-group or out-group member by taking a portion of the pain themselves, aka "costly giving," or tuning out the horror and watching a video of a soccer match instead.

As researchers observed the participants' brain scans using fMRI, depending on whether the person being shocked was a fan of the witnesses' own team or a rival team, different regions of their brain were activated. **When participants saw someone on their own team get a shock, it lit up their empathy brain and they were more likely to step in and take the shocks. When they saw a rival get shocked, it actually lit up a reward center in their brains. It felt good to see an "enemy" suffer, and they were less likely to help.**

This study proves three things: (1) there is a neuroscience basis for being predisposed to help someone we perceive to be on our own team, (2) we have the capacity to feel good about the pain of those we perceive to be our adversaries, and (3) European psychology researchers are obsessed with studying soccer fans.

We are not doomed to *Beyond Thunderdome* bloodlust, clamoring to see our rivals suffer, though. A British study[8] found that if we dig deep and motivate ourselves to be helpful, we will feel more empathy and, in turn, we'll feel good about and be more likely to help and serve in the future, and so on. **The key motivational factor was, going back to the power of imagination, focusing on someone else's feelings. When participants did that, they were more likely to help others than those who remained emotionally detached.** Empathy for others encourages

Live to Give behaviors because we are motivated by how good it feels to help.

GAME THEORY

Psychology researchers have found that a great way to study human behavior is to make it seem like a fun game. We came across a couple of games about empathy that they play. . . .

The Dictator Game: This economic game created by Princeton's Daniel Kahneman, author of *Thinking Fast and Slow*, has two players: Player One is the "dictator" who decides how much money to give (or not give) to Player Two, the recipient. The purpose of the game is to test altruism in different conditions. A Swiss/German study[9] used this game to look at fairness norms and empathy as a motivation for altruism. Before playing the Dictator Game, participants were either given an "empathy induction"—asked to put themselves in the shoes of someone who needs help—or not (the control group). The participants who were primed to be empathetic and "fair" before the game gave significantly more money to the recipients than the control group. Adhering to the norm of fairness along with encouragement to be empathetic can be key motivators for altruistic behaviors. **Be a better Live to Giver by telling yourself, "Helping others is the right thing to do."**

The Prisoner's Dilemma: This is another psychological game that's used to test human behavior, and if you've ever seen a cop show, you get how this works. Two "perps" are in separate interrogation rooms; the detective goes into one of the rooms and says, "If you rat out your friend, we'll go easy on you."

The perp replies, "You got nothing!"

The detective says, "Fine, we'll take the offer to your buddy. Whoever talks first gets the deal. Either way, we've got enough to take you both down."

Or something to that effect.

Maybe the cop is bluffing, in which case, the perp's silence might mean he and his partner in the other room both go free. But if the cop *isn't* bluffing, the perp can save himself by betraying a friend. The optimal situation is that they both stay silent. Can you count on the other perp to stay silent too, and do what's best for you both, or will he stab you in the back and take the deal? Should you beat him to the punch so you don't go down for the crime alone? *That* is the dilemma.

Does *framing* affect one's decision? Are you more likely to do what you can to help your friend depending on "the name of the game"? An Israeli study[10] tested exactly that, whether labeling would influence people's helping behavior in an economic version of the Prisoner's Dilemma.

They ran two experiments, one with Stanford University undergrads and the other with Israeli pilots and their instructors. In both cases, labeling made a huge impact on whether the players cooperated or defected. **When the researchers framed it as "The Community Game" for one group, two-thirds of the players trusted that their friends would have their back. When the researchers called it "The Wall Street Game" for another group, two-thirds of the participants couldn't betray each other fast enough. Same game, different framing, different results.**

The researchers made sure that the Wall Street Game players understood that if they betrayed their friends, they'd still suffer . . . but they'd suffer less than the other guys, and that was what swayed their behavior.

The Live to Give takeaway: In all of these experiments, the key factor was prioritizing empathy. When intentionally and regularly giving yourself "empathy inductions," you will be more community and fairness minded. Then you'll be more likely to give, help, and serve, and get all the benefits. Otherwise, you might veer toward self-focus and emotional detachment, and go it alone, out for yourself only.

A WORD OF CAUTION

Consider how the other person feels, but be careful. Some thinkers on the subject raise a caution flag about being *irrationally* empathetic. Paul Bloom, Ph.D., professor of psychology at the University of Toronto, and the Brooks and Suzanne Ragen professor emeritus of psychology at Yale University, wrote a book called *Against Empathy: The Case for Rational Compassion*[11] that warned readers not to overdo it. Too much empathy can lead to big trouble and nonsensical decisions. For example, if you feel empathy for, say, the victim of a political assassination, a corrupt politician can exploit that empathy, turn it into red-hot "out-group" anger, and all of the sudden, a single criminal incident can start a war. Years later, we would wonder how we got started down the road that cost tens or hundreds of thousands of lives. Bloom makes the argument for "rational compassion" instead, which we interpret to mean, don't use empathy without reason and sound judgment.

Also, it's not enough just to be able to feel what others feel, if your empathy is limited only to people just like you. "Parochial empathy"—that is, empathy limited in range or scope that creates an empathy bias toward the in-group and no empathy for the out-group—creates less altruism overall. A University of Pennsylvania/Harvard University study[12] looked at "empathy failures" between hostile groups that blocked any kind of peaceful interactions. **In three intergroup contexts—Americans regarding Arabs, Hungarians regarding refugees, Greeks regarding Germans—researchers found that out-group empathy (understanding how the other group feels) inhibited harm and promoted helpfulness between groups, but in-group empathy (understanding how people in your own group feel) actually increased intergroup harm and prevented helpfulness.** So empathy in general doesn't do much for you, unless you care about making friends in a larger sense, with people you aren't already predisposed to relate to and feel for.

A University of Houston study[13] looked at this phenomenon in the context of political polarization in America and found that deep concern for people on one's own side was associated with increased polarization. If fact, **the more people cared for "their own," the greater their partisan bias in evaluating political hot-button topics.** So the deeper you love and feel for those you agree with, the more hostile you might become toward those with whom you disagree. Extreme love is sometimes accompanied by extreme hate. If they cancel each other out, that's a problem for everyone.

The Live to Give prescription for finding common ground: We often talk about altruism as turning your light around and shining that beam on others. To be empathetic, we have to turn that light into a lighthouse so that it shines much farther than just on the people right in front of us.

Look for opportunities to be empathetic far and wide, by talking to people you'd otherwise not come into contact with and educating yourself about other cultures, at home and abroad. If you can make at least one friend in an out-group, you'll have more empathy for the entire population, you'll be more helpful and inclusive overall, and you'll think of yourself in a different (better, happier) way.

Assume good intent and seek to understand. Fervent Second Amendment supporters are not in favor of mass murder. Atheists don't want to cancel Christmas. Crack open your mind a sliver to find the positive intent of how the other side feels. You might never agree on certain issues, but at least you're at the table discussing it. Empathy lowers the temperature of our discourse and can lower the stress in your own body.

And please don't throw out a perfectly good hamburger because a fly landed on it. That's just wasteful.

I alone cannot change the world, but I can cast a stone across the waters to create many ripples.

—Mother Teresa

See It

If we pay attention to the news at all, we see stories about human tragedies, natural disasters, and political unrest that cause misery for countless people. When confronted with such distressing images, we can only shake our heads. It can be overwhelming. What can we possibly do to help those suffering both here and abroad?

"Numeracy bias" is the assumption that it's impossible for one person to make a meaningful difference given the scope of need—that is, such an overwhelming number of people that there's no point in even trying. If you believe the numbers are against you, and doing the math makes you feel powerless to make any kind of impact, you are succumbing to this bias. Choosing not to serve others because you can't see how you can make a dent does not serve you well. Turning a blind eye might give you temporary relief of your distress, but every time you look away, you are waging a battle with your own human instinct to help, increasing stress and emotional detachment, and missing out on potential Live to Give benefits.

As you recall, one of the main components of burnout is the feeling that we can't make a difference. When we become aware of people in need, it can lead to burnout if we feel ineffectual. Even if we give to charities that help people in war-torn countries and tornado-ravaged towns, it might not protect us from the distress of seeing the human toll.

If we can't see how our giving makes a positive impact, it's almost like the giving never happened. You give, but you don't get a boost of well-being.

Some scientists call the disheartening lack of feedback "giver burn-out." Others call it "compassion fatigue," which isn't the result of caring and helping too much, but rather what happens when you give and serve to the best of your ability and don't see how you are making a difference.

During the first wave of the pandemic, doctors and nurses were at risk of being sucked into an "impact vacuum." They worked incredibly hard to help COVID-19 patients and advocated for prevention, but the cases kept coming in. Patients died on ventilators despite their best efforts. It was more than disheartening. It was gut-wrenching, and then they'd wake up on too little sleep and do it all over again. If you've wondered why hospital staff made such a big deal celebrating whenever a patient came off a ventilator and was well enough to leave the hospital, it was because they rejoiced in seeing the impact of their efforts for any patient they could. They needed to see (and feel) those individual victories.

Going through the very difficult experience of caring for patients in the pandemic may actually help them become better Live to Givers in the long run. Research shows that going through adversity can teach people to serve others better. A Northeastern University study[1] found that **people who have faced adversity in their lives consequently have more empathy for others, become more resistant to the numeracy bias, and are more likely to take compassionate action to help, even when the numbers of people in need are staggering.** Perhaps it is because people who have gone through struggles understand on a deeper level how much it means to be treated with random acts of kindness in their time of need. Yes, caring for gravely ill patients in the height of the pandemic was difficult and has stayed with many of us even to this day, but those crayon drawings from kids showing doctors as superheroes, people dropping off food to the hospital and banging on pots outside their windows at 7 p.m. every night in support made a meaningful difference to us and kept us going. We know that little things *can* make a big difference, and this prevents us from being sucked into the numeracy bias of believing—falsely—that little things do nothing.

Teachers are another group that can get sucked into the impact vacuum. They work with students for just one school year, pouring their wisdom and good intentions into each child. But they don't always get to see how their efforts to straighten out fourth-grade troublemaker Bart plays out in the longer term . . . unless they are the recipient of a Martin Seligman–style gratitude visit many years later, when a random middle-age man shows up at their door to say, "Hello, Mrs. Krabappel. My name is Bart. You might not remember me, but I drove you nuts with my terrible behavior in fourth grade . . . and now I'm a U.S. senator! All because of you."

In an instant-gratification culture, asking people to measure the impact of giving over a time horizon that stretches years into the future can be a tall order. But that's okay, isn't it? We're not in a race to serve others. It's not a short-term, or short-sighted, mission. Being a Live to Giver is a way of life for your whole life—which, if you overcome the numeracy bias and actively serve others despite overwhelming numbers of people in need—might be longer and happier.

The Live to Give prescription: Feel the benefits of serving others by seeing the impact—either right now with your own two eyes or by envisioning a future impact over a longer time horizon.

SEE IT TO FEEL IT

If you can clearly see how your service benefits others, you're more likely to be enthusiastic and continue doing it. Previously, we mentioned a study that found that college fundraisers worked much harder and more effectively to raise scholarship money if they had just a five-minute interaction with a beneficiary of that fundraising. That short time together made the fundraisers understand the magnitude of the impact, and it became something tangible to them. When you can put a face to your service, it becomes exponentially more meaningful—and therefore, more beneficial to you as well.

In her TED Talk,[2] Elizabeth Dunn explained that giving to charity does make us happy, but to really feel the love, it helps to visualize the tangible benefits for another human being when we give. Seeing a picture of the person you'd be helping makes givers far happier than giving to a faceless charity. As she said, "In my lab, we'd seen the benefits of giving spike when people felt a real sense of connection with those they were helping and could easily envision the difference they were making in those individuals' lives."

In one experiment,[3] Dunn and her team first asked 120 college students to complete a survey on charitable giving (to prime them), and then rated them on a happiness scale. Next, the participants were randomized to an opportunity to donate a sum of money to one of two charities that promote children's health, UNICEF or Spread the Net. The main difference between them is that UNICEF is huge. Some people may visualize donating money to UNICEF as a drop in the ocean, barely making a ripple of impact. Spread the Net, on the other hand, is much smaller, and it makes a concrete promise to donors: for every $10 that donors contribute to the cause, Spread the Net will provide an insecticide-treated bed net to protect children in sub-Saharan Africa from contracting malaria while they are sleeping. Their appeal to donors: "Every two minutes, a child dies from malaria, a disease caused by a single mosquito bite. One bed net can protect up to five children for five years. One net. Ten bucks. Save lives." Instantly, the image of saving a child's life with a simple mosquito net pops into one's mind.

Participants in both groups donated around the same amount (an average of $5) and gave at the same rate overall. However, the Spread the Net donors reported feeling significantly happier in a post-study interview compared to the UNICEF donors. "This suggests that just **giving money to a worthwhile charity isn't always enough. You need to be able to envision how, exactly, your dollars are going to make a difference**," said Dunn. "If we want people to give more . . . we need to create opportunities to give that enable us to appreciate our shared humanity," ideally with visuals of real humans in need. She suggests that charitable organizations stop sending pens or calendars to donors, and instead provide them with proof of impact by showing them in concrete ways how their generosity helps and connecting them with the individuals and communities they're serving. "[Humans] have evolved to find joy in helping others," she said. "Let's stop thinking about giving as just this moral obligation and start thinking of it as a source of pleasure."

Although you will derive some fulfillment from giving to gigantic global charities, if you volunteer at your local food bank or Salvation Army outpost, and interact and connect with the people you're helping, you don't need to imagine the impact of your giving. You'll see it with your own eyes, in vivid detail. It's a whole different experience, and science shows that it can be so much more rewarding for you and perhaps also for those you serve.

APOLOGIES TO MONET: REALISM BEATS IMPRESSIONISM

Jamil Zaki wrote in *The War for Kindness* that a single image of a suffering *individual*—he cited a shocking photo of a dead Syrian boy who fell out of a raft and drowned in the Mediterranean Sea while fleeing his war-torn homeland—can inspire more empathy than the plight of many who are in the same figurative boat. When the image of the child's body washed up on the beach circled the globe via the internet, donations flooded in for Syrian refugee charities. "Laboratory studies [show] people express more empathy for one victim of the tragedy than they do for eight, ten or hundreds," Zaki said.

People give more in response to individuals (the drowned boy) rather than general statistics (*x*-number of Syrian refugees who are killed) because they can identify with one person or one image—this is called the "identified victim effect." According to a Carnegie Mellon study,[4] the "identified intervention effect"—a charity's providing tangible details about its interventions—significantly increases donations to that charity. So the more a charity provides concrete information about how it uses donor money to help, the easier it is for donors to visualize the impact of their contribution. If they can truly envision it, they wind up giving more. The researchers urged charities to remember that the "donor is in the details." The more details they can provide, the more donations they'll receive.

No matter what kind of giver you aspire to be with your time, talent, and treasure, if you have a clear, detailed vision and a specific game plan to turn it into reality, you are more likely to realize your purpose. For a University of Houston series of studies,[5] **participants were randomly assigned either "abstractly framed" prosocial goals (like making someone happy or saving the environment) or "concretely framed"**

prosocial goals (like making someone smile or recycling). The concrete goals group reported feeling happier after they accomplished their objectives compared to the abstract goals group. This relates to visualization because if you were asked to make someone smile, you could easily see the plan to tell a joke or pay a compliment. Participants felt happy to set and meet realistic expectations. In contrast, having the goal of making someone "happy" may seem too big, too fuzzy, to visualize a clear plan of action, so the participants felt frustrated about how to realize their goals and were then disappointed when they failed to do so.

To reap Live to Give benefits, paint a clear, detailed, and realistic mental picture of how to serve and how much good it'll do.

REWIND AND REPLAY

Once you take a mental high-def photo or record a TikTok-length "giving gif" in your head of your own altruistic behavior, you can replay it, relive the experience, and reap additional Live to Give benefits over and over.

A University of California–Riverside study[6] randomized participants into groups assigned to: (1) perform kind acts, (2) recall past kind acts, (3) perform and recall kind acts, and (4) do neither (the control). In terms of well-being gains, it was a tie between the three kindness groups. However, it is easy (and instantaneous) to recall kind acts, so if you are having a bad day and feeling down, and need a quick hit to raise your spirits, research says that you can just flip through your mental photo library and click on a memory of when you made a meaningful difference for others.

Three Simon Fraser University experiments[7] with 680 participants found that **the motives behind doing kind acts determine how happy you'll feel when you remember them. If motives are autonomous (not forced) and authentic (from the heart), the happiness boost is more powerful.** If you served others for selfish ulterior motives (to make yourself look good), thinking back on the experience won't do a lot for you. In fact, it might even make you feel a bit ashamed and embarrassed that you acted selfishly.

Research also supports the idea that if you want to use your memories to motivate yourself to be a better Live to Giver in the future, recall past experiences that put you in the role of "benefactor" instead of the role of "beneficiary" (that is, a giver rather than a receiver). Adam Grant and the University of Michigan's Jane Dutton studied[8] these conditions in a familiar setting: a college fundraiser call center. Thirty-two fundraisers kept daily journals for an average of four months. One group was randomized to write for fifteen minutes per day about a time in their life they were grateful to have *received* help from someone else (the "beneficiary" condition). The other group wrote for the same time period about past experiences of inspiring gratitude in other people by *giving* them help (the "benefactor" condition). Another group, the control, didn't journal at all.

Both journaling groups increased their number of calls per hour and total call volume. But the benefactor group's uptick was significantly greater than the beneficiaries'. Reflecting on times they inspired gratitude in others by their own kind acts felt *so* good, they inspired themselves to really go for it with their fundraising.

Being on the receiving end of help certainly gives us a boost. We fill up with gratitude, which is good for our well-being. But for long-lasting positive affect, reflecting upon giving to others, even years ago, increases our inspiration to give more. The benefits of giving "may encourage prosocial behavior by increasing the salience and strength of one's identity as a capable, caring contributor," wrote Grant and Dutton.

If you see yourself as the person saved by a superhero, you aren't going to have a Live to Give standard of giving behavior to uphold. But if you picture yourself in the superhero role—with the cape and everything—you will live up to your own vision, leaping tall buildings in a single bound or fighting injustice . . . or just putting a smile on someone's face, probably your own.

GROUP PICTURE

In the social science realm, the term "norms" does *not* refer to "normies," or basic mainstream types. Nor does it refer to "normcore" fashion fans who make a math teacher aesthetic look radical and cool. Social norms are standard patterns of behavior that we see every day, everywhere. Unless one is actively trying to subvert norms—which would be very punk rock—most people feel comfortable when their behavior adheres to social standards. But we have to see the norms in order to conform to them. If you have a "line of sight" into the altruism norms of your community, you may realize that people are more giving than you thought, and it'll prod you to become more altruistic yourself.

Harvard's Erika Weisz, Ph.D., has conducted studies on building empathy in teenagers, a population that is particularly sensitive to how they fit into society. Weisz and Jamil Zaki asked one thousand San Francisco Bay Area seventh-graders to write about the importance and usefulness of empathy, and then had them read each other's essays.[9] In exchanging the papers, the teens saw how their peers' personal, positive feelings about giving matched their own (despite whatever they might have assumed about each other's self-focus). The participants also read notes about the importance of altruism from a group the Bay Area teens probably hoped to join one day: Stanford University undergrads. Finally, the teens were asked to imagine bragging about how altruistic, and therefore cool, they were to kids from a different school. The point of the research was to affirm that, **despite what the teens might believe based on the words and actions of the loudest voices in the classroom (the bullies and "popular" kids), the normie students did in fact care about caring. Seeing the proof of that motivated the teens to have more empathy for others and subsequently to be more kind and giving.** When giving was seen as the established norm, teens aspired to conform to it.

In another study,[10] Weisz and colleagues randomized 292 college freshmen into groups: (1) students who were taught that their brain function was malleable (neuroplasticity) and empathy could be enhanced by their behavior, (2) students who learned about the influence of social norms, (3) students who learned both, and (4) the control group who didn't learn squat. **After eight weeks, the students who learned that their brains could be rewired for empathy showed greater empathic accuracy in social situations. Plus, something all college freshmen can appreciate, having more empathy, as they reported, resulted in their having more friends than they did before the study.** Seeing oneself as an empathetic person ultimately nets real-world improvement in one's social life.

So if you can visualize your brain changing to produce a Live to Give mindset, you might as well also visualize yourself letting the good times roll—surrounded by fellow Live to Givers.

IF YOU LOOK, YOU WILL NOTICE

> When I was a boy and I would see scary things in the news, my mother would say to me, look for the helpers. You will always find people who are helping.
>
> —Fred Rogers

If you keep your eyes wide open for examples of people helping people, you will be amazed by the kind acts that are happening all around you, and you will be inspired to join in. Science confirms that people who observe helping and giving wind up doing more of the same themselves, and not just the specific behaviors observed, but all sorts of other kind acts as well.

You've heard the saying: monkey see, monkey do. But for humans (unlike monkeys), watching/doing generous acts goes much deeper than mere imitation. It can also translate to how one *feels* about doing generous acts. According to a Harvard University/Stanford University study[11] about "prosocial conformity," **participants watched others donate to charity, and decided how much to donate themselves. Predictably, those who saw others give a lot gave a lot; those who observed stingy donations gave paltry sums.** But the really exciting finding was this: when they were given an opportunity to write a note of encouragement to another study participant who was going through a tough time, **those who observed the generous donations also wrote notes that showed more empathy and support.** Prosocial conformity went beyond the mirroring of the behavior (monetary donations); it extended to the participants' feelings for others in need. If we see and mirror other-serving behaviors, we are more likely to adopt a Live to Give mindset as well.

The Live to Give prescription for seeing it: To motivate and inspire your own giving behavior, look for individuals to relate to and for proof of the impact of your altruism. The simplest way to get both of those conditions is to serve others in your own community, where you can interact with people directly and see with your own eyes how you are helping them.

Also, you'll be a more effective giver if you have a clear, detailed vision and game plan for how to realize your altruism goals. When things play out the way you saw them in your mind, you get a hit of serotonin just by meeting your own expectations.

Scan your community to find the evidence that empathy and giving really are social norms that we can all conform to, for our own benefit and that of others. Those norms are there, if you look for them. As Mr. Rogers said, it's a beautiful day in the neighborhood when we live up to our Live to Give potential and be good neighbors (cardigans optional).

Your mind shines brightest when you
enlighten others; your heart, when you encourage
others; your soul, when you elevate others; and
your life, when you empower others.

—Matshona Dhliwayo

Elevate

Researchers define "elevation" as an emotional state, a feeling of uplift, that comes about when you bear witness to others' moral excellence, heroism, or virtuous acts. If you happen to spot a Live to Giver in action—helping and serving others with genuine care—you will get a warm, pleasurable sensation in your chest and the sudden motivation to serve others yourself. Consider yourself "elevated."

On the flip side, the opposite of witnessing moral beauty is seeing someone behave hideously to others, and getting a cold, sick feeling in your chest known as "social disgust." Consider yourself degraded.

Professor of ethical leadership at New York University's Stern School of Business Jonathan Haidt, Ph.D., author of *The Happiness Hypothesis: Finding Modern Truth in Ancient Wisdom,* is preeminent in the social psychology field of moral foundations. One of his areas of expertise is how watching the behavior of others (virtuous or atrocious) can motivate one's own behavior. While there had been a ton of research about the effects of altruism on oneself (as we've shown), there wasn't much research about the effects of witnessing another person's altruism. Haidt and scientists like him have endeavored to fill this gap.

Haidt asserts that people can vary along a vertical dimension, which he calls "elevation versus degradation" or "purity versus pollution." **When you are around Live to Givers, you rise on this vertical dimen-**

sion and want to behave with more moral excellence. **When you are around scoundrels, it drags you down the vertical dimension, inch by inch.** The slow fall from moral excellence into the gutter might not be perceptible to you until you wake one day and realize, "Hey, I'm covered in filth."

As the sage of our time, Mazz's mom, would say, "If you lie down with dogs, you get up with fleas."

Carefully pick friends and associates who are upstanding members of society who recognize our moral obligation to serve others and act upon it. Research supports the idea that if you surround yourself with Live to Givers, you will have the best chance of becoming one, consistently, every day. And then your altruistic acts will resonate with those around you, and others will "catch" it from you, spreading other-focus throughout your social network. Small ripples of serving others can come together to form a tsunami of serving. If you think about it, elevation can help bring about the improved health, happiness, and success of an entire community.

The start of the pandemic was a defining time for everyone, especially for those in health care, and most notably for those on the front lines of caring for patients. In that time of crisis, Steve and Mazz consistently experienced elevation as they witnessed their colleagues' heroism on a daily basis. Health care workers described going into the hospital like running into a burning building; their compassion and actions to save the suffering despite the very real danger to their own safety is the essence of heroism. History will tell the story of their selflessness, and their stories will inspire a generation. When civilians watched frontline health care providers' steadfast commitment and self-sacrifice on the news, they were elevated to do their part by practicing prevention protocols. Our collective commitment to slowing the spread by wearing masks, staying home, and social distancing were vital acts of compassion for the most vulnerable among us, and for our frontline health care workers. If the vast majority of Americans hadn't taken those precautions, our health care system could likely have been pushed past the breaking point. Our communities' collective compassion that helped protect frontline health care workers so that they could care for the sick was a virtuous elevation cycle that undoubtedly saved innumerable lives.

> Powerful moments of moral elevation seem to push a mental reset button, wiping out feelings of cynicism and replacing them with feelings of hope, love, and moral inspiration.
>
> —Jonathan Haidt

Watching and modeling service to others is the cure for cynicism, which you might be experiencing right now as we talk about moral beauty and how it can heal the entire world.

But this isn't wide-eyed optimism, nor is it our opinion. The potential power of elevation is evidence-based and grounded in rigorous research.

INSTANT INSPIRATION

Elevation, a response to seeing others' kindness, is all the #inspo you'll need to bring out the Live to Giver in you and in everyone you know (and others you don't know). The way it works: if you see someone do something altruistic, you'll be motivated to follow suit, and if someone sees you behave compassionately, they'll pick up the Live to Give baton, keeping the virtuous relay going ad infinitum. Giving doesn't just multiply, it grows exponentially in social networks. Haidt and others call this "group affect." One person's kindness (and how happy it makes them) spreads across the whole group.

Haidt and his colleague Sara Algoe, Ph.D., of the University of North Carolina, described elevation as one in a family of "other-praising emotions" along with gratitude and admiration. To study[1] its effects, they induced elevation in participants by having them recall times they witnessed others' kind acts, watching videos of people demonstrating moral excellence, and through letter-writing. Sufficiently primed, the participants next filled out a questionnaire about how motivated they were to serve others. Compared to, say, general happiness, the affective state of elevation fired up the participants to get out there and help others, show compassion, and be better people.

Two University of Cambridge experiments[2] showed that elevation was a fast-acting inspiration for helping behavior. **In the first experiment, elevation-induced participants were more likely to sign on to participate in another unpaid research study compared to those in a neutral emotional state (the control). In the second study, the pre-elevated participants spent twice as long helping someone do a "tedious task" compared to the control group.** The researchers concluded that elevation is a distinct emotion, apart from any in the happiness family of emotions, with unique prosocial qualities that lead to tangible increases in altruism.

A UCLA study[3] explored the uniqueness of elevation's inspirational qualities. Researchers had participants watch either: (1) a three-minute version of a Thai TV commercial called "Unsung Hero" (109 million views and counting on YouTube) of a young man giving money to a homeless person, feeding a stray dog, helping a street vendor lift her heavy cart over a curb, plus the positive consequences of his doing all those helpful acts and the recipients' gratitude, (2) a same-length video of high production value of a man running up a wall, doing back flips (the urban sport called parkour), showing extraordinary athletic artistry, or (3) thirty seconds of footage of a commuter train occupied by boring passengers (the control).

Next, the participants were given $5 for taking part in the study and told that they could give that money to the UCLA Children's Hospital. They were given envelopes to make donations, but only if they wanted to, no obligation. The participants who watched "Unsung Hero" were more generous by far than the other groups. As reported by Annie Lowrey in an article in *The Atlantic*, "America's Epidemic of Unkindness," one research assistant thought there was something wrong with their accounting because some of those envelopes were *stuffed* with cash, much more than the money the participants were given. They realized that elevated participants were going into their *own* pockets to put extra money in those envelopes. "It suggests that families or even whole communities could pitch themselves into a kind of virtuous cycle of generosity and do-gooding, and that people could be prompted to do good for their communities even with no expectation of their kind acts redounding to their own benefit," wrote Lowrey.

The researchers were so amazed by how reliably and readily elevation inspired prosocial behavior, they replicated their results in *fourteen more studies* with more than eight thousand participants, just to be sure-sure.

Elevation is so good at making people give, it can be used as a self-administered booster shot to inspire yourself to uphold your own Live to Give values. Back to the U.K.'s University of Cambridge, where researchers tested[4] the effects of "self-affirmation" elevation. First, the participants affirmed their own altruism by saying things like, "I'm a giving person." Then, elevation was induced via recall of witnessing others' kind acts (but not for the control group). The participants who experienced moral elevation after self-affirmation were subsequently more likely to perform kind acts. So it is possible to nudge yourself to be more helpful (and get more Live to Give benefits) if you give yourself a little pep talk and chase that with keeping your eyes fixed on the moral beauty of others.

Speaking of beauty, modeling (demonstrating) Live to Give behavior can elevate an entire community. A University of Illinois meta-analysis[5] of eighty-eight studies with 25,354 participants found evidence of a "prosocial modeling effect" that says when people watch others strutting down the Live to Give runway, they want to follow in those footsteps.

COMMUNITY SPREAD

Two scientists at the forefront of social networks and "group affect" (emotion contagion), the co-authors of *Connected: The Surprising Power of Our Social Networks and How They Shape Our Lives,* are Nicholas Christakis, M.D., Ph.D., physician and sociologist at the Human Nature Lab at Yale University, and James Fowler, Ph.D., professor of political science at the University of California–San Diego. Remember those news stories that reported that if you have obese friends, you're more likely to gain weight, or if your friends quit smoking, you will too? They're responsible for that research, as well as studies about how emotions spread within a group.

In a 2008 longitudinal study,[6] they looked at whether happiness can be passed from one person to the next by analyzing data for 4,739 participants in the Framingham Heart Study from 1983 to 2003. They discovered clusters of happy people—and clusters of unhappy ones—in this large social network. The emotional groupings were not formed because of personality, or like-minded people gravitating toward each other. The clusters were the result of physical proximity. **If an individual had a happy friend very close by (within a mile), his or her happiness probability increased by 25 percent. A similar uptick in happiness probability was seen with a happy spouse, happy nearby sibling, and happy next-door neighbor.** Increasing geographical distance—if one's happy friends, siblings, and neighbors moved away—reduced the probability of happiness.

Emotional spread reaches as far as three degrees of separation between individuals. So if your nearby friend's friend's friend was really happy (or unhappy), you might become happier (or unhappier). Christakis and Fowler found that it's possible to game future happiness by surrounding yourself with as many happy people in your network as possible. Happiness is collective. If we're all happy, we're all happy.

It's also true that the more we can surround ourselves with other-focused people, the more other-focused we are likely to become. And since everything we want in life—good health, happiness, and success—can become more likely by being an other-focused person, we need to seek out those who will inspire and spread that behavior to us, and then we'll spread it right back to them in a virtuous cycle.

Christakis and Fowler studied[7] the social spread—or, more poetically, the *cascade*—of cooperation, a key Live to Give behavior, and whether individuals making sacrifices for the public good would motivate others to pay it forward to people they don't know. The experiment had participants play a "Public Goods Game" with strangers. How it worked: participants could choose to add money into a pot that would then be equally divided and distributed to a group. But individuals could also hold back their own contribution, and still get their share of the divided pot. The "game" would reveal who was generous and who was selfish.

Christakis and Fowler primed the participants with cooperative behavior by giving the opportunity to help each other complete a task, like solving a puzzle. Then they played a version of the Public Goods Game. **The participants who witnessed cooperation were more likely to give their money away to strangers in future rounds of the experiment versus the control group.** (The participants played multiple rounds, but never cooperated with the same people twice to eliminate the possibility of reciprocity or "reputation management"—aka making yourself look good.) Cooperation set off a prosocial spark within individuals that influenced the group, and players in subsequent rounds of the experiment. So the more they played, the more generous they all became, spreading kindness to people they hadn't previously cooperated with or would ever meet. (It wasn't all kumbaya though. Uncooperative behavior among participants was just as contagious as cooperative.)

The Live to Give implications of this research give us great hope for humanity. **It only takes one or two altruistic individuals within a group to "turn" the majority of the community into altruists as well.** In an interview about this research, Christakis said, "There is a deep and fundamental connection between social networks and goodness. The flow of good and desirable properties like ideas, love and kindness is required for human social networks to endure, and, in turn, networks are required for such properties to spread."[8]

Strong evidence of prosocial behavior spread can be found in the workplace too. Research[9] has found that **social proximity to workplace "Givers" predicted boosts in well-being and an increase in their own kind acts, but proximity to "Receivers" predicted a drop in well-being. A third group, "Observers," who witnessed Givers in action and their grateful (we hope) Receivers, were sufficiently elevated by what they saw and increased their own kind acts as well.**

You don't have to be a social scientist to know that being around people who smile and help each other elevates the mood in the room, and that it only takes one toxic egomaniac Me-ness jerk to ruin the party. Per science, if everyone around that person started doing good for each other—and even the jerk (we shouldn't shine our light only on other Live to Givers)— the Me-ness person could "catch" kindness and be inspired to stop being such a jerk. Or the person would flee in terror at being surrounded by Live to Givers. Either way, mood elevated, problem solved.

(DON'T) PASS IT AROUND

Positive feelings and behaviors (happiness, cooperation, selflessness) are contagious within a group, but so are negative ones (unhappiness, division, selfishness, and even burnout[10]). Whatever is out there in the community, we are susceptible to being infected by it.

A University of North Carolina–Wilmington study[11] of eighty-one employees found an association between witnessing a single incident of morning rudeness in the workplace and feeling like everything and everyone sucks for the rest of the day. **Not only did morning rudeness change the participants' perspective (the researchers likened it to putting on "rude-colored glasses"), it predicted lower job performance and led to avoidance and withdrawal.** Essentially, people retreated into their offices and shut their doors. So if someone doesn't hold the elevator for you or grunts obnoxiously when you say, "Good morning," it doesn't turn you into a jerk, but it makes you see jerks wherever you look.

Or maybe it does turn you into a jerk. The same team of researchers also tested whether "catching rudeness" was as easy as catching a cold (shoulder). In a series of studies[12] about behavioral contagion, they found that a single episode of rudeness could trigger a gruff affect. Brain mechanisms are to blame. **Rudeness activates brain networks for hostility, and that neural activity influences behavior. The brain wants what the brain wants, and in response to rudeness, the brain is looking for a fight.** You might prefer not to respond to rudeness with more of the same, but your brain is saying, "Come at me, bro!" Even if you try to suppress rudeness, you can become a "carrier" and transmit it to a third party. It's very much like being an asymptomatic carrier of a virus. It's not obvious you have it, but you still might be spreading it around.

SPARE PARTS

If you had to make a list of the most altruistic things a person can do, donating a kidney to a stranger would have to be very high on

(Cont'd)

the list. What if ten people did it, all in a sequence, to help people they didn't even know? The *New England Journal of Medicine* published a case series[13] about just that circumstance, one of the most radical altruism contagions we have ever heard about.

Most of the time, when a person in end-stage renal failure needs a kidney transplant, they use a "paired donor," where one person volunteers to give a kidney to someone close to them, say a wife giving to a husband, or a related donor like an adult child giving to a parent, a sister giving to a brother. But even if your entire family is willing, they might not be a good match with your blood and tissue, making them incompatible. Incompatible pairs as such can use registries to find other incompatible pairs, and maybe the recipient in pair one and the donor in pair two *are* compatible. That might leave the recipient in pair two without a kidney . . . unless you find a third or a fourth pair or more, and find enough matches so that the dominos line up just right, and everyone who needs a kidney gets one.

It's called "chain donation." The logistics are quite challenging, as you can imagine, with recipients and donors all over the country, surgeries needing to be coordinated ASAP. In theory, you need at least one altruistic donor to tip over the first domino and prevent a situation where someone in this complicated "nonsimultaneous, altruistic, extended donor" chain is left without a kidney if a donor down the line drops out or something goes wrong.

Michael A. Rees, M.D., of the University of Toledo Medical Center in Ohio, and colleagues used two pair-donation registries and computer models to organize five simultaneous organ exchanges and coordinated an additional five transplants over eight months, in six medical centers in five states, to create this long chain. In some cases, a donor gave a kidney to a stranger, but their own mom or husband had to wait five more months for a match of their own. The donors operated in good faith that their supreme act of costly giving would eventually help the person they loved get a kidney, and not die of kidney failure before then.

When news about the ten-link transplant chain got out, more altruistic donors came forward to sign up for registries with no

particular recipient in mind. It affirmed that seeing (or reading about) one person's altruism can motivate and inspire your own and that elevation spreads giving behavior far beyond your own social circles.

This incredible example of extreme altruism started when a twenty-eight-year-old man in Michigan registered as an altruistic donor in 2006. Thanks to the efforts of Dr. Rees and colleagues, the donors and dominos lined up. Two years later, the Michigan man's generosity set off a chain of events that transformed ten lives, spurred technology to help find donor matches that changed our organ donation system for the better, and could potentially wind up helping thousands of people. One generous act can spread far and wide. You might never intend to see far-reaching effects of your Live to Give behavior, but science supports the idea that it can happen anyway.

The Live to Give prescription for elevation: Model moral excellence in service to others and intentionally gravitate toward people and organizations who do the same.

Be very careful selecting who you associate with in both your professional and personal life.

Choose to work for a company that prioritizes people over one that only cares about the bottom line. If you are in a position to do so, focus on hiring people who do the same.

Avoid toxic "it's all about *me*" Live to Getters. Think of them as the Live to Giver's Kryptonite. The more you are exposed to their selfishness, the weaker your altruism will become. And once you hit the bottom on that vertical dimension of moral excellence, you can wave goodbye to your other-serving longevity, happiness, and success benefits.

If you catch rudeness, shake it off by doing kind acts, and you might even cure rudeness in the original offender.

Gravitate toward people who do kind things for others and are happy about it, and you'll boost your own happiness just by being within a mile of them.

And whenever your own giving behaviors seem to slide, self-administer an elevation booster by affirming, "I'm a Live to Giver, dammit!," watch that Thai TV commercial called "Unsung Hero" on YouTube, then go outside and elevate your little corner of the world.

No one is useless in this world who
lightens the burdens of another.

—Charles Dickens

Know Your Power

You don't need to be a boss or in some other position of authority, nor do you need a million Instagram followers or millions of dollars, to have power. These are examples of "outside-in" power that comes from extrinsic forces, like authority, supremacy, influence, or wealth. We can tell you, from our experience as doctors, that rich, "powerful" people have the same brain and body mechanisms as everyone else. If the one-percenters use their riches to pursue only hedonic pleasures or to bury the competition, their outside-in power is scant protection from the ravages of chronic stress and systemic inflammation. People aspiring to these powers might assume a "crush, kill, destroy" tyrant attitude about how to become successful. But science shows that being selfish and status hungry predicts a slower rise up the corporate ladder, less income, dislike from your colleagues, chronic stress, and ill-being. We're not saying *all* outside-in power people are doomed to die young and be miserable. Lots of tyrants seem to be doing okay. But that brand of culturally reinforced power has not been linked to longer life, more happiness, or better health, and it does not do a bit of good for society as a whole.

Examples of "inside-out" power—as a force generated from within— are often alumni from a small British private school named Hogwarts. Or they go to X-Men Academy, hail from Planet Krypton, or are members of an elite squad known as the Order of Jedi Knights. Not to knock witches, wizards, mutants, and aliens, which we'd do at our peril. But most of us can't access inside-out powers as such, try as we might to channel the Force.

Real power—as we call it, "outward" power—has nothing to do with your net worth, title, command over others, or the ability to cast spells.

By being a Live to Giver and using your time, talent, and treasure to serve others, you have unlimited powers to make a real impact on people's lives, including your own.

You may literally prolong your life, because over time altruistic behaviors can reduce chronic stress and inflammation, improve basic human functioning, and help stave off cardiovascular disease and dementia, to remind you of just a few.

You have the greatest power on Earth, the ability to activate the brain's reward center and the Fantastic Four hormones that are the only real source of feelings of pride, euphoria, closeness, and Helper's High we have.

With Live to Give outward power, you will make more friends, strengthen bonds with family, have a happier marriage, and maintain the intimate relationships that are huge factors in your longtime happiness and well-being.

You have the power to inspire and motivate people to do their best work as a "servant leader," earning loyalty and making work better for people while increasing an organization's performance as well.

And all you have to do to access these incredible outward powers is to give till it helps—both yourself and the recipients of your altruism.

The people we should look up to and admire aren't the materialistic land-a-chopper-on-their-yacht types, or the so-called influencers who amass followers but use their platform only to advance their own fame and riches. The real heroes are the Live to Givers who take opportunities to give and help other people through volunteering, charitable donation, or just small random acts of kindness, leveraging their time, talent, and treasure to shine their light on others.

The wealthy can use their outward powers for tremendous social good, and we should all feel grateful when someone uses wealth to serve others. But you don't have to have outside-in power to wield outward power, which is available to every single one of us. We use it whenever we make eye contact and smile at people on the street, wash the dishes without having to be asked, buy an acquaintance a coffee, donate to a worthy cause, or drive a friend home after they get their molars removed.

That person who helps others simply because it should or must be done, and because it is the right thing to do, is indeed without a doubt, the real superhero.

—Stan Lee

Every time we use outward power, we can get a bit stronger physically (through reduced stress and inflammation and a boosted immune system), mentally (by reducing symptoms of anxiety and depression), emotionally (by increasing happiness and well-being), and professionally (by racking up goodwill credits with colleagues, finding joy in our work, and upping our performance).

As Dr. Martin Luther King Jr. told the congregants at Atlanta's Ebenezer Baptist Church on February 4, 1968:

If you want to be important—wonderful. If you want to be recognized—wonderful. If you want to be great—wonderful. But recognize that he who is greatest among you shall be your servant. That's a new definition of greatness. And this morning, the thing that I like about it: by giving that definition of greatness, it means that everybody can be great, because everybody can serve. You don't have to have a college degree to serve. You don't have to make your subject and your verb agree to serve. You don't have to know about Plato and Aristotle to serve. You don't have to know Einstein's theory of relativity to serve. You don't have to know the second theory of thermodynamics in physics to serve. You only need a heart full of grace, a soul generated by love. And you can be that servant.

Here's what else you need to tap your Live to Give outward powers:

HOPE

What is hope? Our favorite definition is this: "Hope is the active conviction that despair will never have the last word."[1] Altruism requires hope (rather than hopelessness). Hope is integral to altruism. An example of the power of hope can be found in patient outcomes. Researchers from Duke University conducted a study[2] of coronary heart disease patients over nearly two decades. The researchers enrolled 2,818 patients who were admitted to the hospital for a coronary event (for example, a heart attack) and underwent cardiac catheterization, a procedure where a cardiologist threads a wire into a patient's heart arteries to assess for blockages.

Prior to discharge from the hospital, the researchers assessed patients' expectations for recovery (that is, their hope for a good outcome) using a well-validated scale. Analyses controlled for age, sex, disease severity, comorbidities, treatments, demographics, depressive symptoms, social support, and functional status. What they found, with up to seventeen years of follow-up assessment, is that **expectation for recovery was strongly associated with survival. At the ten-year mark, mortality in the patients with the lowest recovery expectations—the least hope for a good outcome—was nearly double the mortality compared to patients with the highest recovery expectations (the most hope for a good outcome).**

How patients believe they will do can be a major factor in how they actually do. Therefore, based on these scientific data, one can conclude that hope *matters*. Belief in recovery *matters*.

So what does all this have to do with being a Live to Giver? *Everything.* When patients are struggling with hope, and are far more pessimistic about the trajectory of their health than the medical facts of their illness would support, treating them with compassion can help them see their recovery as something possible. Science shows that hope matters. And science shows that compassion can be a powerful *restorer of hope.*

The power of hope can be harnessed to get better outcomes in any area, not just medical science. It goes back to mindset: if you have hope that things will change for the better, then it's possible they will change. If you have hope that your small donations will make an impact, you're more likely to keep giving. If you have hope that your small investments of volunteering time can make a difference, you'll keep showing up.

WISDOM

As people get older, with the wisdom that being alive for so long brings, they understand that fulfillment comes from helping others. Science has shown an uptick in giving and volunteering as people enter their golden years because they realize it's the best use of the time they have left. Or perhaps it's a reaction to living their whole lives for themselves, waking up at seventy, and realizing that no one cares about them because they didn't care enough about others or that they're leaving their corner of the world in worse shape than when they arrived. If they do begin (or continue) serving others in their advanced years, they'll find that by giving away their precious time, they'll feel like they have more of it. This truly is an outward power: the ability to stretch time.

The great thing is that you don't have to wait until you're at retirement age to use this power. You can, as David Brooks said, bypass the "first mountain" of status and success, and go right to climbing the "second mountain" of significance. Then, when you look back on your life at eighty, you'll feel it was a life well lived, full of eulogy virtues that, at the end, are the only ones that really matter.

INTERDEPENDENCE

Americans mythologize independence. Our national holiday is Independence Day to celebrate going it alone. We're not knocking the Revolutionary War. But we are making the point that the conventional belief that independence is a sign of strength and interdependence (needing each other's help) is a sign of weakness needs an update.

When we help each other, we are stronger. Joining forces increases our collective power, and since we all live on the same planet, we truly are all in it together whether we like it or not.

Live to Givers are more likely to see interdependence as a source of strength. And if we are going to make the world a better place, we need to role model interdependence as a great outward power to harness. If enough of us show others how helping and giving make both the giver and receiver feel better, we can overcome struggles more easily by supporting one another through them. If we are interdependent, we'll unify around a common cause. Any cause. Pick one. We'll be able to see differences of opinion as ways to learn and evolve our approaches.

Going from bare-knuckle independence to share-and-care interdependence can be achieved with passion. Scott Galloway *hates* passion if it's in the context of finding a career path. But to truly enrich your life, his advice is to become "irrationally passionate" for another's well-being, going "all-in" for someone else. Don't just wade into this communal pool. Dive right in. The business model is to "over-index" what you put into other people without any concern for what you'll get back. But also know that when you Live to Give, you do get tons of benefits in return.

GROWTH

As we've mentioned, when people have suffered, their empathy grows. They know that bad things do happen, and that suffering is eased by receiving and giving compassion and support. When people turn their suffering into purpose through helping others, it's called "post-traumatic growth."

By the time we reach middle age, most of us have faced some kind of serious hardship, losing a loved one, a bad diagnosis. Some of us have experienced violence or been victimized in nonviolent but also traumatic ways. Many people who have been through horrific situations don't develop PTSD. Rather, their trauma becomes part of their story and they go on to be stronger, wiser, more purposeful, and more powerful for having survived it.

University of North Carolina–Charlotte psychology professors Richard Tedeschi, Ph.D., and Lawrence Calhoun, Ph.D., who originally coined the term "post-traumatic growth," defined it as positive change as the result of bad experiences,[3] and pinpointed how the growth comes about. It nearly always includes a greater appreciation for life and relationships, seeing new possibilities and purpose

in life, greater understanding of personal strengths, and *increased compassion and altruism*.

Why would someone who'd been victimized become more altruistic? It seems like they should become bitter. But science supports the notion that it can cut the other way—opening doors to learning and serving. We have no idea what we can endure until we do. And then, having survived, we realize we are stronger than we thought. With that new self-awareness, we know we have power and can use it to help others who have been through something similar (or something different but also traumatic). We know something about what they're going through, having been there ourselves; we know they can survive it because we did. By using ourselves as the positive example, we can give them hope (see above). By giving, we become stronger ourselves. The trauma itself can turn into a trampoline that vaults us into seeing and using our outward power.

Growth through adversity doesn't make us feel invulnerable to bad things happening. We know they can happen, but we also know that we will face them and gladly accept help from others—providing others with an opportunity to serve—just as we gladly jump on those opportunities ourselves.

There is a world of empathy, support, and affirmation out there. Ask for help. Giving other people the opportunity to help you is a gift—for both.

—Scott Galloway

MEANING

Meaning is a more valuable search than happiness, per science. People who grow through trauma find meaning in service. Individual happiness, per se, seems like a shoddy goal after surviving trauma and finding transcendent meaningfulness (a deep sense of fulfillment) in service and establishing a new identity as a Live to Giver. Indeed, research supports the idea that satisfying one's individual needs and wants can increase happiness in the short term, but it's got nothing to do with meaningfulness.[4]

Be advised: going the meaningfulness route is not always rainbows and unicorns. A deep commitment to serve can be challenging. That same research links meaningfulness with *temporarily* higher levels of worry and stress. But given the huge benefits of purpose and meaning, and given a choice between happiness in a single moment or enduring transcendence, living in the present and thinking about the future, it's totally worth it.

One of the most widely publicized studies in the late twentieth century was headed up by psychologist Philip Brickman, Ph.D., at Northwestern University. You've probably heard something about it: Brickman and team studied[5] "adaptation level theory" and lasting happiness. Would one life-changing event make us happy (if the event was positive) or miserable (if the event was negative) forever after? They compared the happiness levels of three groups: (1) recent major winners of the Illinois State Lottery, (2) quadriplegics and paraplegics who'd been paralyzed in accidents, and (3) the control group. They asked how much pleasure they took in routine everyday life activities (hanging out with friends, having breakfast, watching TV, joking around). For the lottery winners, the mean happiness score in everyday activities was 3.33 out of 5. For the accident victims it was 3.48. Although the lottery winners said they were more happy in a broad sense than the accident victims, the paralyzed group's ratings of their happiness in any given moment were found to be essentially the same.

The sample size was small, which was controversial: only twenty-two major lottery winners and twenty-nine paralyzed accident victims were included in the study. But the results confirmed something about the lottery winners that we've all experienced: "the hedonic treadmill," that as soon as we reach a level of happiness, we get used to it, and then have to march on endlessly to feel pinnacle happiness again (which won't last). But if we have pleasure in the small things and take opportunities to find meaning in mundane activities, we can get off the hedonic treadmill. When we stop chasing "success" or "happiness," and just appreciate what we have and find joy in service to others, we radiate with an inner glow.

POWER PLAYERS

We've talked about the power of modeling Live to Give behaviors to inspire others. But who can we look to for finding inspiration ourselves?

Science points us toward Disney+, the platform for all Marvel Cinematic Universe movies. In a Hope College study,[6] **246 participants were exposed to either scenes with superhero images or neutral images. Primed by displays of valor, the superhero group reported subsequently doing more helpful interventions in their own lives compared to the control group. This, in turn, gave the superhero group's lives more meaning.** In another experiment, 123 participants were shown a superhero poster (the control group was shown a bicycle poster) and proceeded to be more helpful to another experimenter in a tedious task compared to the control. **The researchers credited the "subtle activation of superhero stimuli" for increasing prosocial intentions and behavior.** Say what you will about the uneven quality of Marvel films, but science has shown that they can inspire Live to Give behavior.

Kids (and kids at heart) are a huge audience for superhero movies and for watching their very own everyday heroes—parents and teachers—for guidance about how to live. For a study[7] of 140 British children from seven to eleven years old, researchers gathered the kids into age groups and read them stories that raised moral issues to prime them. Next, they were told that they could play an electronic bowling game to win tokens. The more tokens they won, the bigger the prizes (like comic books and toys). Or, totally optional, the kids could put their tokens in a bowl under the poster of an impoverished child for the Save the Children Fund. An adult joined the group and was introduced to the kids as a future teacher at their school, but was really a confederate who was in on the experiment. The researcher suggested that the future teacher play first and then left the room.

The faux teacher proceeded to either: (1) "model" and "preach" generosity by donating tokens and saying things like, "It's good to share with kids in need"; (2) model generosity and preach selfishness with comments like, "You should not give to kids like him"; (3) model selfishness and preach generosity; (4) the neutral condition of saying, "This sure is fun!" Then, the teacher left the room and the kids played the game by themselves and made their own decisions. They were called back for a two-month follow-up that re-created the experiment, one that was a replay of the first experiment, and another version that didn't use a teacher to model or preach anything.

As it turned out, "walk the walk" modeling was highly effective at first and two months later at inspiring generosity in kids for the short and long term. "Talk the talk" preaching wasn't as effective, especially when it was inconsistent with the modeling behavior. What matters to kids is what they see adults *do*, not so much in what adults *say*. Attention, parents: kids are looking to us for guidance, and, as parents, we have the power to raise a new generation that cares about caring. Instead of teaching (or preaching to) our kids to be successful, we can help them to be kind by being kind and *showing* them the way.

In this very real way . . .

SERVING OTHERS IS YOUR LEGACY

Legendary poet and memoirist Maya Angelou once said, "People will forget what you said. People will forget what you did. But people will never forget how you made them feel." You were likely familiar with this quote, but did you know that science affirms it? Research from Sweden shows that five years after surviving a traumatic event, in this case a horrific bus crash with fifty-six victims transported to hospitals, patients did not remember the technical aspects of their medical care. What they did remember five years later was how they were treated by the emergency department team, either compassionately—or not compassionately.[8]

When patients and families receive compassion from caregivers, like Mazz and his wife, Joanne, did after the loss of their son, it echoes years later and sometimes forever. Cleveland Clinic neurologist and chief experience officer Dr. Adrienne Boissy explained why **humans can be revisited by experiences of care and compassion over and over again over time. One reason may be that the amygdala, the part of the brain that is responsible for experiencing intense emotions, sits right next to the hippocampus, which is where we build our memories.** The proximity may be evolutionary. When cavemen had the fight-or-flight response from seeing a lion, they would remember that lions are dangerous and run like hell the next time they saw one. But the amygdala being right next to the hippocampus cuts the other direction as well. When we have the intense emotion of receiving compassion in our time of greatest need, it forms very intense memories that will always be with us, for the rest of our lives, no matter what. That is why even small acts of kindness can have amazing—and lasting—power for the receiver when applied at just the right time. People who are at the end of their rope never forget what that feels like, and they never forget when they are met in that moment by somebody who cares.

Steve here.

One final story about something that left a deep impact on me. After twenty years of working in an ICU and meeting patients and their families on the worst days of their lives, I came to the realization that I had every symptom of burnout. Every single one. And I assure you, that's not a good place to be. So, having just synthesized all the evidence that compassion can be beneficial for the giver too, I tried very hard to connect with people more, not less. Not only the patients but their families. Connecting more, not less, leaning in rather than pulling back, helped my burnout to lift. I became very intentional in practicing compassion every chance I could.

Just recently, I had to give awful news to a middle-aged woman whose older brother was a patient fighting for his life in the ICU. We were doing everything we possibly could to try to save him, but he was so critical that it appeared death was imminent. It was devastating news to her because he had been her rock throughout her whole life.

At the end of that very difficult discussion, she said, "You don't remember me, do you?"

I was taken aback. That's a question you don't hear very often in the ICU.

I said, "I'm sorry, I don't."

"I wouldn't think that you would," she said. "You see so many patients here. It's okay. But seven years ago, my mom was in that room right across the hall there. She was dying and you were her doctor. You had to tell me there was nothing else that could be done to save her. You and I have had this talk before."

It took my breath away. But then she told me what she remembered. She said, "I will never forget the kindness of those nurses. They were like angels to me. How they cared for me so that I wouldn't feel alone keeps coming back to me. Every time I think about losing my mom, and I think about it a lot, even now, I think about those nurses and it helps me. It helps me still, even now."

This made me understand the impact that we can have, the echo chamber, reverberating over and over again through the years. Now, I do things differently. I pause every time I go into the room to have a difficult conversation with a patient or family, knowing that my words may reverberate in an echo chamber for years to come, never to be forgotten, with the power to help bring comfort to people even years later when they are revisited by memories and reliving their experience. I now teach this power to my students and trainees.

You don't have to be a doctor in an ICU or ED to wield incredible outward power. Once you fully realize the power you have to impact people's lives with kindness in their time of need, you'll want to use it. And when you fully appreciate how it echoes over time—you'll use it differently and you'll feel humbled and awed by it. It'll change how you experience life. Perhaps before you tapped your outward power, you didn't understand how much you affect people's lives with small acts of kindness and compassion. But when that sinks in, your place in the world, your purpose, becomes clear. By taking on the responsibility and recognizing the power of the Live to Give echo chamber, the benefits for you will be that much more powerful as well.

It's actually an amplification of everything that you've read in this book about the power of serving others to impact your health, happiness, and success. When you realize that science shows that five years from now, the people you help are going to remember the good you did for them and feel elevated by it, you'll be that much more purposeful in serving others. Conviction amplifies intention and the effects. Every time you think about it, no matter what level of power you have put out there, you get a benefit.

Serving others is more powerful than you've ever imagined. And the sheer magnitude of it keeps coming back, to you and to them. It's not like posting a Snapchat, there and gone in seconds. Science supports the idea that a kind act can echo forever. You have done something that another person may never forget.

The Live to Give prescription for knowing your power: Serving others echoes and revisits, and goes on and on, and therefore is more impactful than we even realize. You are *powerful*. Being empathetic, compassionate, grateful, caring, and kind are a human being's greatest strengths. But only if we use them. Don't delay.

NOTES

INTRODUCTION

1. See https://www.ted.com/talks/stephen_trzeciak_healthcare_s_compassion_cri sis_jan_2018.
2. Trzeciak S, Mazzarelli A. *Compassionomics: The Revolutionary Scientific Evidence That Caring Makes a Difference.* Studer | Huron, 2019.
3. Lindauer M, Mayorga M, Greene J, Slovic P, Västfjäll D, Singer P. (May 2020). Comparing the effect of rational and emotional appeals on donation behavior. Judgm Decis Mak. 15(3): 413–20.
4. O'Connor D, Wolfe DM. (1991). From crisis to growth at midlife: Changes in personal paradigm. J Organiz Behav. 12: 323–40.

CHAPTER 1. IT'S NOT YOU, IT'S *ME* CULTURE

1. Clarke TC, Black LI, Stussman BJ, Barnes PM, Nahin RL. (2015). Trends in the use of complementary health approaches among adults: United States, 2002–2012. Natl Health Stat Report. (79): 1–16.
2. Twenge JM, Martin GN, Campbell WK. Decreases in psychological well-being among American adolescents after 2012 and links to screen time during the rise of smartphone technology. Emotion. 2018 Sep;18(6):765–80.
3. See https://www.ted.com/talks/robert_waldinger_what_makes_a_good_life _lessons_from_the_longest_study_on_happiness.
4. Stossel S. "What Makes Us Happy Revisited." *The Atlantic,* May 2013.
5. Chopik W, Joshi D, Konrath S. (2014). Historical changes in American self-

interest: State of the Union addresses 1790 to 2012. Pers Individ Differ. 66: 128–33.

6. Making Caring Common, Harvard Graduate School of Education. (2021). The President and Fellows of Harvard College.

7. Konrath SH, Chopik WJ, Hsing CK, O'Brien E. Changes in adult attachment styles in American college students over time: A meta-analysis. Pers Soc Psychol Rev. 2014 Nov;18(4):326–48.

8. Konrath SH, O'Brien EH, Hsing C. Changes in dispositional empathy in American college students over time: A meta-analysis. Pers Soc Psychol Rev. 15, no. 2 (May 2011): 180–98.

9. Pew Research Center. "A Divided and Pessimistic Electorate," November 2016.

10. Hampton KN. Why is helping behavior declining in the United States but not in Canada?: Ethnic diversity, new technologies, and other explanations. City & Community. 2016;15(4):380–99.

11. Twenge JM, Campbell WK, Freeman EC. Generational differences in young adults' life goals, concern for others, and civic orientation, 1966–2009. J Pers Soc Psychol. 2012 May;102(5):1045–62.

12. Galloway S. The Algebra of Happiness: Notes on the Pursuit of Success, Love, and Meaning. Penguin, 2019.

13. Konrath S. "The Joy of Giving." In Burlingame D, Seiler T, Tempel G (eds.), Achieving Excellence in Fundraising (4th ed., pp. 11–25). Wiley, 2016.

14. See https://www.ted.com/talks/david_brooks_should_you_live_for_your_res ume_or_your_eulogy?language=en#t-27178.1.

15. Achor S. The Happiness Advantage: The Seven Principles of Positive Psychology That Fuel Success and Performance at Work. Broadway Books, 2010.

16. See https://www.ted.com/talks/david_brooks_the_lies_our_culture_tells_us _about_what_matters_and_a_better_way_to_live/transcript?language=en.

17. Brooks D. The Second Mountain: The Quest for a Moral Life. Penguin, 2019.

CHAPTER 2. SURVIVAL OF THE KINDEST?

1. Wilson EO. The Meaning of Human Existence. Liveright, 2014.

2. Aknin LB, Hamlin JK, Dunn EW. Giving leads to happiness in young children. PLOS ONE. 2012;7(6):e39211.

3. Aknin LB, Barrington-Leigh CP, Dunn EW, Helliwell JF, Burns J, Biswas-Diener R, Kemeza I, Nyende P, Ashton-James CE, Norton MI. Prosocial spending and well-being: Cross-cultural evidence for a psychological universal. J Pers Soc Psychol. 2013 Apr;104(4):635–52.

4. Konrath S. "The Joy of Giving." In Burlingame D, Seiler T, Tempel G (eds.), Achieving Excellence in Fundraising (4th ed., pp. 11–25). Wiley, 2016.

5. Schwartz SH, Bardi A. Value hierarchies across cultures: Taking a similarities perspective. J Cross-Cult Psychol. 2001;32(3):268–90.

6. Calvo R, Zheng Y, Kumar S, Olgiati A, Berkman L. Well-being and social capital on planet earth: Cross-national evidence from 142 countries. PLOS ONE. 2012;7(8):e42793.

7. Scheffer J, Cameron C, McKee S, Hadjiandreou E, Scherer A. (2020). Stereotypes about compassion across the political spectrum. Emotion. June 29 (online ahead of print).

8. Klein KJK, Hodges S D. (2001). Gender differences, motivation, and empathic accuracy: When it pays to understand. Pers Soc Psychol Bull. 27(6): 720–30.

9. Kraus MW, Côté S, Keltner D. Social class, contextualism, and empathic accuracy. Psychol Sci. 2010 Nov;21(11):1716–23.

10. Miller DT, Ratner RK. The disparity between the actual and assumed power of self-interest. J Pers Soc Psychol. 1998 Jan;74(1):53–62.

11. See https://www.thecrimson.com/article/2011/9/2/harvard-values-ranked-survey/.

12. Flynn FJ, Bohns V. (2008). If you need help, just ask: Underestimating compliance with direct requests for help. J Pers Soc Psychol. 95(1): 128–43.

13. Zaki J. Catastrophe compassion: Understanding and extending prosociality under crisis. Trends Cogn Sci. 2020 Aug;24(8):587–89.

14. Drury J. (2018). The role of social identity processes in mass emergency behaviour: An integrative review, Eur Rev Soc Psychol. 29(1): 38–81.

15. Philpot R, Liebst LS, Levine M, Bernasco W, Lindegaard MR. (2020). Would I be helped? Cross-national CCTV footage shows that intervention is the norm in public conflicts. Am Psychol. 75(1), 66–75.

16. Manning R, Levine M, Collins A. (2007). The Kitty Genovese murder and the social psychology of helping: The parable of the 38 witnesses. Am Psychol. 62. 555–62.

17. Levine M, Crowther S. (2008). The responsive bystander: How social group membership and group size can encourage as well as inhibit bystander intervention. J Pers Soc Psychol. 95(6): 1429–39.

18. See https://theconversation.com/do-people-become-more-selfless-as-they-age-130443.

19. Cutler SJ, Hendricks J. (March 2000). Age differences in voluntary association memberships: Fact or artifact, J Gerontol: Series B 55(2): S98–S107.

20. Mongrain M, Barnes C, Barnhart R, Zalan LB. (2018). Acts of kindness reduce depression in individuals low on agreeableness. Transl Issues Psychol Sci. 4(3): 323–34.

CHAPTER 3. THE GIVING PARADOXES

1. Grant AM. *Give and Take: A Revolutionary Approach to Success.* Viking, 2013.
2. See https://www.youtube.com/watch?v=rCvhOqThYJ4.
3. Lievens F, Ones DS, Dilchert S. Personality scale validities increase through-out medical school. J Appl Psychol. 2009 Nov;94(6):1514–35.
4. Fritz HL, Helgeson VS. (1998). Distinctions of unmitigated communion from communion: Self-neglect and overinvolvement with others. J Pers Soc Psychol. 75(1): 121.
5. See https://www.ted.com/talks/adam_grant_are_you_a_giver_or_a_taker ?language=en.
6. Jackson M. The pursuit of happiness: The social and scientific origins of Hans Selye's natural philosophy of life. Hist Human Sci. 2012 Dec;25(5):13–29.

CHAPTER 4. HOW SELF-SERVING ARE YOU?

1. Nickell G. (August 1998). "The Helping Attitudes Scale." Paper presented at 106th Annual Convention of the American Psychological Association, San Francisco, CA.
2. Matlock P. (1952). Identical twins discordant in tongue-rolling. J Hered. 43(1): 24.
3. Komai T. (1951). Notes on lingual gymnastics: Frequency of tongue rollers and pedigrees of tied tongues in Japan. J Hered. 42: 293–97.
4. Woods C. "Debunking the Biggest Genetic Myth of the Human Tongue." *PBS News Hour.* Published electronically August 5, 2015.
5. Huml AM, Thornton JD, Figueroa M, Cain K, Dolata J, Scott K, Sullivan C, Se-hgal AR. Concordance of organ donation and other altruistic behaviors among twins. Prog Transplant. 2019 Sep;29(3):225–29.
6. Spalding KL, Bergmann O, Alkass K, Bernard S, Salehpour M, Huttner HB, Boström E, Westerlund I, Vial C, Buchholz BA, Possnert G, Mash DC, Druid H, Frisén J. Dynamics of hippocampal neurogenesis in adult humans. Cell. 2013 Jun 6;153(6):1219–27.
7. Maguire EA, Gadian DG, Johnsrude IS, Good CD, Ashburner J, Frackowiak RS, Frith CD. (April 11, 2000). Navigation-related structural change in the hippocampi of taxi drivers. PNAS 97(8):4398–403.
8. Dweck CS. *Mindset: The New Psychology of Success.* Ballantine, 2008.
9. Schumann K, Zaki J, Dweck CS. Addressing the empathy deficit: Beliefs about the malleability of empathy predict effortful responses when empathy is chal-lenging. J Pers Soc Psychol. 2014 Sep;107(3):475–93.
10. Goleman D, Davidson RJ. *Altered Traits: Science Reveals How Meditation Changes Your Mind, Brain, and Body.* Avery, 2017.

11. Lutz A, Greischar LL, Rawlings NB, Ricard M, Davidson RJ. (November 16, 2004). Long-term meditators self-induce high-amplitude gamma synchrony during mental practice. PNAS 101(46):16369–73.
12. Leung MK, Chan CC, Yin J, Lee CF, So KF, Lee TM. (January 2013). Increased gray matter volume in the right angular and posterior parahippocampal gyri in loving-kindness meditators. Soc Cogn Affect Neurosci. 8(1): 34–39.
13. Weng HY, Fox AS, Shackman AJ, Stodola DE, Caldwell JZK, Olson MC, Rogers GM, Davidson RJ. (July 1, 2013). Compassion training alters altruism and neural responses to suffering. Psychol Sci. 24(7):1171–80.
14. Shin LJ, Layous K, Choi I, Na S, Lyubomirsky S. (2019). Good for self or good for others? The well-being benefits of kindness in two cultures depend on how the kindness is framed. J Posit Psychol. 15(6):795–805.
15. Klimecki OM, Leiberg S, Ricard M, Singer T. (June 2014). Differential pattern of functional brain plasticity after compassion and empathy training. Soc Cogn Affect Neurosci. 9(6): 873–79.
16. Klimecki OM, Leiberg S, Lamm C, Singer T. (July 2013). Functional neural plasticity and associated changes in positive affect after compassion training. Cereb Cortex. 23(7):1552–61.
17. Lim D, Condon P, DeSteno D. Mindfulness and compassion: An examination of mechanism and scalability. PLOS ONE. 2015 Feb 17;10(2):e0118221.
18. Patel S, Pelletier-Bui A, Smith S, Roberts MB, Kilgannon H, Trzeciak S, Roberts BW. Curricula for empathy and compassion training in medical education: A systematic review. PLOS ONE. 2019 Aug 22;14(8):e0221412.

CHAPTER 5. THE BRAIN AND BODY WHEN SERVING OTHERS

1. Lamm C, Decety J, Singer T. Meta-analytic evidence for common and distinct neural networks associated with directly experienced pain and empathy for pain. Neuroimage. 2011 Feb 1;54(3):2492–502.
2. Klimecki OM, Leiberg S, Lamm C, Singer T. Functional neural plasticity and associated changes in positive affect after compassion training. Cereb Cortex. 2013 Jul;23(7):1552–61.
3. Engen HG, Singer T. Compassion-based emotion regulation up-regulates experienced positive affect and associated neural networks. Soc Cogn Affect Neurosci. 2015 Sep;10(9):1291–301.
4. Morelli SA, Sacchet MD, Zaki J. Common and distinct neural correlates of personal and vicarious reward: A quantitative meta-analysis. Neuroimage. 2015 May 15;112:244–253.
5. Goldstein P, Weissman-Fogel I, Dumas G, Shamay-Tsoory SG. Brain-to-brain

coupling during handholding is associated with pain reduction. PNAS. 2018 Mar 13;115(11):E2528-E2537.

6. Cohen S, Janicki-Deverts D, Turner RB, Doyle WJ. Does hugging provide stress-buffering social support? A study of susceptibility to upper respiratory infection and illness. Psychol Sci. 2015 Feb;26(2):135–47.

7. Luks A. "Helper's high: Volunteering makes people feel good, physically and emotionally." *Psychology Today,* October 1988, 34–42.

8. Bachner-Melman R, Gritsenko I, Nemanov L. et al. (2005). Dopaminergic polymorphisms associated with self-report measures of human altruism: A fresh phenotype for the dopamine D4 receptor. Mol Psychiatry. 10: 333–35.

9. Swain JE, Konrath S, Brown SL, et al. Parenting and beyond: Common neurocircuits underlying parental and altruistic caregiving. Parent Sci Pract. 2012;12(2–3):115–23.

10. Bernstein E. "Why Being Kind Helps You, Too—Especially Now." *Wall Street Journal,* August 11, 2020.

11. Szeto A, Nation DA, Mendez AJ, Dominguez-Bendala J, Brooks LG, Schneiderman N, McCabe PM. Oxytocin attenuates NADPH-dependent superoxide activity and IL-6 secretion in macrophages and vascular cells. Am J Physiol Endocrinol Metab. 2008 Dec;295(6):E1495–501.

12. Brown SL, Brown RM. Connecting prosocial behavior to improved physical health: Contributions from the neurobiology of parenting. Neurosci Biobehav Rev. 2015 Aug;55:1–17.

13. Dölen G, Darvishzadeh A, Huang KW, Malenka RC. Social reward requires coordinated activity of nucleus accumbens oxytocin and serotonin. Nature. 2013 Sep 12;501(7466):179–84.

14. Han SH, Kim K, Burr JA. Stress-buffering effects of volunteering on salivary cortisol: Results from a daily diary study. Soc Sci Med. 2018 Mar;201:120–126.

15. Inagaki TK, Bryne Haltom KE, Suzuki S, Jevtic I, Hornstein E, Bower JE, Eisenberger NI. The neurobiology of giving versus receiving support: The role of stress-related and social reward-related neural activity. Psychosom Med. 2016 May;78(4):443–53.

16. Cosley BJ, McCoy SK, Saslow LR, Epel ES. (2010). Is compassion for others stress buffering? Consequences of compassion and social support for physiological reactivity to stress. J Exp Soc Psychol. 46(5):816–23.

17. Field TM, Hernandez-Reif M, Quintino O, Schanberg S, Kuhn C. Elder retired volunteers benefit from giving massage therapy to infants. J Appl Gerontol. 1998;17(2):229–39.

18. DiSalvo D. "Forget Survival of the Fittest: It Is Kindness That Counts." *Scientific American,* September 1, 2009.

19. Kok BE, Fredrickson BL. Upward spirals of the heart: Autonomic flexibility, as

indexed by vagal tone, reciprocally and prospectively predicts positive emotions and social connectedness [published correction appears in Biol Psychol. 2016 May;117:240]. Biol Psychol. 2010;85(3):432–36.

20. Stellar JE, Cohen A, Oveis C, Keltner D. Affective and physiological responses to the suffering of others: Compassion and vagal activity. J Pers Soc Psychol. 2015 Apr;108(4):572–85.

21. Fredrickson BL, Grewen KM, Algoe SB, Firestine AM, Arevalo JM, Ma J, Cole SW. Psychological well-being and the human conserved transcriptional response to adversity. PLOS ONE. 2015 Mar 26;10(3):e0121839.

22. Furman D, Campisi J, Verdin E, et al. Chronic inflammation in the etiology of disease across the life span. Nat Med. 25, 1822–1832 (2019).

23. Nelson-Coffey SK, Fritz MM, Lyubomirsky S, Cole SW. Kindness in the blood: A randomized controlled trial of the gene regulatory impact of prosocial behavior. Psychoneuroendocrinology. 2017 Jul;81:8–13.

24. Pace TW, Negi LT, Dodson-Lavelle B, Ozawa-de Silva B, Reddy SD, Cole SP, Danese A, Craighead LW, Raison CL. Engagement with Cognitively-Based Compassion Training is associated with reduced salivary C-reactive protein from before to after training in foster care program adolescents. Psychoneuroendocrinology. 2013 Feb;38(2):294–9.

25. McClelland DC, Krishnit C. (1988). The effect of motivational arousal through films on salivary immunoglobulin A. Psychology & Health 2(1): 31–52.

CHAPTER 6. PHYSICAL HEALTH THROUGH SERVING OTHERS

1. Arias E, Tejada-Vera B, Ahmad F. Provisional life expectancy estimates for January through June, 2020. Vital Statistics Rapid Release; no 10. National Center for Health Statistics, February 2021.

2. Poulin MJ, Brown SL, Dillard AJ, Smith DM. Giving to others and the association between stress and mortality. Am J Public Health. 2013 Sep;103 (9):1649–55.

3. Brown SL, Nesse RM, Vinokur AD, Smith DM. Providing social support may be more beneficial than receiving it: Results from a prospective study of mortality. Psychol Sci. 2003 Jul;14(4):320–27.

4. Okun MA, Yeung EW, Brown S. Volunteering by older adults and risk of mortality: A meta-analysis. Psychol Aging. 2013 Jun;28(2):564–77.

5. Oman D, Thoresen CE, McMahon K. Volunteerism and mortality among the community-dwelling elderly. J Health Psychol. 1999 May;4(3):301–16.

6. McClellan WM, Stanwyck DJ, Anson CA. Social support and subsequent mortality among patients with end-stage renal disease. J Am Soc Nephrol. 1993 Oct;4(4):1028–34.

7. O'Reilly D, Rosato M, Moriarty J, Leavey G. Volunteering and mortality risk: A partner-controlled quasi-experimental design. Int J Epidemiol. 2017 Aug 1;46(4):1295–1302.

8. Le Nguyen KD, Lin J, Algoe SB, Brantley MM, Kim SL, Brantley J, Salzberg S, Fredrickson BL. Loving-kindness meditation slows biological aging in novices: Evidence from a 12-week randomized controlled trial. Psychoneuroendocrinology. 2019 Oct;108:20–27.

9. Hoge EA, Chen MM, Orr E, Metcalf CA, Fischer LE, Pollack MH, De Vivo I, Simon NM. Loving-Kindness Meditation practice associated with longer telomeres in women. Brain Behav Immun. 2013 Aug;32:159–63.

10. Hainsworth J, Barlow J. Volunteers' experiences of becoming arthritis self-management lay leaders: "It's almost as if I've stopped aging and started to get younger!" Arthritis Rheum. 2001 Aug;45(4):378–83.

11. Arnstein P, Vidal M, Wells-Federman C, Morgan B, Caudill M. From chronic pain patient to peer: benefits and risks of volunteering. Pain Manag Nurs. 2002 Sep;3(3):94–103.

12. Wang Y, Ge J, Zhang H, Wang H, Xie X. Altruistic behaviors relieve physical pain. Proc Natl Acad Sci U S A. 2020 Jan 14;117(2):950–58.

13. López-Solà M, Koban L, Wager TD. Transforming pain with prosocial meaning: A functional magnetic resonance imaging study. Psychosom Med. 2018 Nov/Dec;80(9):814–25.

14. Kochanek KD, Xu JQ, Arias E. Mortality in the United States, 2019. NCHS Data Brief, no. 395. National Center for Health Statistics, 2020.

15. Piferi RL, Lawler KA. Social support and ambulatory blood pressure: An examination of both receiving and giving. Int J Psychophysiol. 2006 Nov;62(2):328–36.

16. Schreier HM, Schonert-Reichl KA, Chen E. Effect of volunteering on risk factors for cardiovascular disease in adolescents: A randomized controlled trial. JAMA Pediatr. 2013 Apr;167(4):327–32.

17. Sneed RS, Cohen S. A prospective study of volunteerism and hypertension risk in older adults. Psychol Aging. 2013 Jun;28(2):578–86.

18. Whillans AV, Dunn EW, Sandstrom GM, Dickerson SS, Madden KM. Is spending money on others good for your heart? Health Psychol. 2016 Jun;35(6):574–83.

19. Scherwitz L, Berton K, Leventhal H. Type A behavior, self-involvement, and cardiovascular response. Psychosom Med. 1978 Dec;40(8):593–609.

20. Scherwitz L, McKelvain R, Laman C, Patterson J, Dutton L, Yusim S, Lester J, Kraft I, Rochelle D, Leachman R. Type A behavior, self-involvement, and coronary atherosclerosis. Psychosom Med. 1983 Mar;45(1):47–57.

21. Scherwitz L, Graham LE 2nd, Grandits G, Buehler J, Billings J. Self-

involvement and coronary heart disease incidence in the multiple risk factor intervention trial. Psychosom Med. 1986 Mar-Apr;48(3 4):187–99.

22. Matthews KA, Xu W, Gaglioti AH, et al. Racial and ethnic estimates of Alzheimer's disease and related dementias in the United States (2015–2060) in adults aged ≥65 years. Alzheimer's Dement. 2019;15(1):17–24.

23. Anderson ND, Damianakis T, Kröger E, Wagner LM, Dawson DR, Binns MA, Bernstein S, Caspi E, Cook SL; BRAVO Team. The benefits associated with volunteering among seniors: A critical review and recommendations for future research. Psychol Bull. 2014 Nov;140(6):1505–33.

24. Corrêa JC, Ávila MPW, Lucchetti ALG, Lucchetti G. Altruistic behaviour, but not volunteering, has been associated with cognitive performance in community-dwelling older persons. Psychogeriatrics. 2019 Mar;19(2):117–25.

25. Fried LP, Carlson MC, Freedman M, Frick KD, Glass TA, Hill J, McGill S, Rebok GW, Seeman T, Tielsch J, Wasik BA, Zeger S. A social model for health promotion for an aging population: Initial evidence on the Experience Corps model. J Urban Health. 2004 Mar;81(1):64–78.

26. Volpi E, Nazemi R, Fujita S. Muscle tissue changes with aging. Curr Opin Clin Nutr Metab Care. 2004;7(4):405–10.

27. Gray K. (2010). Moral transformation: Good and evil turn the weak into the mighty. Soc Psychol Pers Sci. 1(3):253–58.

28. Gruenewald TL, Liao DH, Seeman TE. Contributing to others, contributing to oneself: Perceptions of generativity and health in later life. J Gerontol B Psychol Sci Soc Sci. 2012 Nov;67(6):660–65.

29. Kim ES, Whillans AV, Lee MT, Chen Y, VanderWeele TJ. Volunteering and subsequent health and well-being in older adults: An outcome-wide longitudinal approach. Am J Prev Med. 2020 Aug;59(2):176–86.

30. Cohen R, Bavishi C, Rozanski A. Purpose in life and its relationship to all-cause mortality and cardiovascular events: A meta-analysis. Psychosom Med. 2016 Feb-Mar;78(2):122–33.

31. Alimujiang A, Wiensch A, Boss J, Fleischer NL, Mondul AM, McLean K, Mukherjee B, Pearce CL. Association between life purpose and mortality among US adults older than 50 years. JAMA Netw Open. 2019 May 3;2(5):e194270.

32. Boyle PA, Barnes LL, Buchman AS, Bennett DA. Purpose in life is associated with mortality among community-dwelling older persons. Psychosom Med. 2009 Jun;71(5):574–79.

33. Kim ES, Sun JK, Park N, Peterson C. Purpose in life and reduced incidence of stroke in older adults: "The Health and Retirement Study." J Psychosom Res. 2013 May;74(5):427–32.

34. Kim ES, Kawachi I, Chen Y, Kubzansky LD. Association between purpose in

life and objective measures of physical function in older adults. JAMA Psychiatry. 2017 Oct 1;74(10):1039–45.

35. Kim ES, Strecher VJ, Ryff CD. Purpose in life and use of preventive health care services. Proc Natl Acad Sci U S A. 2014 Nov 18;111(46):16331–6.

36. Kim ES, Hershner SD, Strecher VJ. Purpose in life and incidence of sleep disturbances. J Behav Med. 2015 Jun;38(3):590–97.

37. House, JR, Landis KR, Umberson D. "Social Relationships and Health." *Science,* July 29, 1988, pp. 540–45.

38. Hawkley LC, Thisted RA, Masi CM, Cacioppo JT. Loneliness predicts increased blood pressure: 5-year cross-lagged analyses in middle-aged and older adults. Psychol Aging. 2010 Mar;25(1):132–41.

39. Valtorta NK, Kanaan M, Gilbody S, et al. (2016). Loneliness and social isolation as risk factors for coronary heart disease and stroke: Systematic review and meta-analysis of longitudinal observational studies. Heart. 102:1009–16.

40. Holt-Lunstad J, Smith T. (2016). Loneliness and social isolation as risk factors for CVD: Implications for evidence-based patient care and scientific inquiry. Heart 102(13):987–9.

41. Holt-Lunstad J, Smith TB, Baker M, Harris T, Stephenson D. Loneliness and social isolation as risk factors for mortality: A meta-analytic review. Perspect Psychol Sci. 2015 Mar;10(2):227–37.

42. Lara E, Caballero FF, Rico-Uribe LA, Olaya B, Haro JM, Ayuso-Mateos JL, Miret M. Are loneliness and social isolation associated with cognitive decline? Int J Geriatr Psychiatry. 2019 Nov;34(11):1613–1622.

43. Perissinotto CM, Stijacic Cenzer I, Covinsky KE. Loneliness in older persons: A predictor of functional decline and death. Arch Intern Med. 2012 Jul 23;172(14):1078–83.

CHAPTER 7. MENTAL HEALTH THROUGH SERVING OTHERS

1. See https://www.nami.org/mhstats.

2. See https://www.psychiatry.org/patients-families/depression/what-is-depression#:~:text=Depression%20affects%20an%20estimated%20one,than%20men%20to%20experience%20depression.

3. Miron O, Yu K, Wilf-Miron R, Kohane IS. Suicide rates among adolescents and young adults in the United States, 2000–2017. JAMA. 2019;321(23):2362–64.

4. Czeisler MÉ, Lane RI, Petrosky E, et al. Mental health, substance use, and suicidal ideation during the COVID-19 pandemic—United States, June 24–30, 2020. MMWR Morb Mortal Wkly. Rep 2020;69:1049–57.

5. Mor N, Winquist J. Self-focused attention and negative affect: A meta-analysis. Psychol Bull. 2002 Jul;128(4):638–62.

6. Padilla-Walker LM, Millett MA, Memmott-Elison MK. (2020). Can helping others strengthen teens? Character strengths as mediators between prosocial behavior and adolescents' internalizing symptoms. J Adolesc 79: 70–80, ISSN 0140–1971.

7. Schacter HL, Margolin G. When it feels good to give: Depressive symptoms, daily prosocial behavior, and adolescent mood. Emotion. 2019 Aug;19(5):923–27.

8. Mascaro J, Kelley S, Darcher A, Negi L, Worthman C, Miller A, Raison C. (2016). Meditation buffers medical student compassion from the deleterious effects of depression. J Posit Psychol. 13(2):133–142.

9. Telzer EH, Fuligni AJ, Lieberman MD, Galván A. Neural sensitivity to eudaimonic and hedonic rewards differentially predict adolescent depressive symptoms over time. Proc Natl Acad Sci U S A. 2014 May 6;111(18):6600–5.

10. See https://ourworldindata.org/mental-health#:~:text=Prevalence%20of%20 depressive%20disorders,relative%20to%20other%20age%20groups.

11. Saarinen A, Keltikangas-Järvinen L, Cloninger CR, Veijola J, Elovainio M, Lehtimäki T, Raitakari O, Hintsanen M. The relationship of dispositional compassion for others with depressive symptoms over a 15-year prospective follow-up. J Affect Disord. 2019 May 1;250:354–62.

12. Stirman SW, Pennebaker JW. Word use in the poetry of suicidal and nonsuicidal poets. Psychosom Med. 2001 Jul-Aug;63(4):517–22.

13. Crocker J, Canevello A, Breines JG, Flynn H. Interpersonal goals and change in anxiety and dysphoria in first-semester college students. J Pers Soc Psychol. 2010 Jun;98(6):1009–24.

14. Kashdan TB, McKnight PE. Commitment to a purpose in life: An antidote to the suffering by individuals with social anxiety disorder. Emotion. 2013 Dec;13(6):1150–59.

15. Alden L, Trew J. (2012). If it makes you happy: Engaging in kind acts increases positive affect in socially anxious individuals. Emotion 13(1):64–75.

16. Brown SL, Brown RM, House JS, Smith DM. Coping with spousal loss: Potential buffering effects of self-reported helping behavior. Pers Soc Psychol Bull. 2008 Jun;34(6):849–61.

17. Wilkinson H, Whittington R, Perry L, Eames C. Examining the relationship between burnout and empathy in healthcare professionals: A systematic review. Burn Res. 2017 Sep;6:18–29.

18. McKee A, Wiens K. "Why Some People Get Burned Out and Others Don't." Harvard Business Review, November 23, 2016.

19. Taylor SE. (2006). Tend and befriend: Biobehavioral bases of affiliation under stress. Curr Dir Psychol Sci. 15(6):273–77.

20. von Dawans B, Fischbacher U, Kirschbaum C, Fehr E, Heinrichs M. The social dimension of stress reactivity: Acute stress increases prosocial behavior in humans. Psychol Sci. 2012 Jun;23(6):651–60.

21. Pagano ME, Friend KB, Tonigan JS, Stout RL. Helping other alcoholics in alcoholics anonymous and drinking outcomes: Findings from project MATCH. J Stud Alcohol. 2004 Nov;65(6):766–73.

22. Raposa EB, Laws HB, Ansell EB. Prosocial behavior mitigates the negative effects of stress in everyday life. Clin Psychol Sci. 2016 Jul;4(4):691–98.

23. Doré BP, Morris RR, Burr DA, Picard RW, Ochsner KN. Helping others regulate emotion predicts increased regulation of one's own emotions and decreased symptoms of depression. Pers Soc Psychol Bull. 2017 May;43(5):729–39.

24. Musick MA, Wilson J. Volunteering and depression: The role of psychological and social resources in different age groups. Soc Sci Med. 2003 Jan;56(2):259–69.

CHAPTER 8. HAPPINESS THROUGH SERVING OTHERS

1. Steger MF, Kashdan T, Oishi S. (2008). Being good by doing good: Daily eudaimonic activity and well-being. J Res Pers 42: 22–42.

2. Csikszentmihalyi M. *Flow: The Psychology of Optimal Experience.* Harper Perennial, 2008.

3. See https://www.ted.com/talks/martin_seligman_the_new_era_of_positive _psychology/transcript?language=en.

4. Brooks D. *The Second Mountain: The Quest for a Moral Life.* Penguin, 2019.

5. Goleman D, Davidson RJ. *Altered Traits: Science Reveals How Meditation Changes Your Mind, Brain, and Body.* Avery, 2017.

6. Kahneman D, Deaton A. (September 2010). High income improves evaluation of life but not emotional well-being. Proc Natl Acad Sci U S A 107(38): 16489–93.

7. Kashdan TB, Breen WE. (2007). Materialism and diminished well-being: Experiential avoidance as a mediating mechanism. J Soc Clin Psychol. 26(5): 521–39.

8. Borgonovi F. Doing well by doing good: The relationship between formal volunteering and self-reported health and happiness. Soc Sci Med. 2008 Jun;66(11):2321–34.

9. Dunn EW, Aknin LB, Norton MI. Spending money on others promotes happiness. Science. 2008 Mar 21;319(5870):1687–88.

10. Aknin L, Dunn E, Norton M. (2011). Happiness runs in a circular motion: Evidence for a positive feedback loop between prosocial spending and happiness. J Happiness Stud. 13. 347–55.

11. Aknin LB, Barrington-Leigh CP, Dunn EW, Helliwell JF, Burns J, Biswas-Diener R, Kemeza I, Nyende P, Ashton-James CE, Norton MI. (2013). Prosocial spending and well-being: Cross-cultural evidence for a psychological universal. J Pers Soc Psychol. 104(4): 635–52.

12. See https://www.ted.com/talks/elizabeth_dunn_helping_others_makes_us_happier_but_it_matters_how_we_do_it/footnotes.

13. Park SQ, Kahnt T, Dogan A, Strang S, Fehr E, Tobler PN. A neural link between generosity and happiness. Nat Commun. 2017 Jul 11;8:15964.

14. Moll J, Krueger F, Zahn R, Pardini M, de Oliveira R, Grafman J. (2006). Human front-mesolimbic networks guide decisions about charitable donation. Proc Natl Acad Sci U S A. 103: 15623–28.

15. Kumar A, Killingsworth M, Gilovich T. (2020). Spending on doing promotes more moment-to-moment happiness than spending on having. J Exp Soc Psychol. 88. 103971.

16. Nelson SK, Layous K, Cole SW, Lyubomirsky S. (2016). Do unto others or treat yourself? The effects of prosocial and self-focused behavior on psychological flourishing. Emotion. 16(6):850–61.

17. Mongrain M, Chin JM, Shapira LB. (2011). Practicing compassion increases happiness and self-esteem. J Happiness Stud. 12:963–81.

18. Thomas PA. Is it better to give or to receive? Social support and the well-being of older adults. J Gerontol B Psychol Sci Soc Sci. 2010 May;65B(3): 351–57.

CHAPTER 9. SUCCESS THROUGH SERVING OTHERS

1. Gini A. (1998). Work, identity and self: How we are formed by the work we do. J Bus Ethics. 17: 707–14.

2. See http://www.apaexcellence.org/assets/general/phwp_fact_sheet.pdf.

3. See https://www.ted.com/talks/shawn_achor_the_happy_secret_to_better_work?language=en.

4. Caprara GV, Barbaranelli C, Pastorelli C, Bandura A, Zimbardo PG. Prosocial foundations of children's academic achievement. Psychol Sci. 2000 Jul;11(4): 302–6.

5. Vergunst F, Tremblay RE, Nagin D, Algan Y, Beasley E, Park J, Galera C, Vitaro F, Côté SM. Association between childhood behaviors and adult employment earnings in Canada. JAMA Psychiatry. 2019 Oct 1;76(10):1044–51.

6. Jones D, Greenberg M, Crowley D. (2015). Early social-emotional functioning and public health: The relationship between kindergarten social competence and future wellness. Am J Public Health. 105. e1-e8.

7. Layous K, Nelson SK, Oberle E, Schonert-Reichl KA, Lyubomirsky S. Kind-

ness counts: Prompting prosocial behavior in preadolescents boosts peer acceptance and well-being. PLOS ONE. 2012;7(12):e51380.

8. Eskreis-Winkler L, Milkman KL, Gromet DM, Duckworth AL. (2019). A large-scale field experiment shows giving advice improves academic outcomes for the advisor. Proc Natl Acad Sci U S A. 116(30):14808–10.

9. Anderson C, Sharps DL, Soto CJ, John OP. (September 2020). People with disagreeable personalities (selfish, combative, and manipulative) do not have an advantage in pursuing power at work. Proc Natl Acad Sci U S A. 117(37): 22780–86.

10. Hollander EP. (1958). Conformity, status, and idiosyncrasy credit. Psychol Rev. 65(2):117–27.

11. Hardy CL, Van Vugt M. Nice guys finish first: The competitive altruism hypothesis. Pers Soc Psychol Bull. 2006 Oct;32(10):1402–13.

12. Kim E, Glomb TM. Get smarty pants: Cognitive ability, personality, and victimization. J Appl Psychol. 2010 Sep;95(5):889–901.

13. Grant A, Campbell E, Chen G, Cottone K, Lapedis D, Lee K. (2007). Impact and the art of motivation maintenance: The effects of contact with beneficiaries on persistence behavior. Organ Behav Hum Decis Process. 103: 53–67.

14. Grant AM. The significance of task significance: Job performance effects, relational mechanisms, and boundary conditions. J Appl Psychol. 2008 Jan;93(1):108–24.

15. Stavrova O, Ehlebracht D. Cynical beliefs about human nature and income: Longitudinal and cross-cultural analyses. J Pers Soc Psychol. 2016 Jan;110(1):116–32.

16. Eriksson K, Vartanova I, Strimling P, Simpson B. Generosity pays: Selfish people have fewer children and earn less money. J Pers Soc Psychol. 2020 Mar;118(3):532–44.

17. Brooks AC. (2007). Does giving make us prosperous? J Econ Finan. 31: 403–11.

18. Brooks AC. "Why Giving Matters." Y Magazine, summer 2009.

19. De Dreu CK, Weingart LR, Kwon S. Influence of social motives on integrative negotiation: A meta-analytic review and test of two theories. J Pers Soc Psychol. 2000 May;78(5):889–905.

20. Hougaard R, Carter J, Chester L. "Power Can Corrupt Leaders. Compassion Can Save Them." Harvard Business Review, February 15, 2018.

21. Owen D, Davidson J. (May 2009). Hubris syndrome: An acquired personality disorder? A study of US Presidents and UK Prime Ministers over the last 100 years. Brain. 132(5):1396–1406.

22. Tyran K. (2000). When leaders display emotion: How followers respond to negative emotional expression of male and female leaders. J Organ Behav. 21: 221–34.

23. Zengler J, Folkman J. "Your Employees Want the Negative Feedback You Hate to Give." *Harvard Business Review,* January 15, 2014.

24. Boehler ML, Rogers DA, Schwind CJ, Mayforth R, Quin J, Williams RG, Dunnington G. An investigation of medical student reactions to feedback: A randomised controlled trial. Med Educ. 2006 Aug;40(8):746–49.

25. Westberg J, Hilliard J. *Fostering Reflection and Providing Feedback: Helping Others Learn from Experience.* Springer, August 22, 2001.

26. Webster J, Duvall J, Gaines L, Smith R. (2003). The roles of praise and social comparison information in the experience of pride. J Soc Psychol. 143: 209–32.

27. Banerjee R, Bennett M, Luke N. Children's reasoning about the self-presentational consequences of apologies and excuses following rule violations. Br J Dev Psychol. 2010 Nov;28(Pt 4):799–815.

28. Baumeister RF, Bratslavsky E, Muraven M, Tice DM. (1998). Ego depletion: Is the active self a limited resource? J Pers Soc Psychol. 74(5):1252–65.

29. Konrath S, Handy F. (2020). The good-looking giver effect: The relationship between doing good and looking good. Nonprofit and Voluntary Sector Quarterly 50(2):283–311.

30. Grant A, Berry J. (2011). The necessity of others is the mother of invention: Intrinsic and prosocial motivations, perspective taking, and creativity. Acad Manag J 54: 73–96.

31. Chancellor J, Margolis S, Jacobs Bao K, Lyubomirsky S. Everyday prosociality in the workplace: The reinforcing benefits of giving, getting, and glimpsing. Emotion. 2018 Jun;18(4):507–17.

32. Flynn L, Liang Y, Dickson GL, Xie M, Suh DC. Nurses' practice environments, error interception practices, and inpatient medication errors. J Nurs Scholarsh. 2012 Jun;44(2):180–86.

CHAPTER 10. MOTIVES MATTER

1. Savary J, Goldsmith K. (2020). Unobserved altruism: How self-signaling motivations and social benefits shape willingness to donate. J Exp Psychol. Appl 26(3):538–550.

2. Susewind M, Walkowitz G. Symbolic moral self-completion: Social recognition of prosocial behavior reduces subsequent moral striving. Front Psychol. 2020 Sep 4;11:560188.

3. Ariely D, Bracha A, Meier S. (2009). Doing good or doing well? Image motivation and monetary incentives in behaving prosocially. American Economic Review. 99(1):544–55.

4. Qu H, Konrath S, Poulin M. (2020). Which types of giving are associated with reduced mortality risk among older adults? Pers Indiv Diff. 154: 109668.

5. Brown AL, Meer J, Williams JF. (2019). Why do people volunteer? An experimental analysis of preferences for time donations. Manag Sci. 65(4): 1455–68.

6. Tashjian SM, Rahal D, Karan M, Eisenberger N, Galván A, Cole SW, Fuligni AJ. Evidence from a randomized controlled trial that altruism moderates the effect of prosocial acts on adolescent well-being. J Youth Adolesc. 2021;50(1):29–43.

7. Harbaugh WT, Mayr U, Burghart DR. Neural responses to taxation and voluntary giving reveal motives for charitable donations. Science. 2007 Jun 15;316(5831):1622–25.

8. Nonaka K, Fujiwara Y, Watanabe S, Ishizaki T, Iwasa H, Amano H, Yoshida Y, Kobayashi E, Sakurai R, Suzuki H, Kumagai S, Shinkai S, Suzuki T. Is unwilling volunteering protective for functional decline? The interactive effects of volunteer willingness and engagement on health in a 3-year longitudinal study of Japanese older adults. Geriatr Gerontol Int. 2019 Jul;19(7):673–78.

9. Weinstein N, Ryan RM. When helping helps: Autonomous motivation for prosocial behavior and its influence on well-being for the helper and recipient. J Pers Soc Psychol. 2010 Feb;98(2):222–44.

10. Stukas AA, Hoye R, Nicholson M, Brown KM, Aisbett L. Motivations to volunteer and their associations with volunteers' well-being. Nonprofit Volunt Sect Q. 2016;45(1):112–32.

11. Konrath S, Fuhrel-Forbis A, Lou A, Brown S. Motives for volunteering are associated with mortality risk in older adults. Health Psychol. 2012 Jan;31(1):87–96.

12. Cutler J, Campbell-Meiklejohn D. A comparative fMRI meta-analysis of altruistic and strategic decisions to give. Neuroimage. 2019 Jan 1;184:227–41.

13. Hein G, Morishima Y, Leiberg S, Sul S, Fehr E. (2016). The brain's functional network architecture reveals human motives. Science. 351:1074–78.

14. Kahana E, Bhatta T, Lovegreen LD, Kahana B, Midlarsky E. Altruism, helping, and volunteering: Pathways to well-being in late life. J Aging Health. 2013;25(1):159–87.

15. Gleason ME, Iida M, Bolger N, Shrout PE. Daily supportive equity in close relationships. Pers Soc Psychol Bull. 2003 Aug;29(8):1036–45.

16. Batson CD, Duncan BD, Ackerman P, Buckley T, Birch K. (1981). Is empathic emotion a source of altruistic motivation? J Pers Soc Psychol. 40(2):290–302.

17. Morelli SA, Lee IA, Arnn ME, Zaki J. Emotional and instrumental support provision interact to predict well-being. Emotion. 2015;15(4):484–93.

18. Sonnentag S, Grant AM. (2012). Doing good at work feels good at home, but not right away: When and why perceived prosocial impact predicts positive affect. Pers Psychol. 65:495–530.

19. Jordan J, Yoeli E, Rand DG. Don't get it or don't spread it? Comparing self-

interested versus prosocial motivations for COVID-19 prevention behaviors. Sci Rep. 2021;11(1):20222.

20. Larson EB, Yao X. Clinical empathy as emotional labor in the patient-physician relationship. JAMA. 2005 Mar 2;293(9):1100–6.

21. Shin LJ, Layous K, Choi I, Na S, Lyubomirsky S. (2019). Good for self or good for others? The well-being benefits of kindness in two cultures depend on how the kindness is framed. J Posit Psychol. 15(6): 795–805.

CHAPTER 11. START SMALL

1. O'Connor D, Wolfe D. (1991). From crisis to growth at midlife: Changes in personal paradigm. J Organ Behav. 12: 323–40.

2. Mogilner C, Chance Z, Norton MI. Giving time gives you time. Psychol Sci. 2012 Oct 1;23(10):1233–38.

3. Fogarty LA, Curbow BA, Wingard JR, McDonnell K, Somerfield MR. Can 40 seconds of compassion reduce patient anxiety? J Clin Oncol. 1999 Jan;17(1):371–79.

4. Fujiwara Y, Sugihara Y, Shinkai S. [Effects of volunteering on the mental and physical health of senior citizens: Significance of senior-volunteering from the view point of community health and welfare]. Nihon Koshu Eisei Zasshi. 2005 Apr;52(4):293–307.

5. Windsor TD, Anstey KJ, Rodgers B. Volunteering and psychological well-being among young-old adults: How much is too much? Gerontologist. 2008 Feb;48(1):59–70.

6. Booth J, Park K, Glomb T. (2009). Employer-supported volunteering benefits: Gift exchange among employers, employees, and volunteer organizations. Hum Resour Manag J. 48(2):227–249.

7. Kim ES, Whillans AV, Lee MT, Chen Y, VanderWeele TJ. Volunteering and subsequent health and well-being in older adults: An outcome-wide longitudinal approach. Am J Prev Med. 2020 Aug;59(2):176–86.

8. Park SQ, Kahnt T, Dogan A, Strang S, Fehr E, Tobler PN. A neural link between generosity and happiness. Nat Commun. 2017 Jul 11;8:15964.

9. Cialdini R, Schroeder D. (1976). Increasing compliance by legitimizing paltry contributions: When even a penny helps. J Pers Soc Psychol. 34: 599–604.

10. Aknin LB, Sandstrom GM, Dunn EW, Norton MI. It's the recipient that counts: Spending money on strong social ties leads to greater happiness than spending on weak social ties. PLOS ONE. 2011;6(2):e17018.

11. Kogan A, Impett E, Oveis C, Bryant HUI, Gordon A, Keltner D. (2010). When giving feels good. Psychol Sci. 21(12):1918–24.

12. Dew J, Wilcox W. (2013). Generosity and the maintenance of marital quality. J Marriage Fam. 75:1218–28.

13. Stavrova O. Having a happy spouse is associated with lowered risk of mortality. Psychol Sci. 2019 May;30(5):798–803.

14. Rowland L, Curry OS. A range of kindness activities boost happiness. J Soc Psychol. 2019;159(3):340–43.

15. Joiner T. *Why People Die by Suicide.* Harvard University Press, 2007.

CHAPTER 12. BE THANKFUL

1. Ma LK, Tunney RJ, Ferguson E. Does gratitude enhance prosociality?: A meta-analytic review. Psychol Bull. 2017 Jun;143(6):601–35.

2. Karns CM, Moore WE, Mayr U. The cultivation of pure altruism via gratitude: A functional MRI study of change with gratitude practice. Front Hum Neurosci. 2017 Dec 12;11:599.

3. Bartlett M, Condon P, Cruz J, Wormwood J, DeSteno D. (2011). Gratitude: Prompting behaviours that build relationships. Cogn Emot. 26: 2–13.

4. Bartlett M, DeSteno D. (2006). Gratitude and prosocial behavior: Helping when it costs you. Psychol Sci. 17: 319–25.

5. DeSteno D, Bartlett MY, Baumann J, Williams LA, Dickens L. Gratitude as moral sentiment: Emotion-guided cooperation in economic exchange. Emotion. 2010 Apr;10(2):289–93.

6. Froh J, Bono G, Emmons R. (2010). Being grateful is beyond good manners: Gratitude and motivation to contribute to society among early adolescents. Motiv Emot. 34: 144–57.

7. Kumar A, Epley N. (2018). Undervaluing gratitude: Expressers misunderstand the consequences of showing appreciation. Psychol Sci. 2018;29(9): 1423–1435.

CHAPTER 13. BE PURPOSEFUL

1. Chau VM, Engeln JT, Axelrath S, Khatter SJ, Kwon R, Melton MA, Reinsvold MC, Staley VM, To J, Tanabe KJ, Wojcik R. Beyond the chief complaint: Our patients' worries. J Med Humanit. 2017 Dec;38(4):541–47.

2. Darley JM, Batson CD. (1973). "From Jerusalem to Jericho": A study of situational and dispositional variables in helping behavior. J Pers Soc Psychol. 27(1):100–8.

3. Van Tongeren DR, Green JD, Davis DE, Hook JN, Hulsey TL. (2016). Prosociality enhances meaning in life. J Posit Psychol. 11(3):225–36.

4. Broadfoot M. "Teens and Other Volunteers Help Seniors Find Scarce COVID Shots." *Scientific American,* March 3, 2021.

CHAPTER 14. FIND COMMON GROUND

1. Kalmoe N, Mason L. (2018). Lethal mass partisanship: Prevalence, correlates, and electoral contingencies. Paper presented at the 2018 American Political Science Association's Annual Meeting, Boston, MA.
2. Vavreck L. "A Measure of Identity: Are You Wedded to Your Party?" *New York Times,* January 31, 2017.
3. Depow GJ, Francis ZL, Inzlicht M. (December 11, 2020). The experience of empathy in everyday life. Psychol Sci. 2021;32(8):1198–1213.
4. Levine M, Prosser A, Evans D, Reicher S. Identity and emergency intervention: How social group membership and inclusiveness of group boundaries shape helping behavior. Pers Soc Psychol Bull. 2005 Apr;31(4):443–53.
5. Batson CD, Polycarpou M, Harmon-Jones E, Imhoff H, Mitchener E, Bednar L, Klein T, Highberger L. (1997). Empathy and attitudes: Can feeling for a member of a stigmatized group improve feelings toward the group? J Pers Soc Psychol. 72:105–18.
6. Nai J, Narayanan J, Hernandez I, Savani K. People in more racially diverse neighborhoods are more prosocial. J Pers Soc Psychol. 2018 Apr;114 (4):497–515.
7. Hein G, Silani G, Preuschoff K, Batson CD, Singer T. Neural responses to ingroup and outgroup members' suffering predict individual differences in costly helping. Neuron. 2010 Oct 6;68(1):149–60.
8. Pavey L, Greitemeyer T, Sparks P. "I help because I want to, not because you tell me to": Empathy increases autonomously motivated helping. Pers Soc Psychol Bull. 2012 May;38(5):681–89.
9. Klimecki OM, Mayer SV, Jusyte A, Scheeff J, Schönenberg M. Empathy promotes altruistic behavior in economic interactions. Sci Rep. 2016 Aug 31;6:31961.
10. Liberman V, Samuels SM, Ross L. The name of the game: Predictive power of reputations versus situational labels in determining Prisoner's Dilemma game moves. Pers Soc Psychol Bull. 2004;30(9):1175–85.
11. Bloom P. *Against Empathy: The Case for Rational Compassion.* Ecco, 2016.
12. Bruneau EG, Cikara M, Saxe R. Parochial empathy predicts reduced altruism and the endorsement of passive harm. Soc Psychol Pers Sci. 2017;8(8):934–42.
13. Simas E, Clifford S, Kirkland J. (2020). How empathic concern fuels political polarization. Am Political Sci Rev. 114(1):258–69.

CHAPTER 15. SEE IT

1. Lim D, DeSteno D. (2020). Past adversity protects against the numeracy bias in compassion. Emotion. 20(8):1344–56.

2. See https://www.ted.com/talks/elizabeth_dunn_helping_others_makes_us _happier_but_it_matters_how_we_do_it/transcript?language=en.
3. Aknin LB, Dunn EW, Whillans AV, Grant AM, Norton MI. (April 2013). Making a difference matters: Impact unlocks the emotional benefits of prosocial spending. J Econ Behav Org. 88: 90–95.
4. Cryder C, Loewenstein G, Scheines R. (2013). The donor is in the details. Org Behav Human Decis Process. 120: 15–23.
5. Rudd M, Aaker J, Norton MI. (2014). Getting the most out of giving: Concretely framing a prosocial goal maximizes happiness. J Exp Soc Psychol. 54: 11–24.
6. Ko K, Margolis S, Revord J, Lyubomirsky S. (2019). Comparing the effects of performing and recalling acts of kindness. J Posit Psychol. 16(1):73–81.
7. Wiwad D, Aknin LB. (2017). Motives matter: The emotional consequences of recalled self-and other-focused prosocial acts. Motiv Emot. 41(6):730–40.
8. Grant A, Dutton J. Beneficiary or benefactor: Are people more prosocial when they reflect on receiving or giving? Psychol Sci. 2012;23(9):1033–39.
9. Zaki J. The War for Kindness. Crown, 2019.
10. Weisz E, Ong DC, Carlson RW, Zaki J. Building empathy through motivation-based interventions. Emotion. 2021;21(5):990–999.
11. Nook EC, Ong DC, Morelli SA, Mitchell JP, Zaki J. Prosocial conformity: Prosocial norms generalize across behavior and empathy. Pers Soc Psychol Bull. 2016 Aug;42(8):1045–62.

CHAPTER 16. ELEVATE

1. Algoe SB, Haidt J. Witnessing excellence in action: The "other-praising" emotions of elevation, gratitude, and admiration. J Posit Psychol. 2009;4(2):105–27.
2. Schnall S, Roper J, Fessler DM. Elevation leads to altruistic behavior. Psychol Sci. 2010 Mar;21(3):315–20.
3. Sparks AM, Fessler DMT, Holbrook C. Elevation, an emotion for prosocial contagion, is experienced more strongly by those with greater expectations of the cooperativeness of others. PLOS ONE. 2019 Dec 4;14(12):e0226071.
4. Schnall S, Roper J. (2012). Elevation puts moral values into action. Soc Psychol Pers Sci. 3: 373–78.
5. Jung H, Seo E, Han E, Henderson MD, Patall EA. Prosocial modeling: A meta-analytic review and synthesis. Psychol Bull. 2020 Aug;146(8):635–63.
6. Fowler JH, Christakis NA. Dynamic spread of happiness in a large social network: Longitudinal analysis over 20 years in the Framingham Heart Study. BMJ. 2008 Dec 4;337:a2338.
7. Fowler JH, Christakis NA. Cooperative behavior cascades in human social networks. Proc Natl Acad Sci U S A. Mar 2010, 107 (12):5334–5338.

8. See https://www.eurekalert.org/news-releases/869835.

9. Chancellor J, Margolis S, Lyubomirsky S. (2016). The propagation of everyday prosociality in the workplace. J Posit Psychol. 1–13.

10. Bakker AB, Le Blanc PM, Schaufeli WB. Burnout contagion among intensive care nurses. J Adv Nurs. 2005 Aug;51(3):276–87.

11. Woolum A, Foulk T, Lanaj K, Erez A. (2017). Rude color glasses: The contaminating effects of witnessed morning rudeness on perceptions and behaviors throughout the workday. J Appl Psychol. 102(12):1658–72.

12. Foulk T, Woolum A, Erez A. Catching rudeness is like catching a cold: The contagion effects of low-intensity negative behaviors. J Appl Psychol. 2016 Jan;101(1):50–67.

13. Rees MA, Kopke JE, Pelletier RP, Segev DL, Rutter ME, Fabrega AJ, Rogers J, Pankewycz OG, Hiller J, Roth AE, Sandholm T, Unver MU, Montgomery RA. A nonsimultaneous, extended, altruistic-donor chain. N Engl J Med. 2009 Mar 12;360(11):1096–101.

CHAPTER 17. KNOW YOUR POWER

1. Booker C. *United: Thoughts on Finding Common Ground and Advancing the Common Good.* Ballantine, 2016.

2. Barefoot JC, Brummett BH, Williams RB, Siegler IC, Helms MJ, Boyle SH, Clapp-Channing NE, Mark DB. (May 23, 2011). Recovery expectations and long-term prognosis of patients with coronary heart disease. Arch Intern Med. 171(10):929–35.

3. Tedeschi R, Calhoun L. (2004). Posttraumatic growth: Conceptual foundations and empirical evidence. Psychol Inq. 15: 1–18.

4. Baumeister RF, Vohs KD, Aaker JL, Garbinsky EN. (2013). Some key differences between a happy life and a meaningful life. J Posit Psychol. 8(6):505–16.

5. Brickman P, Coates D, Janoff-Bulman R. Lottery winners and accident victims: Is happiness relative? J Pers Soc Psychol. 1978 Aug;36(8):917–27.

6. Van Tongeren DR, Hibbard R, Edwards M, Johnson E, Diepholz K, Newbound H, Shay A, Houpt R, Cairo A, Green J D. (2018). Heroic helping: The effects of priming superhero images on prosociality. Front Psychol. 9, Article 2243.

7. Rushton JP. (1975). Generosity in children: Immediate and long-term effects of modeling, preaching, and moral judgment. J Pers Soc Psychol. 31: 459–66.

8. Doohan I, Saveman BI. Need for compassion in prehospital and emergency care: A qualitative study on bus crash survivors' experiences. Int Emerg Nurs. 2015 Apr;23(2):115–19.

ACKNOWLEDGMENTS

Mutually, we want to express our deep gratitude for all of the people who made this book possible.

We thank our colleagues at Cooper University Health Care. It is an honor to work with such an impressive group of people. We are continually inspired by their commitment to serve others, and there was no greater display than during the pandemic. They were heroes to us well before COVID. Every day, they remind us that caring makes a difference. In particular, we want to thank the physician and nursing leaders at Cooper for their dedication to patients and to one another's success.

We also thank our Board of Trustees, particularly our chairman, George E. Norcross, III. His efforts to serve the people of Camden and his dedication to Cooper are prime examples of a giving mindset.

Our medical school, Cooper Medical School of Rowan University (CMSRU), is truly special because of its spirit of service, and in particular, its commitment to serving the people of Camden. We are so fortunate to have a dean, Annette Reboli, M.D., who leads by example. Dean Reboli has not only been a supporter of the concepts in this book from the beginning, but also she has a deep understanding of these concepts from her own experience as a physician and leader. In the future, we believe that CMSRU students, trainees, and faculty will be on the forefront of the science of service, and it will be in large part because of her vision. We truly appreciate all she has done for us.

We are incredibly grateful for the talents and commitment of Valerie Frankel, who was with us every step of the way in writing this book. Val is absolutely brilliant, and her intellect is matched only by her wit. We could not have done this without her. Few people get the opportunity to be Val's collaborators, and we consider ourselves very fortunate to be among those people.

We'd like to thank Michael Carlisle from InkWell Management. He not only believed in us to make this book possible, but also supported us throughout the whole process. Along with Michael Mungiello, the InkWell Michaels patiently put up with our endless questions to understand an industry that sometimes still feels foreign to us. We just know we are in good hands with them.

Of course, none of this would be possible without Elizabeth Beier from St. Martin's Press. She is the one who believed in our message and took the leap of faith to allow all of this to unfold. We'd like to thank everyone at St. Martin's Press for their work on this book. We'd especially like to thank Liana Krissoff, for her excellent work in copyediting and polishing the manuscript, and Hannah Phillips and Brigitte Dale, for walking us through the process of bringing the book to market.

We are very grateful for the team at Chartwell Speakers. Ellis Trevor and Francis Hoch helped us to see our work as a "Big Idea" that needed to be shared, and accordingly they introduced us to the people who could make this book happen. We also thank Chartwell's Catherine McQueen, Mackenzie Coke, and Sandra Fant for helping us spread the message.

Many thanks to Craig Deao from Huron Consulting, not only for nudging us at the very beginning and helping us believe that we could write books, but also for being one of the first to give us advice on this one. He is a tireless champion for all of its principles.

We are grateful for Brian Roberts, M.D., MSc, who directs our compassion science research program at Cooper. He is an invaluable resource for us, and he graciously helps us interpret statistics when we need his analytical chops. Brian is a brilliant scientist, and in the years to come we have no doubt that he will leave an indelible mark on the field. At the end of our careers, we predict that our main "claim to fame" will be that we once worked with the famous Dr. Roberts.

If we ever need a jolt of inspiration to be a better Live to Giver, we need to look no further than the example set by Cooper's Chief Physician Executive, Eric Kupersmith, M.D. For Eric, it's never about him; it's always about the other person. Giving is in his DNA. That's a big part of what makes him such an effective leader. Eric is a Jedi Knight in the science and the art of serving others, and because of that he is a role model we both look up to immensely.

We also thank Cooper's Tom Rubino for his tireless support of our work and for helping us amplify the message.

For each person we have named here, there are many more who have helped in so many ways. We are grateful to all of you.

Lastly, we are indebted to the hundreds of researchers whose collective studies comprise this book. The works of these scholars and scientists opened our eyes to the true power of serving others and compelled us to tell this story.

PERSONAL ACKNOWLEDGMENTS FROM STEPHEN TRZECIAK

First and foremost, I am forever thankful for my amazing wife, Tamara, the ultimate Live to Giver. Tamara is the most giving person I have ever known, and she has taught me more about serving others than anyone else ever could. She was, and always will be, my inspiration for this work. Every day, she sets a shining example for our family to follow.

I thank my parents, Vi and Walt Trzeciak, for starting me on this journey, and for encouraging me and supporting me unconditionally every step of the way. Decades ago they instilled in me values that have now culminated in this work and this book.

I also thank Lydia and David Lyzinski for showing our whole family what it means to love and serve one another over a lifetime. Julie and Bob Nettleton, you guys supported me through the writing of this book and were a great sounding board for ideas. I am grateful for that.

I am especially grateful for everyone in Cooper's internal medicine residency program, the crown jewel of our department of medicine. You guys are awesome and very, very special. The way you serve your patients, and one another, inspires me every day. And you have been heroes through the pandemic. I am so proud of you.

I also want to thank my Cooper critical care family for all of their support, especially: Nitin Puri, Phil Dellinger, Christa Schorr, Jason Bartock, Emily Damuth, Lars Peterson, Lindsey Glaspey, Sebastien Rachoin, Toni Spevetz, Toni Piper, Sergio Zanotti, Nancy Loperfido, and so many others. As Nitin always says: such a special group of people.

I thank all of the nurses that I have been so fortunate to work alongside in the ICU at Cooper for the past twenty years. They put their hearts and souls into caring for the critically ill. They have been a wellspring of compassion for patients and continue to amaze me to this day. My medical training and textbooks taught me how to treat patients, but these nurses have helped me understand what it really means to *take care of* patients.

I owe a special debt of gratitude, one I could not possibly repay, to the patients and families I have had the privilege of caring for in the Cooper ICU. The lessons they taught me were part of the genesis of this book, and a common thread through all of its pages.

I am so fortunate to be part of an incredible team in the Adult Health Institute (AHI) at Cooper, especially: Pam Ladu, Megan Avila, Sue Kreh, Jim Haddock, Sunil Marwaha, Briana Thomas, and so many others. Thank you for helping our health care providers serve their patients. I look forward to collaborating with you to infuse the principles from this book into everything we do.

I am especially thankful for Rebecca Smith, my awesome assistant. I would love to say that Rebecca and I make a great team, but that would be giving me too much credit. She is responsible for so much of our success. In addition, Rebecca is a true Live to Giver, and she shows great kindness to everyone we collaborate with. That sets a great example for me and the whole AHI team to follow. I also thank Dan Hyman, Tony Rostain, and Phil Koren for their constant support, sage advice, and friendship.

I am eternally grateful to my whole Notre Dame family, for always supporting me and encouraging me to dream big, especially: Uncle Ed, Fr. Andre Leveille, Matt Jenkins, J. P. McNeill, Dan Kruse, Bill Spellacy,

Geoff Robertson, and so many others. Special thanks to Dominic Vachon, Ph.D., for building a truly special program in the science of compassion at Notre Dame, and for continuing to collaborate with me from afar.

There are dozens of people in my church family who have encouraged and supported me through this project, but I especially want to thank my Deep Waters crew: Lorenzo Eagles, Brian Catanella, Tom Grant, Manny Delgado, Dave Fauvell, Wes Allen, Carl Krott, and Greg Harr. I admire you all, and I greatly value your friendship and fellowship. I also thank my great friend Larry Dunne, who gave me a lot of support through the pandemic and is always looking out for me.

Lastly, I thank my wonderful children: Christian, Isabel, Bethany, and Jonathan. You all are amazing and you continue to inspire me every day. This book will be marketed far and wide for anyone who wants to start living their best life through serving others, but the secret of this book is that it's actually written for *you*.

PERSONAL ACKNOWLEDGMENTS FROM ANTHONY MAZZARELLI

Above all I would like to thank my wife, Joanne. I am incredibly lucky to have such a supportive partner and friend. As a practicing cardiologist and medical educator, she is not only clinically excellent but beloved by her patients as well as recognized by those whom she teaches. She has made a life of being other-focused, which is all too often focused on helping me. She is always unbelievably supportive no matter the endeavor. There were many nights when I'm sure Joanne just wanted to go to sleep, but I kept her up to get her opinion. I still wonder how she is so patient with me.

I would also like to thank my parents, Joe and Virginia, who have always supported everything I have done. As incredible as they are as parents, they are even more impressive as grandparents. As my children grow older I wonder how I could ever measure up to be even a fraction as supportive and loving as they are.

To my children—Sophia, JP, Leo, and forever in our hearts Joseph—you have all inspired me not only to write this book but to want people to read it. Once again, please don't let on to our publisher, but I don't really care about how many books we sell. I do, however, care deeply about increasing the number of people in the world who are other-focused. We hope you contribute to and benefit from such a world.

My most heartfelt thanks again go to Michael Smerconish, whose mentorship, guidance, and influence over the years is likely the reason I wrote one book, let alone two. "You need to write a book," was his advice for years. In our first conversation about the first book he was already asking what would be in the second book. He has always motivated me to do more, think more, and reach further than I ever thought possible, and his enduring support is greatly appreciated. Those who know him well will notice his influence throughout the pages of this book.

I need to thank TC Scornavacchi. Her encouragement, support, and work on *Compassionomics* has carried right over into her encouragement and support of this book as well. She is a perfect specimen of a Live to Give mindset, as those who listen to her podcast, TC After Dark, are reminded in every episode.

I am very grateful to Rich Zeoli. Not only did Rich read early drafts of the book to offer guidance, but his continual counsel has been invaluable. Rich has become a radio star, but he remembers his Jersey roots and is always willing to take time to help no matter the project.

I also want to thank Sacha Montas, M.D., J.D., M.B.E. If you are thinking, "What a nerd with all those degrees," I completely agree. Sacha is the person who first got me interested in the academic side of medicine many years ago in college, when he introduced me to the world of bioethics. He continues to be the best sounding board a friend can have.

I would be remiss if I did not give a special thanks to Jennifer Knorr. In the world of executive assistants she has few, if any, equals. Her job would be exponentially easier if she did not choose to show kindness to others when dealing with them. She has never wavered from this practice, on good days and bad, which I appreciate almost as much as the fact that without her I would be completely lost.

Thank you to the senior leadership team at Cooper. I know how hard you work to serve our patients and our employees, and your desire to have a culture of compassion and support within our organization. There were many times I thought of each of you in the writing of this book.

I especially want to thank my co-president, Kevin O'Dowd, with whom I have the pleasure to work closely every day. We have faced together what I hope will be the biggest challenge health care faces in our lifetime. But, frankly, it doesn't matter what the world throws at our industry moving forward: I'm confident that with his skill, thoughtfulness, intelligence, and enduring calmness, we will be able to face it. He has made a career of service his entire professional life and I don't think a day goes by when I don't learn something in that regard from him.

Lastly, I would like to thank all of the past, present, and future patients I have ever been given the privilege to take care of in the emergency department. I hope I continue to grow in my journey to provide more compassionate care so that I can serve you better.

INDEX

ABOUT THE AUTHORS

STEPHEN TRZECIAK, M.D., M.P.H., is a physician scientist, professor, and chair of medicine at Cooper Medical School of Rowan University, and the chief of medicine at Cooper University Health Care. Dr. Trzeciak is a practicing intensivist (specialist in intensive care medicine), and a clinical researcher with more than 120 publications in the scientific literature, primarily in the field of resuscitation science. Dr. Trzeciak's publications have been featured in some of the most prestigious medical journals, such as: *Journal of the American Medical Association, Circulation,* and *The New England Journal of Medicine.* His scientific program has been supported by research grants from the American Heart Association and the National Institutes of Health, with Dr. Trzeciak serving in the role of principal investigator.

© JONATHAN KOLBE

Dr. Trzeciak is a graduate of the University of Notre Dame. He earned his medical degree at the University of Wisconsin-Madison, and his Masters in Public Health at the University of Illinois at Chicago. He completed his residency training at the University of Illinois at Chicago Medical Center, and his fellowship training in critical care medicine at Rush University Medical Center. He is board-certified in internal medicine and critical care medicine.

ANTHONY MAZZARELLI, M.D., J.D., M.B.E., is co-president/CEO of Cooper University Health Care and the associate dean of clinical affairs for Cooper Medical School of Rowan University. Prior to his current role, Dr. Mazzarelli served as Cooper's chief physician executive where he oversaw the physician practice, as well as quality/patient safety and continuous process improvement efforts for the health system, the same topics for which he teaches within the medical school and residency programs. Dr. Mazzarelli has been named one of the fifty most powerful people in New Jersey health care by NJ Biz and NJ ROI. Dr. Mazzarelli has also received numerous commendations for his leadership and he speaks regularly on several local and national media outlets.

© JONATHAN KOLBE

Dr. Mazzarelli received his medical degree from Robert Wood Johnson Medical School, his law degree from University of Pennsylvania Law School, and his master's degree in bioethics from the Perelman School of Medicine at the University of Pennsylvania. He trained in emergency medicine at Cooper University Hospital, where he also served as chief resident. He is board-certified in emergency medicine, and is actively practicing in the emergency department at Cooper.